CUTTIN' UP

CultureAmerica

Erika Doss
Philip J. Deloria
Series Editors

Karal Ann Marling
Editor Emerita

CUTTIN' UP
How Early Jazz Got America's Ear

COURT CARNEY

 University Press of Kansas

Published by the

University Press of Kansas

(Lawrence, Kansas 66045),

which was organized by the

Kansas Board of Regents and

is operated and funded by

Emporia State University,

Fort Hays State University,

Kansas State University,

Pittsburg State University,

the University of Kansas,

and Wichita State University

A version of chapter 2 was published as Court Carney, "New Orleans and the Creation of Early Jazz," *Popular Music and Society* 29, no. 3 (July 2006): 299–315. Reprinted by permission of the publisher (Taylor & Francis Ltd, http://www.tandf.co.uk/journals).

Library of Congress Cataloging-in-Publication Data

Carney, Court.
  Cuttin' up : how early jazz got America's ear / Court Carney.
    p.   cm. — (CultureAmerica)
  Includes bibliographical references and index.
  ISBN 978-0-7006-1675-6 (cloth : alk. paper)
  1. Jazz—1921–1930—History and criticism. 2. Dissemination of music—United States—History—20th century. I. Title.
  ML3508.C37 2009
  781.65'20973—dc22   2009024290

British Library Cataloguing-in-Publication Data is available.
Printed in the United States of America

10 9 8 7 6 5 4 3 2 1

The paper used in this publication is recycled and contains 30 percent postconsumer waste. It is acid free and meets the minimum requirements of the American National Standard for Permanence of Paper for Printed Library Materials Z39.48–1992.

For my parents and grandfather,
Pat and Rosemary Carney
and Harold Rethmann

Contents

Acknowledgments

First, I would like to thank Kalyani Fernando, my editor at the University Press of Kansas, for her unwavering patience in navigating the publishing process for me. I thank, too, Susan Schott, Jennifer Dropkin, and Kay Kodner for their considerable work in making this project come together in terms of editing and marketing. In addition, I thank the outside readers of my manuscript, as they provided valuable and constructive criticism in how the book could be made better.

In terms of research assistance, I would like to thank Amy Baptist, at the Williams Research Center in New Orleans, for her help with the Jelly Roll Morton files in the William Russell Collection. Also, I would like to acknowledge Deborah Gillaspie and Ray Gadke at the University of Chicago for their help with the Chicago Jazz Archive. In addition, I received a great many comments from papers related to this project that I presented at the American Historical Association, the Experience Music Project, and at the Hagley Museum and Library. These comments (both formal and informal) proved especially useful in framing some of the larger arguments of the study.

On a more personal note, I must thank Rand Dotson and Ben Cloyd for their continued friendship. Both Rand and Ben have been with this project since the beginning, and I am honored to count both of these scholars, rogues though they are, as friends.

Though many of these people have scattered since my time in Baton Rouge, I would like to thank my friends from Louisiana State University who helped keep me sane during my research: John Sacher, Matthew Reonas, Ava and Phil Johnson, the entire Kimbrell family, Tiwanna Simpson, Nichole Staab, Chris Leahy, John and Sylvia Rodrigue, Heather Morrison, and Michael Steinberg. I would like to thank Joseph "Chip" Dawson, Andy Kirkendall, David Vaught, and R. J. Q. "Quince" Adams at Texas A&M University for their interest in the project and some much-needed happy hours. Also, in other cities and at other universities, George Rable, Jonathan Phillips, Gerald Betty, Mark Boulton, George Williamson, Heather Lundine, Kelly Crager, Derek Mallett, and John Beeler deserve my thanks for their friendship and guidance. Thanks also to Troy Davis and my colleagues at Stephen F. Austin State University for their support as I readied this manuscript for publication.

I especially wish to thank my parents and grandfather, to whom this book is dedicated, for their unfailing enthusiasm for my project and financial and emotional support for my education and through numerous visiting positions. Their generosity and understanding can never be fully repaid

It is without exaggeration to say that this project could not have been completed without the help and support of two individuals. Charles J. Shindo, my mentor and friend, has been a constant source of encouragement for over a decade, and, simply put, this book exists because of him. Finally, I am indebted to Charity Rakestraw for her heart, her strength of character, and her steadfast companionship on this journey. I thank her, in particular, for insisting that I keep the focus on what matters. This book is as much hers as it is mine.

Nacogdoches, Texas
May 2009

CUTTIN' UP

Publicity still from Howard Hawks's 1948 film, *A Song Is Born*, featuring the musicians (from left to right) Charlie Barnet, Tommy Dorsey, Benny Goodman, Louis Armstrong, and Lionel Hampton. Note the chalkboard behind Hampton that illustrates the "origins of jazz" as conceptualized by the musicians for their contribution to the encyclopedia of music being compiled by Professor Hobart Frisbee (played by Danny Kaye). (Underwood & Underwood/CORBIS)

INTRODUCTION

A Song Is Born

In 1948, Howard Hawks directed *A Song Is Born*, a late-period screwball comedy about an out-of-touch music professor's introduction to jazz music.[1] A near scene-by-scene remake of Hawks's 1941 film, *Ball of Fire*, the film gathered together a group of well-known jazz musicians known primarily for their music popular a decade earlier.[2] The film's story centers on Hobart Frisbee (Danny Kaye), a naive music professor contracted to write an encyclopedia of music for the privately funded Totten Institute. Seven older professors—each an expert in a particular field of musical history—assist in the production of the encyclopedia. The scholars work diligently on their project, isolating themselves from the outside world. Early in the film, however, two black window washers, played by Buck and Bubbles, an African American comedy team, enter the institute and ask the professors to help them with a radio quiz concerning music. One of the window washers sits at the piano and begins to play along with the professors, ad-libbing a boogie-woogie tune as an accompaniment to a classical piece by Bach. Stunned by the performance, Professor Frisbee realizes that his section on folk music would be incomplete without the inclusion of this jazz vernacular, and he scurries off into a variety of nightclubs to recruit an array of jazz musicians to elucidate this mysterious music for him and his colleagues. Frisbee eventually compels a number of famed jazz musicians, including

Louis Armstrong, Tommy and Jimmy Dorsey, Louis Bellson, Mel Powell, and Lionel Hampton, to sketch a general history of jazz music.

Although unfamiliar to Frisbee, by the late 1940s, this group of musicians represented some of the most famous jazz performers of the last fifteen years. In one scene, the jazz musicians teach Frisbee the convoluted interconnections of jazz styles—a chalkboard behind Frisbee lists a number of subcategories, such as Dixieland and Swing—and then the musicians perform a short improvised jazz piece to illustrate their pedagogical point. Despite the history lesson, the film disregards the larger shift in values that provided the context for the creation of jazz as well as the resultant controversy stemming from the music's popularity. The director even portrays the underworld connections to jazz comedically, and Honey Swanson, a gangster's moll played by Virginia Mayo, appears more for the romantic subplot than as an indicator of the immoral elements of jazz music. In addition, the elderly housekeeper for the musicologists disapproves of Swanson's temporary tenure at the institute but has no real qualms with the music performed by the professors aside from the volume. Although the movie was filmed only a few years removed from jazz music's prime (and all of the controversy that attended the new popular musical form), it presents jazz as a foregone conclusion, simply another logical step in a broader musical evolution. Illustrating this point, Hawks cast Benny Goodman, the symbol of popular jazz in the 1930s, in the role of Professor Magenbruch, a classical clarinet virtuoso inherently able to adapt his classical training to the syncopated rhythms of jazz. The King of Swing thus plays the square, and the film detaches jazz absolutely from its historical context.

Overall, the film avoided any comment on the issue of race, perhaps the defining element in the development (and subsequent controversy) of jazz during this period. A casual integrated spirit frames the musical numbers in the film—and a firm connection to Africa organizes the history segments—but, aside from Armstrong, the most prominent black characters in the film are the two window washers performing a comedic role, speaking in slang and expressing an innate ability to play music. By removing the issue of race from the jazz narrative and downplaying black involvement in the construction of the music, the film deftly avoids a discussion of the larger debates that accompanied jazz throughout the 1920s and 1930s. In 1948, Howard Hawks could produce a film centered on jazz and expect the audience to accept the music as an unquestioned aspect of American musical culture. Produced a decade after the peak of the Swing Era, *A Song Is*

Born posited jazz as a perfectly acceptable subject for both films and academic pursuits. Twenty years earlier, however, jazz music represented the most polarizing form of musical expression in America, and in large measure, jazz reflected the cultural transformation that drastically altered the nation during the early twentieth century.

Between the 1890s and the 1930s, the United States developed into a modern nation, and throughout this period a number of demographic, political, and economic changes greatly impacted American culture and society. Together, increased urbanization, regional mobility, technological innovation, and a rapidly expanding economy eroded the Victorian moorings that underpinned American culture. Much of this change emerged on a national scale in the 1920s, and in many ways this decade signified a period of transition as Americans attempted to reconcile the traditional Victorian values of commercial thrift, emotional repression, and hard work with modernism's thirst for fulfillment and interconnection. Aside from this shift in social and cultural values, America in the 1920s experienced a further transformation in economic principles and political ideals through the development of a vibrant consumer-centered culture. Overall, a marked sense of ambivalence defined much of this period as Americans came into contact with modernity. By the 1930s, these pressures had molded America into a more interconnected and homogeneous nation. Within this period, three specific tensions—of culture, of race, and of music—contributed to a new modernist perspective and challenged and redefined the nation as Americans confronted new social configurations.

Cultural forces created an interconnectedness that American society had never experienced before and also led many Americans to raise critical questions about the changing national environment. The development of mass culture, which is the framework I will most employ in this book, tremendously shaped the years immediately after World War I and brought commercial and technological possibilities that were both powerful and frightening.[3] Warren Susman pinpoints this decade as the period in which Americans experienced, and slowly came to grips with, a new cultural order. "By 1922," Susman argues, "an exceptional and ever-growing number of Americans came to believe in a series of changes in the structure of their world, natural, technological, social, personal, and moral."[4] Technology played a large role in this transformation, and radio in particular connected millions of Americans through regular national broadcasts that often included an increasingly popular jazz music. The creation and eventual popularization of jazz reflects much of the larger pattern of cultural change impacting America during the early twentieth century. Cultural historian Lawrence Levine used jazz to examine the broader historiographical themes of America in the 1920s. "Jazz tells us much about what was original and dynamic in American culture," Levine argues, "even as it reveals to what extent our culture, or more correctly, our cultural attitudes had not yet weaned themselves from the old colonial patterns of the past."[5] As a nation largely (and self-consciously) defined by its culture during this period, a detailed examination of the cultural forms prominent in America during the 1920s represents a necessary avenue of inquiry, and the lens of culture allows for a more complete examination of the myriad new associations that drew the nation into the modern era.

Entwined with this discussion of culture is the second major tension of this period: race and its impact on American music and society. The late nineteenth and early twentieth centuries constituted a volatile period in terms of race relations, as the Great Migration redirected demographic trends and tested racial hierarchies and identities. With its origins in New Orleans, jazz music mirrored many of the ongoing revolutions in racial discourse and effectively pushed the conversation to a national audience via mechanical reproduction. Many contemporary listeners, of course, were aware of the racial undercurrents of the jazz craze—whether positively or negatively, based on stereotype or personal experience—and scholars over the years became increasingly interested in this dynamic. In 1962, scholar Neil Leonard published *Jazz and the White Americans*, one of the first books underscoring the larger social (and racialized) implications of jazz in the 1920s.[6] Since then, historians have developed even further this line of inquiry, and some of the most interesting work on racial identity generally has emerged from jazz historiography.[7] Many of these racial issues developed in urban areas, as many African Americans left the rural South for the cities of the Midwest and Northeast in the first decades of the twentieth century. Much of this study thus centers on the development of cities and the cultures that materialized as diverse racial identities collided with one another in the 1920s.[8]

The third major tension involved the evolution of various musical forms and the rapid growth of an industrial entertainment complex that could effectively broadcast these new sounds to a national audience. This book does not set out to retell the totality of the early jazz narrative; a number of scholars have already ably traced the particular origins of the music. Burton

Peretti's superb *The Creation of Jazz* and Ted Gioia's commendable *The History of Jazz*, for example, provide nice overviews of both the historical structures of jazz music as well as the sounds of the era.[9] Other scholars, such as Kathy Ogren and David Ake, have crafted excellent studies on the cultural reactions and reverberations jazz made as it infiltrated modern America. Charles Hersch's recent work on New Orleans and Lawrence DeGraaf's writing on Los Angeles have explored many of the racial entanglements present in early jazz.[10] Still, this early period has received comparatively less attention than later eras, such as the Bebop and Free Jazz years, though many of the racial issues made so explicit by musicians such as Charles Mingus, Dizzy Gillespie, and Miles Davis had their roots in the complicated experiences of Jelly Roll Morton and King Oliver.[11] Finally, a large number of jazz biographies have helped flesh out the careers of many of the protagonists of this period. Thomas Brothers's recent study of Louis Armstrong, for example, is a model for future work combining the personal with the social in a jazz biography.[12] My work uses these studies as a starting point in exploring some of the larger questions that percolated beneath the surface during the creation of a jazz nation.

With a particular focus on the way various tensions within American society merged to help create both a new music and a new audience for this music, this book is necessarily selective, with certain elements of the story of jazz in the 1920s emphasized over others. What I have aimed to construct is a conceptual framework that addresses the cultural contours of the 1920s and the creation of the American modern age by focusing on the development of the racialized culture of jazz music and the complex mechanizations that led to its national dominance.[13] By focusing on the mechanics of diffusion, my focus has necessarily been on Chicago, New York City, and Los Angeles. Jazz, of course, existed outside of these cities, and some of the crucial evolutionary stages within the music's history surfaced in places like Kansas City, Oklahoma City, and dozens of other areas across the southern and midwestern landscape.[14] My point is not to diminish the vastness of the jazz story but rather to pinpoint the specific cultural turns that resulted in the emergence of a national music. Likewise, I emphasize the role played by the development of the phonograph, radio, and motion picture industries on the dispersion of jazz in the 1920s. Other technological innovations and advancements, of course, functioned as transmitting agents. Riverboats, in particular, helped bring jazz out of New Orleans to an extent rivaling only the railroads.[15] In an effort to keep my focus as concise and concentrated as possible, however, I have maintained an emphasis on the larger context of diffusion in an effort to highlight the mechanics of the process of bringing jazz not simply to a specific region but also to a national audience.

At the center of this book is the complex notion of modernity and its dual (and sometimes competing) roles within a national as well as racial context. A focus on jazz music allows for a unique emphasis on both the creation of a modernist spirit and the actual *process* of a modernist development. As jazz musicians developed a new musical language, for example, this self-aware and self-reflexive crafting of identity redefined the cultural conversation of expression. Placing this process within the context of America in the early twentieth century underscores the function of music as individuals began challenging and redefining their place within a heterogeneous society. My understanding of the contours of African American modernism within the context of musical expressive culture has been shaped dramatically by the works of Paul Gilroy, Houston Baker, Samuel A. Floyd, Guthrie P. Ramsey Jr., Joel Dinerstein, and Ingrid Monson. Gilroy's work on the hybrid and Creole nature of black music, Baker's study of black intellectuals' impact on culture, Floyd's examination of the role music plays within the development of ideas, Ramsey's discussion of Afro-modernism, Dinerstein's rooting of African American modernism within the context of mechanization and technological development, and Monson's perspective on music as discourse have greatly shaped my thinking on the way music reflects these larger patterns.[16] My musical map of African American modernism begins with the emergence of black composers in the late nineteenth century, then shifts to the development of proto-jazz forms in New Orleans in the first decades of the twentieth century, the emergence of recorded jazz in the 1920s, and the rise to prominence of jazz as a complex art music in the early 1930s. This study forms an arc, then, stretching from Scott Joplin to Duke Ellington via Jelly Roll Morton and Louis Armstrong. The story of jazz in the 1920s combines the interconnected dynamics of race, gender, identity, mechanization, communication, urbanization, and production. And within this context emerged a new way of looking at the musical instrument, the musicians, the music—and by extension American music, American culture, and America.

Within the specific context of this book and with the particular history of jazz music, the concept of modernity relates directly to African American concepts of expression and culture. As Guthrie Ramsey has argued, the concept of Afro-modernism as a sociopolitical force dominated the postwar Bebop scene, but its roots evolved over the course of the previous decades, as Louis Armstrong and Duke Ellington echoed in music what Alain Locke and W. E. B. Du Bois were exploring in literature and history.[17] In many ways, Armstrong's "West End Blues" stands at the center of this modernist narrative as it signifies the culmination of expression within the context of African American music in the first half of the twentieth century. Armstrong's achievement ushered in a new era of musical expression that exemplified the modernist spirit of African American life. Declarative and dramatic, Armstrong's playing on "West End Blues" cut up expectations of tone and time. The title of the book, *Cuttin' Up*, relates to the spirit of this process and the culture of modernity by emphasizing the fractured and creative elements involved in this period of monumental transformation. Named for a 1930 song recorded by Paul Howard's Quality Serenaders, *Cuttin' Up* refers to the impact jazz and jazz diffusion had on the nation as well as reflects the ambiguity of much of this change. The phrase "cuttin' up" thus references the way in which jazz music crossed geographic and social boundaries; the idea of integrating various musical elements into a hybrid form of performance; the fracturing of accepted modes of transmission and culture; and, of course, the slang for dancing and having a good time. Americans confronted the modern age with ambivalence as much as anything else, and the harmony as well as the discord attending a new culture illustrates the degrees to which modernity affected the nation.

Overall, to establish an emphasis on the shifts in American culture as well as the process of diffusion, this book is organized in three parts: Creation, Dispersion, and Acceptance. In the first part, Creation, chapters 1 and 2 focus on the various moments of creation within the jazz story as musicians began to experiment with new sounds in the late nineteenth and early twentieth centuries. Chapter 1, "Ragtime, the Blues, and the Reorientation of American Life," illustrates the twisted roots of jazz, showing how ragtime and the blues slowly synthesized into a novel form of syncopated music connected to a particular audience. From its beginnings, jazz has straddled both urban and rural identities, as midwestern city music merged with a southern sound connected to the country. Furthermore, this chapter explores some of the issues related to the concept of "double consciousness" as African American musicians began to enter into a national economy. Chapter 2, "New Orleans and the Creation of Early Jazz," examines the role of New Orleans as an incubator for this new, still nameless configuration of rhythm, melody, and musical expression. The peculiar arrangement of New Orleans with its unique demographics maintained a tangible connection to the past while simultaneously obliterating any easy conceptions of historical memory. As the unreliable narrator of the early history of jazz, New Orleans stood at the center of a complex blending of sources, both musical and social, that slowly became identified as jazz music. This chapter, then, underscores the cultural fractures that eventually helped drive the creation of a new sound that came to define many of the same tensions that impelled its birth. In addition, this chapter illustrates the complexity of labels as jazz emerged as a "folk" music—defined generally here as a noncommercial musical performance that maintained a pattern of transmission and reception thoroughly circumscribed by a particular cohort—and highlights the porous nature of music in New Orleans in regard to classification. As seen in the film *A Song Is Born*, the terms "folk" and "jazz" (within many early contexts of the music) were somewhat interchangeable, but this casual correspondence began to dissolve as both terms played increasingly politicized roles in later academic and musicological debates.

The second part of the book, Dispersion, spans three chapters that each take as their bifurcated points of convergence a jazz city and its connected process of mechanical diffusion. Chapter 3, "Chicago and the Recording of Jazz in the 1920s," considers the role of Chicago in formulating jazz as an identifiable sound within the context of preserving the music on phonograph records. Highlighting the process of cultural diaspora in the age of mechanical reproduction, this chapter provides a study of the various forces that both drove jazz into the urban Midwest and compelled businesses to capitalize on the music through various means. Similarly, chapter 4, "New York City and the Broadcasting of Jazz in the 1920s," illustrates the way jazz began to infiltrate the national consciousness as jazz attracted larger audiences through the emergence of radio networks committed to the sounds being performed in the city's ballrooms. Musical innovation (with larger bands playing more complicated arrangements) coupled with greater exposure due to new technology provided New York City with a thriving musical culture that reverberated across the nation. This section culminates with chapter 5, "Los Angeles and the Diffusion of Early Jazz," and the examination of the West Coast expansion of the jazz story. Hollywood turned a cultural expression into a consumerist mode of production, translating a particular form of jazz to national audiences through a number of films related to the singular developments occurring in Los Angeles in the late 1920s and early 1930s.

The national audience created by the various mechanizations of urban America in the decade prior to the Great Depression underscores the vastness of the jazz landscape just a few years removed from its creation. In the third part, Acceptance, the final chapter of this book, "An American Music," outlines the process of acceptance as different groups of Americans began to encounter the new soundtrack for modern America. This acceptance did not happen immediately, and some of the most full-throated condemnations of the music continued in various guises for some time after this period. Still, by the early 1930s, the widespread reception of jazz had a profound impact on the national culture as Americans came into contact with new expressions of identity. Created out of the various agitations that defined Victorian America, jazz helped usher in the modern age of American culture through its incorporation of disparate sources and its ability to connect large groups of people across long distances. Integrating the tensions of the modern age into a music that engaged consumers on a number of levels, jazz exploded cultural boundaries and signified a new articulation of American life.

Maintaining a focus on the larger historical issues impacting the nation between the 1890s and the 1930s, this book combines historical and musical analysis to provide a more complete view of American culture during the 1920s. During this period, jazz emerged as a particular form of black folk music from the rural South. Black migration out of the South, increased urbanization, technological innovation, and a developing commercial entertainment—the same mechanisms promoting the process of modernization—helped create a national audience for jazz music. On the cusp of modernity, many Americans embraced jazz as a music symbolic of a new age. "In fact," Charles Nanry argues, "jazz as a child of the new order uniquely represents both its own development as an art and, at the same time, reflects the eclectic coming-of-age of all of America."[18] Others remained unimpressed, and the debate over the supposed immorality of jazz generally mirrored the larger concerns over the direction of American society. These tensions dissipated throughout the 1930s and 1940s, and by 1948, when a number of Americans flocked to the theater to see *A Song Is Born,* jazz signified a safe and uncontroversial form of popular music. Twenty years from its contentious adolescence, jazz seemed perfectly harmless and perfectly American in a postwar society concerned more with consumption than fretting over the social impact of a music years past its prime. As nonthreatening as jazz seemed in 1948, a half century earlier, a number of musicians scattered throughout the Midwest and South began an ever-evolving experiment in rhythm, melody, and harmony. This new music, which eventually found a national audience, signified a revolution in sound related intrinsically to the massive transformation of values connected to the generation of modern America.

PART ONE

CREATION

1

Ragtime, the Blues, and the Reorientation of American Life

At the 1893 World's Columbian Exposition in Chicago, Scott Joplin, a young black piano player, introduced ragtime to America. Maybe. No real evidence exists to prove that Joplin, then in his early twenties, actually played along the Midway, nor can scholars conclusively place him in Chicago during that year. Despite these murky origins, ragtime and its musical successor, the blues, came to dominate American popular culture during the late nineteenth century and served as the major musical antecedents for jazz music in the 1920s. Like jazz, ragtime and the blues correlate directly to the economic, social, and cultural transformation of American life that characterized the late nineteenth and early twentieth centuries. The years between 1890 and 1920 were a volatile and contradictory era that signified a crucial period of change in American culture. A number of factors, including increased urbanization, a shift away from Victorianism, rapid industrialization, and the construction of a large corporate bureaucratic order, challenged and redefined the way Americans connected to one another. These larger changes in American society augmented a period of tremendous technological innovation. With the advent of the player piano, piano rolls, the sheet music industry, the phonograph, and the radio, the music of the early twentieth century could be recorded, preserved, and transmitted on a larger scale than ever before. Ragtime and the blues emerged from this transformative tableau as the most prominent genres of black music produced in America, exemplifying distinct elements of African American culture. These musical forms exposed the tensions inherent in American life, and much of this cultural friction found expression in the entwined histories of ragtime and the blues.[1]

Both ragtime and the blues emerged at the same time that modernism—with its decidedly urban, secular, industrial representation of identity—began to infiltrate American life in the late nineteenth century. If, as Paul Gilroy argues, the sailing ship stood as a chronotype of the Black Atlantic, then the northbound train could serve a similar purpose for the transitional period between the 1890s and 1920s when the nation transformed into the modern age.[2] The train, with its energy and motion, marked the nation through physical networks of transportation as well as a large-scale transfer of populations. Ambiguous in its fusion of diasporic, connective, dialytic, and restorative properties, the image of the train delineated American modernism in the late nineteenth century as African Americans fractured traditional cultural pathways by abandoning the South. American life during this period witnessed a massive transformation as Victorianism—with its restraint and moralizing—gave way to the more integrating and raucous spirit of a world in transition.[3] Ragtime and the blues developed within this culture of transition and redefinition, and each genre also related directly to the expansion of rail routes, corporate growth, and the accretion of entertainment markets. The northbound train eventually splintered the southern landscape as the Great Migration developed, and with this transference of population came a new musical culture, at once more integrated in spirit and reliant on new forms of media than earlier forms of entertainment. Music defined by train travel—from the ragtime clubs made possible by the midwestern rails to the syncopated chug of southern bluesmen echoing the sound of the steam engine—came to dominate the nation in the opening years of the twentieth century.

Within these years, major shifts in economics, society, and culture unleashed a number of changes that would have tremendous consequences for the twentieth century. Urbanization—attended by shifting populations, the extension of corporate culture, and the redefinition of spatial life in America—introduced city life to what had been a predominantly rural country and individual cities doubled, tripled, and even quadrupled their populations over a relatively short period of time. Increased industrialization soon followed this urban stimulus, and within a few short years factory growth and corporate concerns eclipsed traditional agrarian foundations of the economy. This transformation fomented a new bureaucratic order and encouraged an emerging middle class. Immigration from Europe and Asia expanded an already diverse population at the same time that many black southerners left for better—if still limited—employment opportunities in the West, Midwest, and urban North. Cultural newness often produced stresses and strains that threatened national cohesion. As Paul Gilroy has demonstrated, the cultural ramifications of black movement across the nation were immense as the "color line" spelled out a warped narrative of men and women forced between two worlds: one still deeply defined by kinship and images (and reimagining) of Africa, and one increasingly defined by predominantly white notions of consumer capitalism. Still, this demographic change radiated some salutary repercussions as Americans came into contact with the strange and the unfamiliar. The pattern of black migration, in particular, led to a greater incorporation of African American culture into American life, especially as new technology transmitted that culture to the nation.[4]

Events during the 1890s demonstrated both the peril and promise of these substantial shifts as an agrarian-centered society dissolved and a more urban and corporate atmosphere developed. The year 1893, alone, illustrates the vacillating timbre of this period as a major economic panic abutted a celebration of national achievements. That year the failure of a number of large corporations generated a succession of business closings, bank foreclosures, and falling farm prices, which eventually precipitated a stock market crash. By December as many as one-quarter of American workers remained idle. After a dizzying period of economic growth, the depression of the 1890s—the worst in U.S. history before the twentieth century—caused four years of financial chaos and disorder.[5] The same year as the stock market crash, Chicago hosted the World's Columbian Exposition in commemoration of the 400th anniversary of Christopher Columbus's voyages to North America. To honor the past, Chicago looked to the future. Thus at the dawn of a massive economic depression, a number of Americans marveled at the wonders of electricity and chewing gum, Cream of Wheat and Pabst Blue Ribbon Beer. More significantly, at the annual meeting of the American Historical Association (also in Chicago that year), historian Frederick Jackson Turner delivered an address positing the frontier as the fundamental characteristic of American identity. Indeed the frontier, to Turner, represented the central process of America, with the nation's culture, society, and politics emerging from the peculiar existence of a definable frontier. Turner's address, "The Significance of the Frontier in American History," rejected openly the germ theory consensus that maintained Eurocentric parameters for American development and placed greater emphasis on the exceptional qualities of the United States.[6] The paradoxical juxtaposition of the fears generated by economic disaster and the hopefulness inherent in the Columbian Exposition provided a unique backdrop for the musical culture of the 1890s.[7] Arriving on the American scene amid this period of transition, ragtime reflected this duality of turmoil and potential.[8]

Like the Columbian Exposition, ragtime exemplified Americans' newfound fascination with all things modern and cosmopolitan. Yet, ragtime was Turnerian in its insistence on invented American newness, and it also had strong ties to European art music, blurring any germ theory of musical composition. Within this context, ragtime brought together a diverse array of sources in a new package including marches, cakewalks, quadrilles, coon songs, and various forms of dance music popular in the Caribbean. This mottled ancestry cohered through the use of a strongly syncopated rhythm, allowing for a definitive sound regardless of the instrumentation involved. Both proponents and opponents of ragtime pointed to this quality when explaining why they enjoyed or despised the music. The name itself referred to the "ragged" nature of the music's beat, and the controversy over ragtime usually revolved around the music's rhythm as critics routinely referred to the music as maddened or hysterical. This pronounced emotional response resonated particularly with Americans critical of the repression reinforced by Victorian values. The suddenness of ragtime's popularity was mired in controversy as commentators associated the ragged style that characterized the music with its black origins. Syncopation itself fell under attack as the uncommon rhythmic pulse of ragtime stemmed from the supposed inability of African American musicians to play printed music correctly or smoothly. In a related attack, some moralistic detractors complained that syncopated dance music allowed for a loosening of values in young people. These same arguments would surface decades later at the apex of the jazz craze during the 1920s. Jazz appropriated more from ragtime than a broad repertoire of songs and a certain rhythmic intensity—the music also shared ragtime's involvement in national questions of moral decency and racial separation. A similar controversy concerning that curious amalgam of imposed morality and overt racism unsurprisingly materialized over the fears associated with jazz, since many Americans exhibited a marked propensity to tolerate intolerance.[9]

Born in 1868 in the piney woods of northeastern Texas near the Arkansas border, Scott Joplin grew up amid the hope and ultimate betrayal of the Reconstruction-era South.[10] Joplin's mother, Florence Givens, was a free-person of color from Kentucky, and his father, Giles Joplin, was a North Carolina slave freed before the Civil War. They provided their son with at least the potential of escaping the web of racially constructed obstacles. Shortly before Joplin's birth, Arkansas ratified the Fourteenth Amendment granting the rights of citizenship to all Americans, white and black. Texas delayed ratification until 1870, but neither state delivered much substance beyond political promises. In fact, during the supposed period of reconciliation, various terrorist groups, including most prominently the Ku Klux Klan, reasserted through violence white authority over African Americans. Replacing lumberyards with railroad yards, the Joplin family moved to Texarkana in the late 1870s, a transition that mirrored the migration of thousands of other American families as urban areas consumed the national culture. City life afforded the Joplin family with previously unheard of educational and occupational opportunities, and the education Joplin received, though limited, separated him from the vast number of African Americans who remained illiterate.[11] Joplin's broad repertoire stemmed from his lessons with a German music teacher in Texarkana. His combined knowledge of classical sources, church hymns, and popular dances allowed Joplin the opportunity to play in an assortment of venues that further diversified his music.

A self-consciously urban music, ragtime echoed the ordered chaos of city life in the nineteenth century and emerged from the stages, theaters, and clubs of urban America. Attracted to city life himself, in 1885, Joplin moved to St. Louis and began playing in various saloons and clubs where he encountered a number of influential people. In particular, the young piano player met John Turpin, a popular African American man with political connections in the area. Turpin ran the Silver Dollar Saloon, a venue that hosted local and itinerant piano players. Turpin's son, Tom, also played piano, and Joplin spent much of his time in St. Louis at the Silver Dollar with the Turpin family.[12] Turpin became close friends with Joplin, and their playing preceded the supposed introduction of ragtime at the Chicago world's fair by at least one year. Again, little evidence exists that the world's fair included ragtime, though the lack of an established genre name would explain at least in part the absence of any overt mention of this new music.[13] Regardless of the details of origin, sheet music companies began churning out printed rags within a few years of the Chicago exposition. In 1897, the first instrumental rag appeared in print, and later that year, Turpin published "Harlem Rag"—the first published ragtime composition by an African American.[14] Due to its small print run, however, "Harlem Rag" reached few piano players outside of St. Louis. Turpin's real fame in the city stemmed from his ownership of the Rosebud Bar, where he and Joplin routinely played piano. The block-long Rosebud allowed a patron to pursue a variety of interests, whether dining, drinking, playing cards, or playing piano—and the rooms upstairs guaranteed further illicit behavior. For piano players, however, the magnetism of the Rosebud derived solely from the ragtime emanating from its walls.

Despite the obvious musical charms of St. Louis, Joplin—for reasons not entirely clear—moved to Sedalia, a railroad town in the middle of Missouri. Although St. Louis or Chicago would have offered more business opportunities for a young composer, Sedalia drew Joplin in. He soon published two original compositions through local distributors in 1895—"Please Say You Will" and "A Picture of Her Face." Although not technically ragtime—neither tune featured a syncopated construction—these pieces helped introduce Joplin to the commercial side of songwriting.[15] Now a published composer, Joplin still spent a considerable amount of his time playing in clubs throughout the area, including the recently opened Black 400 and Maple Leaf clubs.[16] In 1898, Tony Williams, a vaudeville performer, opened the Black 400 Club in an attempt to provide respectable entertainment for Sedalia's black community. A short time later, the brother partnership of Walker and Will Williams (two men unrelated to the director of the Black 400) inaugurated the Maple Leaf Club, further expanding the black performance options in the city.[17] Within a year the two clubs came under attack by the black religious community as well as local law enforcement officials, and in two separate arrests, city officials charged both Tony Williams and Walker Williams with selling unlicensed liquor. In early 1900 Sedalia officials closed down the two clubs.[18] Ragtime, of course, did not encourage club owners to use shady business practices, but social critics tended to lump the music into an insalubrious category of vice and cultural degradation. Burdened with this inauspicious history, the Maple Leaf Club would achieve some amount of prominence years later as the titular inspiration for one of Joplin's more enduring rag compositions.

During his tenure as club entertainer in Sedalia, Joplin wrote a number of rags and attempted to publish at least three compositions in 1898.[19] Carl Hoffman, a music publisher in Kansas City, bought "Oriental Rags" from Joplin in 1899, but it was Joplin's second published rag that would have a national impact. Joplin's "Maple Leaf Rag"—the title a gesture to his friends in Sedalia—both summed up ragtime's past and pointed toward a more complex future. Joplin used an established ragtime structure but also modified certain elements of the rag; specifically, he lopped off the standard introduction and launched directly into the unambiguous syncopation of the first strain.[20] Joplin's "Maple Leaf Rag" reflected a much more complex and mannered structure. The piece boasted a strong melody, evident from the beginning, but the rhythmic pulse of the song was more pronounced and central to the mood of the composition.[21] A further change in structure concerned Joplin's addition of a fourth strain (most other rags contained only three), and as with the greater syncopated intricacy of the rag, this subtle variation made "Maple Leaf Rag" familiar to listeners and also fascinatingly new. The result cemented his growing reputation as a ragtime piano player, brought him a steady royalty-based income, and eventually made him famous.

Joplin may have written "Maple Leaf Rag," but music publisher John Stark made it a sensation. Writers have often blurred the circumstances behind the first meeting between Joplin and Stark perhaps in order to preserve the supposed artistic integrity of the piano player. The most popular story maintains that Stark, in search of a beer, stumbled upon Joplin midway through the performance of "Maple Leaf Rag." This romanticized tale (with its explicit rejection of commercial motives) notwithstanding, Joplin more likely sought out the publisher in an attempt to increase potential sales.[22] However the two men met, Stark agreed to publish the piece and signed Joplin to a five-year contract in 1900. In addition to giving the piano player a publishing outlet, the contract provided Joplin with a royalty claim of one cent for each copy sold. Negligible as it may seem, Joplin's royalty agreement with Stark represented a major advance over the standard practice of extending black songwriters no more than a flat fee.[23] Of course, this royalty arrangement would grant Joplin only a symbolic victory if the rag had not sold well. Within a few years, not only did "Maple Leaf Rag" rack up sales, it came to embody all of the definitive attributes of ragtime music. "Maple Leaf Rag" was Joplin's most popular piece during his life, and music dealers sold several thousand copies of the piece each month.[24] By 1909, Joplin earned roughly $600 annually from the royalties of that composition alone.[25]

After the publication of "Maple Leaf Rag," Joplin continued to compose and entertain. Over the next few years he wrote a number of tunes that would later become ragtime standards—including "Elite Syncopations" and "The Entertainer"—but he was never able to duplicate his earlier success. After perfecting a short-form style of ragtime, Joplin committed himself to a large-scale "ragtime opera" entitled *Treemonisha*. An ambitious, if ultimately unsuccessful, composition, *Treemonisha* only contributed to Joplin's personal and financial dilemmas as he devoted all of his energies to this one work. Furthering Joplin's problems, the public clamored for "ragtime songs" instead of the richly textured rags that he composed. The confusing nature of this ragtime syntax relates to the somewhat arbitrary use of the term "ragtime" as well as the existence of two distinctive styles. Joplin composed "classic ragtime," a primarily piano-based music, but many music publishers also produced "ragtime song," a genre connected closely to Tin Pan Alley, the center of the music publishing business in New York City. Related only ostensibly to the music Joplin produced, ragtime songs discovered a much larger audience by combining lyrics to a simplified ragtime beat.[26] Many of these songs—written mainly by white musicians— also incorporated some of the racist imagery of minstrel songs. Ragtime songs emphasized lyrical content and entertainment over technical proficiency or instrumental prowess; thus, the greatest success of the ragtime era proved not to be "Maple Leaf Rag" but "Dill Pickles," a song that attracted an audience because it was "noisy, easy, and great fun to play fast."[27] The sensation caused by ragtime song unleashed a myriad of compositions throughout the 1910s that made commercial ragtime the most popular music of the period. In general, this period witnessed the promotion of a music with explicitly black origins finding genuine, if limited, success. White sheet-music publishers exaggerated the syncopated nature of the music to the point of novelty, added racially skewed artwork or lyrics, and found, for a few years anyway, a massive white audience across the nation— a pattern of cultural absorption that would be repeated in different contexts throughout the twentieth century from jazz to rock 'n' roll to hip-hop.

As Americans obsessed over ragtime song, Joplin's health and career began to decline. Misfortune added to misfortune when the piano player contracted syphilis, which bankrupted both his finances and physical energy and forced him into various hospitals throughout the early months of

1917. Scott Joplin died that April, and his death coincided with the end of ragtime's decade of glory—the waning of a music that he had almost single-handedly created. The composer's last printed rag, "Magnetic Rag," appeared in 1914 when the country was beginning to pick up on a stylized form of the blues. And two months before his death, the Original Dixieland Jazz Band, a group of white musicians, entered a Victor Records studio and recorded "Livery Stable Blues," one of the first songs expressly marketed as jazz. Joplin may not have recognized the music as having anything to do with his compositions—in many ways, it connected more to the hokum passed off as ragtime song—but ragtime music helped provide early jazz with a strong rhythmic form. Many musicians remembered the composer, but the listening public and, significantly, the black community, looked elsewhere for entertainment and inspiration. A modern, urban triumph for a few short years, ragtime seemed hopelessly old-fashioned and obsolete by the late 1910s.

Ragtime's popularity peaked between the years 1897 and 1917, and a number of technological and business changes—along with larger historical developments in the country—made ragtime a national musical phenomenon. Manufacturers of musical instruments took advantage of new construction techniques to reach a larger group of consumers. Piano production in particular increased dramatically after the Civil War, and by the 1920s American businesses produced roughly 400,000 of the instruments each year. New business practices increased the supply of instruments and helped create a nation of piano-owning families. The introduction of a corporate-centered business model in America had obvious effects on industrialization and national economics, but this production-based system also played an important role in the construction of a new musical culture. Ragtime composers understandably garnered new business, and music-publishing companies began producing large amounts of sheet music to attract the amateur musician. At the center of this potentially lucrative commercial situation stood the vaudeville stage. This particular brand of late-nineteenth-century American theater served as a key marketing tool for a number of publishing houses. Audiences would go to the theater and hear new ragtime compositions performed by traveling musicians. Local stores would then advertise these new songs in the hope of enticing a few pennies away from this burgeoning nation of piano enthusiasts.[28]

More than simply capitalizing on a musical trend, the association between vaudeville and ragtime had important social implications as well, especially in terms of vaudeville's use of minstrelsy. As ragtime rhythms infused national entertainment, American race relations reached their nadir as the Supreme Court codified Jim Crow in the *Plessy v. Ferguson* decision in 1896, a year before the appearance of the first printed rag. This backdrop of racial antagonism and confusion provided the social context for ragtime, especially as the music filtered through minstrel performers on the vaudeville stage. One of the most popular forms of entertainment in the nineteenth century, minstrel shows offered predominantly male audiences a bawdy form of musical theater. The shows—typically housed in saloons—featured singing, dancing, and a number of short skits often centered on stereotypical accounts of the actions and language of black Americans. Throughout the early 1800s, white performers blackened their faces and delivered parodies of black life in America, portraying African Americans as buffoons and clowns. These crude impressions became refined throughout the first half of the century, and by the Civil War these false stage images became the most popular representation of black people. Further complicating matters, black musicians and actors found employment in minstrel shows and followed stage conventions and their white counterparts by blackening their faces with cork and exaggerated their lips with grease paint. The appearance of black actors and musicians on stage seemingly mocking their own race affected white audience members, many of whom (especially in the North) had little contact with black people in real life. These stereotypes would dramatically influence race relations during the late nineteenth century, as many white people viewed African Americans as Zip Coons and Uncle Toms instead of human beings.[29] Ragtime's popularity had unmistakable roots in minstrel performance, and this taint of blackface infected public debate over the music. Although direct connections do not necessarily exist between the music played in minstrel shows and ragtime and the blues, this nexus of racist comedy, blackface caricature, and musical entertainment would impact the reception of newer musical forms. Minstrelsy's insistence on representative duality (with the boundaries of racial identities intentionally smudged) also foreshadowed W. E. B. Du Bois's concept of "double consciousness" and the modern age of identity confusion.[30]

During the late nineteenth century, vaudeville cast off some of the coarser elements of the skits and toned down the overt racism of its comedy—while retaining the "coon songs" and the blackface buffoonery—to produce a more refined entertainment spectacle. The changes attracted larger, more diverse crowds and vaudeville quickly replaced minstrelsy as America's most popular form of public leisure. Vaudeville shows represented a more genteel form of entertainment, with gilded theaters replacing malodorous saloons, and these new shows brought more women and children to the performances than did minstrels. Commerce trumped racial ideology as large profits confirmed vaudeville's success. Theater owners realized that by omitting the more outrageous racial elements they could reach a much larger potential audience (especially by designating segregated sections in the theater). This shift from the lewd to the more conspicuous lured more black musicians and actors to the stage, granting employment opportunities for black actors and musicians to a larger degree than had minstrelsy. One of the largest vaudeville organizations had a chain of roughly four hundred theaters spread throughout the East and Midwest by the onset of World War I. A network of vaudeville theaters provided a large number of Americans with the opportunity to hear some form of ragtime music across the nation. Although not yet mass culture—a situation only made possible through large-scale mechanically reproduced distribution methods—ragtime music had the ability to reach more people in more places than any previous type of music.[31]

This web of vaudeville theater chains emerged when it did because of a large number of advancements made in both transportation and the corporate world during the late nineteenth century. As railroads increasingly connected cities and businesses learned efficiency, more and more Americans came into contact with the same product. The railroad allowed musicians to travel farther and more quickly than before, contributing to the dynamic nature of vaudeville shows. Minstrel shows rarely changed and had a small travel circuit. Vaudeville, in contrast, could attract larger audiences because they offered much more diversity and a quicker turnaround in acts. In addition, vaudeville offered vast opportunities for music publishers to hawk their wares as the recent flood of vaudeville musicians demanded fresh material.[32] Commerce merged with art as a sizable group of amateur musicians—including women, who rarely went to minstrel shows—heard ragtime on the vaudeville stage and then went out and purchased ragtime sheet music. The advent of chain stores strengthened this arrangement and increased the availability of sheet music for customers. Vaudeville presented new rags to the audience every few weeks, and chain stores then sold the listeners the sheet music for those songs. This combination of vaudeville theater and music publishing allowed ragtime to flourish, providing musicians with fairly steady employment and encouraging the popularity of ragtime. Although limited in size and scope in comparison to the record, radio, and film industries of the 1920s, music publishing generated a national audience for ragtime, especially as vaudeville saturated America.[33]

Although relatively few academic writers have focused on the development of ragtime, the blues has generated a complex and dynamic historiography as literary critics analyzed lyrics, scholars of race and ethnicity placed the blues within the framework of modern black identity, ethnomusicologists discussed the compositional mechanics and improvised nature of the music, and cultural historians argued about how the spirit and contours of the blues mirror American society generally. Unlike ragtime, however, with its relatively clear musical origins, the history of the blues remains hidden behind a shadowy curtain of rumor and speculation supported by scant documentary evidence. Nonetheless, sometime in the 1890s a new style of music emerged from the rural South. African American in origin, this music had its rhythmic and lyrical antecedents in work songs, slave tunes, ballads, and spirituals, musical forms with a heritage of African tribal songs and rituals. Work songs, in particular, had a tremendous effect on what would become the blues as later musicians adopted the improvised call-and-response introduced by the style.[34] These work songs received no musical accompaniment save for the blow of the hammer or stroke of the axe; in the evenings, black southerners used these songs as a form of leisure entertainment. "Somehow, somewhere," James Collier writes, "there began to grow out of this leisure music a new form, one more strict than the work song, whose function was to talk about the things that a working man or woman felt about his or her life."[35] Work songs and the blues retained an intersecting thematic and compositional devices, and the blues incorporated many of the feelings, values, and musical constructions inherent in work songs.[36] More important, like work songs, blues music related directly to the experience of black people in America. Although a predominantly African American music, writers in the last half of the twentieth century usually connected ragtime (especially in its more popular, Tin Pan Alley incarnation) with white listeners. The lyrical format of ragtime song, composed predominantly by white songwriters, contrasted with the primarily instrumental structure of classic ragtime. Thus, the relationship between classic ragtime and the African American experience remained somewhat obfuscated. In contrast, the blues—regardless of form—maintained a close affiliation with the black community.[37] Black musicians created ragtime, but the music spoke to the black community in limited terms. Born in the fields, the blues maintained a closeness and proximity to black life in the early twentieth century.

Complicating the early history of the blues is the division that scholars have determined for the styles that surfaced in the early twentieth century, a delineation not unlike that between piano ragtime and ragtime song: classic (or vaudeville) blues and country (or "downhome") blues. Classic blues (which emerged in some measure from the stage songs of vaudeville acts and both black and white minstrel performances) were much more formalized than the country blues and became quite popular in the early 1920s through the recordings of Bessie Smith, Ma Rainey, Ethel Waters, and Mamie Smith among others. This style of the blues incorporated band arrangements and was grounded in a long history of showmanship and public entertainment. The country blues, in contrast, featured more improvisation and maintained a less structured form. Associated primarily with solo performers (usually on guitar), this music emphasized the emotional nature of the blues. The lack of a band allowed for a more extemporaneous structure, and solo blues performers could stretch and mutate the beat freely without making concessions to other musicians. This style had strongly gendered implications—men generally performed country blues and women typically sang vaudeville blues. Compounding these gender differences, men primarily wrote and performed their own material whereas women usually sang songs written by men. Nonetheless, both classic and country blues shared a common structure with three lines of verse (the second line normally repeating the first line) and twelve-bar stanzas. The beat in these early blues songs fluctuates.[38] The traits that made the blues distinctive—blue notes, a fluctuating rhythm, and a unique vocal performance—could not be adequately notated in printed music.[39] What popularized the blues tended not to be sheet music sales but record sales since the audience preferred an individual performance to an amateur reproduction. Recordings, rather than sheet music, proved to be the medium capable of transmitting the intricacies of blues performances since blue notes and timbre could not be transcribed accurately in print. A nascent recording technology, which would eventually create a national audience for jazz music, provided the blues with a widespread regional prominence at least in black communities.

In 1920, Mamie Smith and Her Jazz Hounds entered an OKeh studio and recorded Perry Bradford's "Crazy Blues"—a recording routinely regarded as the first blues record.[40] Bradford had already published "Crazy Blues" under three different titles for three different companies, but Smith's recording became a hit, selling 75,000 copies in its first month of release. Bradford's song, and in particular Smith's recording of it, introduced America to the classic blues.[41] Recordings allowed listeners to experience a specific performance repeatedly, and the uniqueness of Smith's record attracted a large audience. Somehow an unremarkable, almost formulaic composition, with lyrical connections to vaudeville, came to life in the studio. On the printed page, for example, "Crazy Blues" differed little from other blues-themed songs with its opening lines: "I can't sleep at night / I can't eat a bite." Mamie Smith's voice, however, explodes the boundaries of this song and elevates "Crazy Blues" past minstrelsy cliché and into performance art. Mirroring the growling slur of Dope Andrews's trombone, Smith's voice competes with a whining clarinet for the listener's ear and shatters the relative safety of the printed lyrics. The record attracted audiences not for any inherent compositional exceptionalism but rather because of the audacious timbre of the recording. With ragtime, consumers wanted the notes, the concreteness of the composition. With the blues, however, the raw immediacy of the recording, the emotional nature of the singing, and the blistering near-cacophony of the instruments overshadowed the compositional intentions of the song.

Mamie Smith and Perry Bradford scored a hit, but W. C. Handy stood as the most important figure in popularizing the early blues. A preacher's son from Alabama, Handy saw the pecuniary potential of the blues and almost single-handedly brought an African American folk music to the nation.[42] William Christopher Handy, a trained musician, played the cornet in a number of marching and dance bands and committed himself to performing respectful music. In 1903, however, Handy's attention to classical parlor music drifted toward a rawer, more unkempt sound, when the young musician—then traveling with a minstrel group—happened upon a black guitar player in Tutwiler, Mississippi. While waiting for a long-delayed train, Handy overheard the guitar player singing a song about the "Yellow Dog," the Mississippi colloquialism for the Yazoo-Delta Railroad. "As he played," Handy later noted in his memoirs, "he pressed a knife on the strings of the guitar in a manner popularized by Hawaiian guitarists who used steel bars." This version of the Ur-story of the blues—with its rural (expectant) train, the shock of the new, the aural oddities, the improvisational slant—would be echoed by many other musicians throughout the early history of the genre. Each listener who experienced his or her own personal moment of musical unbelief felt this similar moment of electricity and curiosity. Handy wrote that it was "the weirdest music I had ever heard."[43]

Later, while playing a concert in Cleveland, Mississippi, Handy received a request to allow a local black band to play a few numbers. The band performed an improvised dance tune not far removed from what the Tutwiler guitarist had played, but a less than enthusiastic Handy later wrote that the "strumming attained a disturbing monotony." Once they finished, however, Handy realized that the young band had thoroughly impressed the audience. The dancers began showering the musicians with coins. "A rain of silver dollars began to fall around the outlandish, stomping feet," Handy wrote. "Dollars, quarters, halves—the shower grew heavier and continued so long I strained my neck to get a better look. There before the boys lay more money than my nine musicians were being paid for the entire engagement." He may not have fully appreciated the music performed by the guitar player in Tutwiler or the band in Cleveland, but Handy immediately understood its commercial power. "Then," Handy wrote without irony or self-consciousness, "I saw the beauty of primitive music."[44] Forty years later in his autobiography, Handy wrote in epiphanic terms about the change that occurred in him after witnessing this event. "That night," he wrote, "a composer was born, an *American* composer."[45] With his first tentative steps down the blues road to Damascus via Tutwiler, Handy at the age of thirty fabricated a new career.

In 1909, Handy wrote a piece called "Mr. Crump," a song written ostensibly in support of E. H. Crump's candidacy for mayor in Memphis. The lyrics of the song alluded to problems between the city's black community and the white power structure. Still, Crump (in all probability unaware of the actual lyrics) used the song to court black voters. Handy later altered the song and retitled it "Memphis Blues," a song he claimed "was the first of all the many published 'blues.'" "It set a new fashion," Handy maintained, "in American popular music and contributed to the rise of jazz."[46] For his part, Handy usually did not claim to have invented the blues, only to have popularized it and brought the music to a larger audience— although he did entitle his autobiography *Father of the Blues*. In the 1930s, Jelly Roll Morton, himself the self-proclaimed creator of jazz, would lambaste Handy as a thief, but at least publicly (and Handy, the businessman, was nothing if not conscious of his public persona) Handy argued that he served only as the promoter of the form.[47] Despite questions surrounding his role in its creation, Handy's publications gave the blues an identity firmly grounded in the African American experience. Handy described his blues compositions as an attempt "to combine ragtime syncopation with a real melody in the spiritual tradition."[48] Regardless of these musical motivations, the composer understood and promoted the publication of blues songs as a capitalist venture. In some ways, then, Handy's intentions were not too far removed from Crump's. Handy's music may have had "little, if anything, to do with legitimate [downhome] blues," as Amiri Baraka pointedly argued, but by refining the idiosyncrasies of the country blues and standardizing its form, he made it palatable to a white audience eager to pay for the experience.[49] As with ragtime, the commercial possibilities and a desire to capitalize on them led to changes in the musical form.

Handy's "Memphis Blues" established the popular blues form, but Handy's largest success, and the song most associated with the musician, was "St. Louis Blues." In a sense the song represented to the blues what Joplin's "Maple Leaf Rag" represented to ragtime—the one composition that would define both a style and a career. Handy completed "St. Louis Blues" in 1914, two years after publishing "Memphis Blues." The song had an unusual arrangement and, in some ways, "St. Louis Blues" has more explicit compositional ties to ragtime than to the country blues.[50] The song is far removed from the Mississippi Delta—the guitar player in Tutwiler would probably not even recognize "St. Louis Blues" as having anything in common with his own songs—but in a sense, that confirmed Handy's objective.[51] Though later blues purists would dismiss this intention in Handy's work, the composer consistently argues in his autobiography that he endeavored to make the blues respectable. A businessman and entertainer, Handy wrote the song with the public (essentially the white dancing public) in mind, and the composition hit big. It sold well on its own as sheet music, but various recordings of the tune extended its reach. In fact, by 1925, at least five full-band versions could be purchased. In 1916, the Prince Orchestra recorded the song as an instrumental, and three years later, singer Al Bernard released the first vocal rendition of the song. Unlike the sheet music–driven ragtime craze, the recording industry fueled the nation's infatuation with the blues. By the early 1920s, Victrolas had begun to seep into the marketplace, allowing these early blues records to amass a large number of willing listeners. Again, like ragtime, the most popular blues pieces tended toward vaudeville, but the success of Handy and others underscored the emergent scope of the entertainment industry.[52] Early copies of

Handy's "St. Louis Blues," for example, clearly labeled it "the most widely known ragtime composition," underscoring the conflation and obfuscation of two distinct genres that emerged from the African American musical community.[53]

The vast number of available blues recordings tends to obscure the role ragtime played in the creation of jazz. As the less noisy cousin of the blues, ragtime failed to sustain much popularity after World War I. The near disappearance of true ragtime after World War I and the increased appearance of the blues through phonograph records helped to skew the historical record. Furthermore, outside of Joplin and a few others, the popular rags of the day tended to be composed by white musicians for Tin Pan Alley. Part of the racial, social, and musical confusion stems from the promotional labels applied to different pieces of music, and music marketers routinely shoehorned songs into vaguely defined categories. Many jazz songs, for example, were sold as rags, and a number of titular blues pieces were essentially pop songs. Likewise, the distinction between blues singers and jazz singers proved to be considerably subjective in terms of marketing. As the issue of race clouded the history of jazz, a number of scholars wrote ragtime out of the narrative. Amiri Baraka, for example, declared ragtime "a pitiful popular debasement that was the rage of the country for about twenty years," implying that the blues connected directly to the black experience whereas ragtime served the needs of white music entrepreneurs.[54] Activists attempting to promote jazz as primarily black in origin found a supporter in Gunther Schuller, a prominent white musicologist who published *Early Jazz* in the late 1960s. "Every musical element [of jazz]," Schuller contends, "is essentially African in background."[55] By defining jazz as quintessentially African, these writers have removed the idea of cultural collaboration that represents one of the most remarkable aspects of early jazz. "Ragtime music," music historian Ted Gioia writes, "rivals the blues in importance — and perhaps surpasses it in influence — as a predecessor to early jazz."[56] Even writers who acknowledge ragtime's importance tend to do so somewhat tentatively. Jazz epitomizes the convergence of black and white culture as the ragtime elements of harmony and composition merged with the timbre, syncopation, and improvisational qualities of the blues to produce a uniquely American form of musical expression.

The piano player and composer Jelly Roll Morton, for example, defies easy classification and illustrates the arbitrary rigidity of defining the different styles that emerged in the early twentieth century. Although

Morton's legacy collars him as a jazz artist, the pianist played all genres of music, including ragtime, the blues, and popular songs, as well as jazz. He serves as a reminder that the creation of jazz was not a singular event nor did the music follow a straight developmental trajectory from one particular source.[57] As if to underscore this very point, Morton performed Joplin's "Maple Leaf Rag" as a rag, as blues, and as jazz for Alan Lomax in the 1930s. Morton's discourse may have lacked historical accuracy as he tended to equate ragtime only with fast tempos when Joplin, in particular, preferred slower tempos marked accordingly on his piano rolls.[58] Still, by slowing down the tempo dramatically and incorporating trills, blue notes, and glissandos, Morton underscored the seeds of jazz with a musical form that entwined blues timbre with ragtime syncopation. Always mindful of his place in jazz history, Morton maintained that he had invented out of whole cloth this new style of playing. Morton's bravado notwithstanding, the piano player illustrates the connections between seemingly disparate styles of music. Translating urban America into a rhythmically inventive compositional form, ragtime performers created a music that reflected the superficial verve and excitement of industrial growth in the late nineteenth century. In contrast, the blues fused a striking emphasis on timbre with a rural identity rooted in the lives of southern African Americans. Together, as Jelly Roll Morton implicitly understood, these musical idioms anticipated the artistic innovation and national popularity of jazz music.

During the period that Americans embraced ragtime and the blues, a new, yet related, form of music—eventually known as jazz—began to percolate out of the South. Both ragtime and the blues prefigured the syncopated rhythms and harmonic construction of the jazz music of the 1920s. Also, the commercial elements of ragtime and the blues, though somewhat limited to the sale of sheet music, piano rolls, and phonograph records, would provide a market context for jazz. This profitability would soon characterize jazz music, but ragtime and the blues existed apart from the national commercial culture that developed alongside jazz in the 1920s. Whereas the ragtime and blues crazes proved to be short-lived, the popularity of jazz came to parallel the national tenor of American life in the 1920s. Although certain precursors of jazz appeared throughout the United States, it was in New Orleans that the music found a home. By the late 1920s jazz had infiltrated most of urban America, but in New Orleans in the early 1900s musicians such as Jelly Roll Morton conjured up a music unlike anything Americans had encountered before.

2 New Orleans and the Creation of Early Jazz

In early 1938, Jelly Roll Morton, self-proclaimed "Originator of Jazz and Stomps" and "World's Greatest Hot Tune Writer," wrote a rambling letter to the jazz magazine, *Down Beat,* announcing that "New Orleans is the cradle of jazz, and I, myself, happened to be the creator [of jazz] in the year 1902." This year-specific boast had as its impetus an episode of Robert Ripley's popular *Believe It or Not* radio series that claimed W. C. Handy as the "originator of jazz and the blues." Full of vitriol, Morton's letter was an attempt by the New Orleans piano player to place his hometown (and himself) at the center of the creation of jazz. "My contributions were many," Morton wrote, "first clown director, with witty sayings and flashily dressed, now called master of ceremonies; first glee club in orchestra; the first washboard was recorded by me; bass fiddle, drums—which were supposed to be impossible to record."[1] He even claimed to have invented the style of playing drums with brushes instead of sticks. A critique of Handy coursed through the letter, and Morton claimed that Handy's "Memphis Blues" borrowed (or stole) heavily from one of Jelly Roll's own compositions. A controversial letter in jazz circles, Morton's not entirely unfounded rant inspired a folklorist working for the Library of Congress to contact the pianist for a series of interviews.[2]

Conducted over the course of four weeks that May, Alan Lomax's interviews with Morton represented the first extensive oral history of

New Orleans jazz. In these interviews, Morton's well-lubricated narrative (Lomax provided the alcohol) is interspersed with random piano chords that accompanied the musician's dubious story of the creation of jazz. Several years later, Lomax published these reminiscences in a book entitled *Mister Jelly Roll.* A braggart and a pimp, Morton also was one of the first real composers of jazz music, and his career points to the large variety of musical antecedents of jazz as well as the importance of New Orleans, the most cosmopolitan of southern towns, to the creation of the music. Boasting a diverse lineage of French, Spanish, African, and Caribbean influences, New Orleans also developed a complex social order of white, black, and Creole residents. Each of these groups maintained unique—if related—musical performance styles and took advantage of the large number of various venues that dominated and defined the city. Although other cities maintained dynamic musical scenes, only New Orleans fostered an environment that encouraged rapid musical fusion and evolution within the span of a few years at the dawn of the twentieth century. Or as Jelly Roll Morton remarked to Alan Lomax during one of his interviews, "I thought New Orleans was the whole world."[3]

Born Ferdinand Joseph LaMothe in 1890, Jelly Roll Morton constantly changed his name, family history, and date of birth throughout his career to provide evidence of his role in the creation of jazz music.[4] The trickster hero of early jazz, Morton persistently presented himself as the founding father of jazz music. As a New Orleans Creole with an African American heritage, Morton lived and worked within the fluid middle community of the city. This environment obviously affected the musician, who throughout his interviews with Alan Lomax discoursed regularly about his ancestry and racial identity. Morton's own name underscores the diversity of his Creole existence as well as the importance of self-invention even in the early years of jazz. His given name, LaMenthe or LaMothe, relates directly to his French ancestry, and Morton often referenced and emphasized this fact. In one interview with Lomax, for example, the piano player avers, "Of course, I guess you wonder how the name Morton come in. Why, the name Morton being a English name, it wouldn't sound very much like a French name. But my real name is Ferdinand Lamothe."[5] Overall, his invented sobriquet belies his mixed ancestry as well as his determination to project himself as American, rather than some specific ethnic group. He muted the French overtones of LaMothe with the less foreign-sounding Morton, but his acquired first name connects back to his undeniable African ancestry.[6]

Replacing Ferdinand—a reference to the king of Spain—with Jelly Roll, Morton chose a name ripe with sexual connotations that relates clearly to the African American vernacular. A number of blues songs employ the term "jelly roll" in reference to both the sexual organ (of men and women) as well as to the act of sexual intercourse itself. Morton also referred to himself as the "winin' boy," an epithet that connotes someone with a prodigious sexual appetite.[7] A blend of cosmopolitan pretension and sexual innuendo, Morton created a new American identity that blurred certain components of his ancestry while implicitly stressing other, more desirable features.

Just as his invented name compounded black and white cultures, Morton's music borrowed liberally from a variety of diverse sources. Morton's main innovation concerned the merging of ragtime syncopation with the tonalities and harmonies of the blues.[8] Improvisation played a role in Morton's music, but the piano player also liked the written composition. Seemingly informal, Morton's music was based on a complex understanding of rhythm, melody, and harmony. The Creole musician borrowed from a variety of styles, including Latin American music, which he referred to as the "Spanish tinge" in his songs. Still, his sound remained rooted in the basic ragtime and blues arrangements of Scott Joplin and W. C. Handy. One influence on Morton's musical synthesis was the number of piano players active in New Orleans, especially in the area known as Storyville, the local vice district where Morton professed to have found employment in 1902 (when he was twelve years old).[9] Though perhaps the most infamous area of late-nineteenth-century New Orleans, the connection of Storyville to jazz history remains rather elusive. Early jazz scholars tended to overemphasize the role of the district perhaps because of a salacious interest in whorehouse jazz, but also because many early jazz musicians cited the area as a place known for jazz performance.[10] Although few if any jazz bands actually played in the district—due to limited sizes of venues, noise restrictions, and lack of available monetary compensation—solo piano players, including Morton's mentor Tony Jackson, certainly found some employment opportunities at various brothels. Despite the exaggerated descriptions of Storyville in jazz historiography, the district and the city of New Orleans served as an urban catalyst for the development of jazz music.

New Orleans played a rather unusual role as the first "jazz city." Although both Chicago and New York would produce jazz scenes that depended on an urban culture, New Orleans jazz never developed a strong urban identity. Vague divisions defined much of the culture in New Orleans, with race serving as the visible marker of these boundaries. The racial classifications in the city were clouded by a middle grouping of Creoles. A port city in a state with a complex history affected by international imperialism, New Orleans differed from most other southern cities by maintaining a diverse, cosmopolitan, and racially mixed population. In 1900, New Orleans stood as the twelfth-largest city in the nation with just over 287,000 inhabitants, 27 percent of whom were considered black.[11] These numbers, however, obfuscate the racial and ethnic groupings of the city. In broad strokes, three basic groups of people lived in New Orleans: white citizens from a variety of ethnic and religious backgrounds; English-speaking, predominantly Protestant, black Americans; and a middle group of French-speaking, mostly Catholic, Creoles. The general fan-shaped geography of the city—bordered to the north by Lake Pontchartrain and to the south by the Mississippi River (which runs roughly northwest to southeast near the city)—gave physical markers for the neighborhoods in which these groups were concentrated. Most Creoles, for example, resided southeast of Canal Street in the downtown area whereas the majority of the African American community lived west of Canal Street in the uptown area of the city. Many ethnic whites lived parallel to the river near the Magazine Street area. Wealthy whites lived primarily on or near St. Charles Avenue in the Garden District.[12] "The city was split by Canal Street," Creole guitarist Danny Barker remembers, "with one part of the people uptown and the Creoles downtown." Despite this geographical arrangement, the three-tiered divisions of New Orleans provided the city with a remarkable degree of racial fluidity, mitigating at least in part the strictures placed on southern society by Jim Crow. The complex mixture of New Orleans society with its white, black, and Creole identities; European, African, and Caribbean influences; and Catholic, Protestant, and non-Christian worship practices contributed to the musical culture of a cosmopolitan city still heavily connected to a rural existence. Although race constituted a major defining issue dividing blacks, whites, and Creoles, the other issues of class, background, and religion played an equally important role in the stratification of New Orleans society. Race, however, played only a partial role in differentiating the groups as class, social background, education, and religion all played roles in constituting the middle ground between black and white.[13]

Unique in its demographic composition, the city's Creole community existed in between urban and rural society, providing an opportunity for the development of a varied and distinct culture.[14] Perhaps the most complicated (and controversial) aspect of New Orleans history concerned the definition and role of the Creole community. Embracing a variety of working definitions, the term "Creole" relates to descendents of three groups: first-generation French and Spanish settlers (nonracial heritage); the small nonslave portion of black Louisianans (racial, nonmixed heritage); and the children born out of the union of French or Spanish men and Louisianan black women (racial, mixed heritage).[15] Each of these definitions has been the focus of debate throughout the state's history, but by the late nineteenth century, the third category, centered on the idea of a racially mixed identity, had the largest social impact on the eventual creation of jazz music. A complex jumble of cosmopolitan pretensions and rural ancestry, Creole society provided a cultural synthesis as the improvised rural blues of black Americans merged with the harmonic structure of urban American song to produce a new musical form.[16]

If Creoles associated themselves with Europe and a cosmopolitan lifestyle, then African Americans related more to former slave culture, the rural region of the Mississippi Delta, and, to some degree, the continent of Africa itself. In large measure, rural society and experience proved rather indissoluble, and many African Americans identified more readily as rural white immigrants than black Creoles. Most southern cities during this period existed somewhere along this rural–urban continuum with a permeable boundary distorting the difference between city and countryside. The unique racial divisions of New Orleans, however, amplified this rural identity, allowing for a diversity uncommon in other cities. These various divisions played out in a number of ways, but in terms of the creation of jazz music this rural–urban dichotomy allowed for a wide range of related and contradictory musical influences to permeate the city. Connecting this rural identity to the musical culture of the city, Burton Peretti argues that jazz facilitated the urbanization of rural Americans, as its attendant "male-oriented jazz fraternity" served as "a mechanism for socializing young migrants to new urban ways."[17] "By 1917," he continues, "New Orleans jazz signified, among other things, a conjunction of rural and urban culture, Africa and Europe, individual skill and communal fraternization, Protestant and Creole sensibilities, and the violent past and an encouraging future."[18] This intricate array of identities created a unique cultural environment in New Orleans, the city that came to represent a microcosm of late-nineteenth-century American musical trends.

Early jazz in New Orleans served a variety of functions unlike what developed later in the 1920s when jazz primarily served the needs of dancers and record buyers. New Orleans musicians performed for private parties, dances, funerals, marches, and other informal events in bars and honky-tonks. Although the settings differed, in general New Orleans jazz signified a compromise somewhere between the folk dynamics of the blues and the commercial leanings of ragtime. Jazz was not purely "folk music"—early jazz musicians performed for paying audiences not entirely composed of their own specific social and class groups.[19] Yet jazz also failed to be defined simply as commercial music. The ragtime songs of Tin Pan Alley, for example, existed in order for music publishers to sell sheet music, and the music played an essential role in the process of commercialization. Early jazz, however, sold no such products and was still inherently limited to the groups—black, white, and Creole—that produced the music. Not quite folk, not quite commercial, New Orleans jazz can be more easily understood as an example of a music produced outside the framework of mass culture. Not preserved on record or in print, and not transmitted through radio, early jazz maintained the identity of the groups from which it originated. In this way, New Orleans jazz related more to the blues improvisations of the Mississippi Delta than the jazz heard on the radio in the 1920s. This blending of folk music and commercialism characterized early jazz at its creation as a number of New Orleans musicians began adapting and transforming ragtime, the blues, music for dancing, and music for marching into something unique to the city.[20]

The careers of three local musicians—Alphonse Picou, Jack Laine, and Buddy Bolden—demonstrate the racial, social, cultural, and musical differences represented in the New Orleans scene in the late nineteenth century and serve as reminders that jazz emerged from a variety of sources. Alphonse Picou, a Creole clarinetist, signified the important role Creole musicians played in New Orleans as well as the often-ambiguous boundaries between classical music, ragtime, and the blues. "Papa" Jack Laine, a white bandleader and entrepreneur, helped structure and popularize white brass bands in the city. And Charles "Buddy" Bolden, a black trumpet player, prefigured the age of the soloist and serves as perhaps the most significant figure in the prehistory of New Orleans jazz. Together, the careers of these musicians underscore the diversity of both New Orleans society and its jazz scene. No single New Orleans musician created jazz—though not a few have claimed to have done so—but the city did foster a fertile environment for musical development and presented a microcosm of late-nineteenth-century music. Jazz, the modernist soundtrack of the 1920s, originated in turn-of-the-century New Orleans, and this new, weird noise had as its antecedents the primeval rhythms and myths of southern Louisiana.

Born in 1878 in New Orleans, Alphonse Picou played in a variety of brass bands throughout his career in the city. What differentiated Picou from other musicians in the area (and certainly compared to later jazz players) was his musical training. As a teenager in the Creole neighborhood of the city's Seventh Ward, Picou began to practice the clarinet and maintained a confidence and pride in his music-reading abilities throughout his life. "The ability to read and write music and [the] accuracy and finesse that went with it," Picou maintained, "was highly valued by the old musicians."[21] As a trained musician (he notes in one interview that he "took lessons for about eighteen months"), Picou gravitated to more formalized music and often had problems improvising during performances. Writer Charles Hersch, in his discussion of the role of music within Creole culture, underscores the degree to which improvisation was "unfamiliar" to Picou and other Creoles in the city. "Playing without music," Hersch quotes Picou as saying, "was a very new style to me. I think it was impossible to me! It seemed a sort of style without notes."[22] Picou's career illustrates some of the parameters of the Creole musical tradition in New Orleans during the late nineteenth century—his adherence to reading and practice, but also the balancing of a music career with a day job (in his case, tinsmithing).[23] The hybridity of his career and the hybridity of his influences illustrate the social world that made Alphonse Picou such a transitional figure within the eventual creation of jazz.

As a light-skinned Creole, Picou experienced the racial and social fluidity that marked New Orleans during this period. This mixed background provided Picou with a number of opportunities in New Orleans as he played with both black and Creole ensembles. In addition to his ability to navigate racial lines, three foundational moments illustrate the centrality of Picou's contributions to the early narrative of jazz history. First, Picou knew and apparently performed with Buddy Bolden, the enigmatic cornet player. In an interview with Alan Lomax, Picou insists that when he played with Bolden "we never did use a piece of music at all"—an obvious moment of pride for the improvisationally challenged clarinetist.[24] The second moment involved his clarinet solo on "High Society," a march tune written by Porter Steele. Recognized by many jazz historians throughout the twentieth century as one of the central evolutionary transitions from brass band/ragtime music to identifiable jazz, Picou's solo was actually the transcription of a piccolo solo. The piece became synonymous with Picou and was one of the most recognizable solos of early jazz.[25] The third moment relates to Picou's discovery of the blues and his subsequent interaction with the black culture of New Orleans.[26] With its use of ambiguous intonation and improvisation, the blues idiom represented a sound far removed from the sheet music of Picou's brass band training. Yet, this combination of brass band composition and blues tonality would make a tremendous impact on the development of jazz.[27]

Whereas Picou's career spoke to the relative fluidity of life as a Creole, Jack Laine's experiences attest to the exceedingly more capacious boundaries affecting white New Orleans. Born in 1873, George Vital "Papa Jack" Laine represents the most important and influential white musician performing in nineteenth-century New Orleans. Sometimes referred to as the "father of white jazz," Laine served less as a jazz innovator than a musical organizer. Although not based in improvisation, Laine's brass bands provided white New Orleanians (and some lighter-skinned Creoles) opportunities to learn an instrument as well as acquaint themselves with a repertoire of marching band standards. Practically every major white New Orleans jazz musician of the 1910s and 1920s fulfilled tenure in one of Laine's bands, creating a legacy of brass band performance and instruction in early jazz. An entrepreneur, Laine organized as many as five different bands all under the "Reliance" moniker, a system that allowed Laine to employ groups throughout the city for a variety of events.[28] These brass bands performed a wide range of material—religious songs, minstrel songs, and ragtime songs—for a variety of events—parades, civic ceremonies, dances, community concerts, and funerals. Many American cities had brass bands, but few communities rivaled New Orleans in terms of size and available venues for music. "The key factor," Thomas Hennessey notes, "was simply the size of New Orleans that allowed it to support many competing brass bands instead of just one or two community groups."[29] The city's size and diversity allowed for Laine's success, too, as he found it commercially viable to disperse four or five bands throughout different areas of New Orleans. Laine's bands represent the strongest link between the brass bands of the nineteenth century and the early jazz of the early twentieth century.

The Reliance bands led by Laine corresponded with a larger tradition of public entertainment found in American cities, especially in late-nineteenth-century New Orleans.[30] Brass bands, usually associated with the military, appeared in cities and towns throughout America in the late 1700s, but the "golden age of brass bands" occurred a century later and lasted roughly from 1880 to the early 1900s.[31] Laine created the first Reliance band in the early 1890s. Maintaining a membership of about ten players, brass bands like the Reliance provided early jazz with several qualities that would come to define in part this new style of music. The instrumentation of brass ensembles, for example, with their line-up of cornets, trombones, baritone horns, clarinets, tuba, and percussion, served as the template for later jazz bands.[32] Brass bands usually performed with military-style outdoor instruments—horns with larger tubing and wider, deeper mouthpieces—allowing for more volume and range.[33] Later jazz musicians adopted these outdoor instruments, partly due to their apprenticeship with them in marching bands as well as their brash noisiness. The members of brass bands relied on the bandleader to teach the material through rehearsals rather than sheet music.[34] These bands played arrangements rather than purely improvised pieces, but this method of instruction would allow jazz bands to rehearse a tune and at the same time establish a precise pattern of short solos and accompaniment. This teaching style also underscores the importance of ensemble playing in the city. The cornet player, for example, might spell out the melody, but the harmonies and counterpoint of the ensemble were just as significant. These ensemble arrangements featuring light syncopation, melodic counterpoint, and harmonic overtones rarely included extended solos, improvised or not. The collective sound of the band, in other words, took precedence over individual performances, and although some of Laine's players went on to become important soloists, the bandleader always emphasized the collective components of his bands.[35]

Although Jack Laine and Alphonse Picou emerged from different social backgrounds, both musicians helped bring ragtime, brass band, and dance music into the early models of jazz. Both Picou and Laine stressed the importance of compositional integrity with a small ensemble performing rehearsed arrangements. Picou and Laine thus combined in varying degrees the arrangement acuity of Scott Joplin with the business acumen of W. C. Handy to create a unique style of New Orleans music. This connection was made even more explicit by black New Orleanians as they provided a key link between the blues music of the rural Mississippi Delta and the more ragtime-influenced syncopation of the city. Born on September 6, 1877, Charles "Buddy" Bolden personified this synthesis of urban and rural aesthetics and represents "the key figure in the formation of classic jazz."[36] In many ways, Bolden's life signified late-nineteenth-century African American life in New Orleans, with its diversity of influences, constant economic and social obstacles, and the lack of certainty that often accompanied the black experience. The grandson of a slave, Bolden received some education and acquired a degree of literacy, but his occupational options remained limited.[37] Like many other black New Orleanians, Bolden was familiar with both the formality of church with its spirituals and hymns as well as the informal themes of black folk culture rooted in field hollers and the blues. Like Morton, but unlike most of the players that followed him, Bolden had much experience in various string bands, not simply brass bands.[38] String bands allowed for a looser, less brass-heavy arrangement as well as served as a less brash complement to Bolden's playing. The most important element of Bolden's style, however, concerned his powerful solo technique.[39]

With a loud, penetrating tone, Bolden enlivened his musical surroundings and broke free of the restraints placed on ensemble-driven bands like Laine's Reliance groups. Whereas Laine emphasized the collective ensemble, Bolden created the role of jazz soloist, with his commanding solos influencing most other black cornetists in the city. His neighborhood fame lasted only a few years. By 1906 Bolden began suffering from severe headaches and within a few months the cornet player slipped into dementia, a condition apparently caused by acute alcoholism. The next year, the state declared Bolden insane, and he was transferred to the mental hospital in Jackson, Louisiana. Bolden remained there until his death almost a quarter century later.[40] A black man born in Reconstruction-era New Orleans who performed a style of music that escaped preservation and became a formidable legend that imparted a shadow across the entire history of early jazz, Bolden "may well be the most enigmatic figure the music has ever produced."[41] Although he was a marginalized figure in his time, Bolden became perhaps the most important single musician in early jazz history as the music began flowing from the black community. The lack of recordings prevented Bolden from achieving fame during his lifetime, but innumerable New Orleans musicians consistently posited the horn player as the "the man who started the big noise in jazz."[42] Never recorded, Bolden's legacy relates both to the heroic, paternalistic elements of jazz history as well as to the significance of myth, rumor, and speculation in the creation of that history.[43]

Bolden's peculiar placement within the jazz story—simultaneously at the center of the action as well as on the periphery of documented history—illustrates the difficulties involved in defining New Orleans music during the late nineteenth and early twentieth centuries. The complexity of black life during the 1890s coupled with the mythomania of early-twentieth-century New Orleans produces a number of complications for historians, both in terms of generating a sensible narrative of early New Orleans jazz as well as describing an unpreserved sound. Connected to Bolden's mysterious career, for example, stood the formational myth of Place Congo (Congo Square). As with Storyville, historians have overstated the importance of Place Congo, overlooking its real impact in favor of a somewhat romantic tale of cultural continuation. The setting for dancing and drumming by enslaved Africans and immigrant black Haitians living in the city, Place Congo served as a weekly meeting place for black New Orleanians to find camaraderie and informal entertainment. More than any other event, then, the actions in Place Congo represent the vestigial connection to Africa and the Caribbean. One of the few surviving Africanisms maintained in slave culture, the dancing, drumming, and singing in Place Congo lasted from the early years of the nineteenth century until the mid-1830s when the city closed down the area. The dancing resumed ten years later, in 1845, as a way to confine the actions of slaves on Sundays, the traditional day of lessened work for slaves in the city. This second period of Place Congo activity lasted only a short time and ended well before the Civil War.[44] Still, various histories throughout the mid-twentieth century routinely associated Place Congo with Bolden. This near caricature of African American life in New Orleans helped foster a romantic tale that compressed the complexity of black identities within the city into a usable (if flawed) discourse for early jazz historians.[45]

Together, the music and careers of Alphonse Picou, Jack Laine, and Buddy Bolden form a composite of New Orleans jazz, society, and myth in the late nineteenth century. These men represent the diversity of New Orleans life as well as the constancy of musical development within the city. The individual circumstances varied, but Picou, Laine, and Bolden each represent a key element of early jazz development. Later musicians who discovered more immediate financial success and fame would reference their contributions implicitly and explicitly. All three musicians performed music deeply connected to nineteenth-century musical styles, and this musical form would soon come to define American culture. None of these men achieved much lasting fame within their hometown, but their musical innovation, repertoire, and instruction helped create a distinctive New Orleans musical identity adopted by subsequent jazz musicians. The next group of jazz musicians also emerged from New Orleans, but these players encountered a city that looked remarkably different from the one inhabited by Picou, Laine, and Bolden only a few years earlier. The racial, social, and class confusion spawned by the events of the late 1890s and early 1900s altered the structure of the city, a situation that would have a major impact on the evolution of jazz music.

Although the story of jazz in the late nineteenth century tends to focus on the mythic and picturesque, the 1890s represented one of the most volatile and violent periods in New Orleans history.[46] Throughout this decade, a series of state laws, national court rulings, and racially motivated assaults transformed the relative social fluidity experienced by many New Orleanians into a strict arrangement based upon the assumption of black inferiority. Jim Crow affected all black southerners, but the unique social gradations of New Orleans presented particular dilemmas to African Americans living in the city. For most of the nineteenth century, black New Orleanians (both free and enslaved) lived under the constrictions of the oft-updated Code Noir first enacted in 1724 by the founding governor of New Orleans. This series of laws attempted to regulate every aspect of a slave's life, including his or her religious practices, marriage, and ownership of weapons. Though emancipation severely undercut the power of these "black codes," white New Orleans still maintained control through other methods, especially through the legal system. In 1896, for example, the United States Supreme Court decided a New Orleans lawsuit concerning segregated streetcars and formally established the legal precedent for separate facilities and services for black people. Two years later, the Louisiana legislature barred black people from the polls through constitutional disfranchisement. By 1900, only 4 percent of black Louisianans could vote.[47] White society compounded these legal measures with the quotidian threat of physical and mental brutality.[48]

Although New Orleans experienced fewer incidents of racial violence compared to other areas, there were some outbreaks that quickly contributed to local social tensions and fed local lore. The killing of a policeman by a black resident touched off a five-day riot that threatened to unhinge the relatively nonviolent coexistence of black and white New Orleanians. In July 1900, Robert Charles, a black man in his mid-thirties, shot a policeman and fled to his home neighborhood on Saratoga Street, between Clio and Erato streets. The police department began harassing other black New Orleanians as they searched the area for Charles. These actions coupled with the frenzied fear that the white community had of their black neighbors set off a race riot as hundreds of innocent African Americans became the targets of white mob violence. Over the course of five days, mobs murdered dozens of African Americans and injured hundreds more. The police, tipped off by a member of the black community, finally surrounded Charles on July 27 and laid siege on the humble wood house where he had found asylum. Charles continued to shoot down police officers and angry bystanders until officers torched his house, which finally impelled him to attempt an escape before being shot dead by several policemen. After his death the mobs disappeared and New Orleans regained its superficially pacific social environment.[49]

The Robert Charles incident underscores a number of pressures that impacted New Orleans society in the late nineteenth and early twentieth centuries. Although his death occurred in the streets of New Orleans, Charles began his life in Copiah, Mississippi, as the son of a sharecropper and maintained strong relationships with his family throughout his life. Charles amended this affinity for his rural roots with more urban concerns stemming from his literacy and his exposure to contemporary political ideas. Charles, in particular, became intensely interested in the extension of colonization efforts in Liberia.[50] The news of recent lynchings and the disfranchisement of black Louisianans only heightened his racial consciousness, and when accosted by a white police officer on a July evening, Charles snapped. Although the explicit use of violence differentiated Charles from other black New Orleanians, his background and concerns reflected the strange mixture that made up New Orleans society. Charles's rural identity, which he maintained "until the very end of his life," combined with his political activism to serve as a reflection of the diverse influences acting on the city's black community at the turn of the century.[51] The riot surrounding his death also illustrates to some degree the racial stratification that had already occurred as the city divided itself into two basic factions: a white community and an embattled black community. A certain amount of solidarity existed as black New Orleanians—save one—hid Charles from the white mobs and afterward the black community saw Charles as a folk hero.

A song honoring Charles gained some popularity and notoriety in the years following his death. Jelly Roll Morton recalls that he "once knew the Robert Charles song, but I found out it was best for me to forget it and that I did to go along with the world on the peaceful side."[52] In his interviews with Lomax, Morton also segued his discussion of Robert Charles—and other "swell people"—into his thoughts on Buddy Bolden. On one level, Morton the Creole identifies with the careers and activities of Charles and Bolden, but the piano player also subtly distances himself from these two men. Morton can simply forget the Robert Charles song and continue on with his life, an ability that signified the differences between the Creole and black communities. These differences affected the creation of jazz music as black culture and Creole culture became conflated by New Orleans society during the Jim Crow era. A simplified explanation of the origins of jazz emphasizes the synergy of urban, ragtime-influenced Creoles coming into contact with black musicians more connected to the rural sounds of the blues.[53]

The developments of the 1890s along with the Robert Charles incident of 1900 impacted greatly the rather laissez-faire racial attitudes of the city. By the early 1900s New Orleans society had lost the racial fluidity that had marked much of its history, and over the course of a few years the unique middle caste of black Creoles disappeared as the city narrowed the definition of race down to the two categories of black and white. This constriction of Creole culture and the construction of a two-tiered racial system stemmed from a number of larger forces rather than one single legislative act, but by the early twentieth century the complex diversity of New Orleans devolved into a simplified racial caste system composed of white and black New Orleanians. No longer a vaunted, mysterious middle class, Creoles became identified simply as African Americans by the white community. If white New Orleans came to see Creoles as black, the Creole community still attempted to maintain a dual identity. During the Robert Charles affair, for example, one historian argues that Creoles and blacks shared a common disdain for the overbearing (and violent) white community.[54] Other historians focus on different divisions within New Orleans society, arguing instead that Creoles and whites "increasingly perceived the entire colored population as a common enemy, and temporarily subordinated the Creole/American opposition for the sake of fighting together for white supremacy."[55] Instead of contradicting one another, these writers underscore the racial, social, and class complexities impacting New Orleans at the dawn of the twentieth century. In large measure, turn-of-the-century New Orleans was a city in turmoil.[56]

A second group of musicians came of age in New Orleans following this period of racial and social confusion and experienced a social scene and musical culture much different from the one encountered by earlier musicians. These players—most notably Sidney Bechet, the Original Dixieland Jazz Band (ODJB), and Joe Oliver—helped develop the sound first brought together by earlier artists, but their main contribution to the history of jazz concerned their diffusion of the form. Through their widespread traveling and various recordings, Bechet, the ODJB, and Oliver brought the proto-commercial folk music of New Orleans into the national musical culture. None of these men experienced much success until after leaving New Orleans, and each of these musicians traveled a great deal. Bechet played throughout the country (and eventually Europe), the ODJB popularized jazz in New York City, and Oliver spurred the burgeoning jazz scene in Chicago. If Picou, Laine, and Bolden provided a bridge from the past to the future, then Bechet, the ODJB, and Oliver expanded the path of the music to bring jazz to a national audience. Diffusion coupled with innovation thus defined the essence of the contributions of this second group.

Born in New Orleans on May 14, 1897, Sidney Bechet blended ragtime with the blues and developed a striking clarinet technique built around his strong vibrato. As a Creole growing up in New Orleans in the late 1890s, Bechet experienced few of the bourgeois elements that marked earlier Creole life as the city crept toward a newly compressed society. According to one biographer, "The changing laws and restrictions introduced in the 1890s meant that the Bechets found themselves reclassified in a way that they themselves considered to be a form of relegation."[57] One obvious change involved music education as Creole instructors began teaching black students. Although Bechet himself rarely took formalized lessons, this convergence of black and Creole musical cultures would have an impact on early jazz. The amalgamation of different styles, the hallmark of early jazz in New Orleans, only increased during the early 1900s. In general, Bechet merged the musical background of Alphonse Picou with the ragtime rhythms of Jelly Roll Morton and the brash soloing of Buddy Bolden to represent "probably the greatest instrumentalist to come out of New Orleans after Louis Armstrong."[58] Although his playing style defied easy characterization, Bechet helped shape further the role of jazz soloist and encouraged the dissemination of early jazz throughout the world.

A fife player as a child, Bechet soon graduated to the clarinet, the instrument most associated with the musician. Although he received only a few formal lessons, Bechet listened to and learned from a number of older clarinetists active in the city. In particular, Bechet repeatedly heard Picou, George Baquet, Lorenzo Tio Jr., and Louis "Big Eye" Nelson. Both Baquet and Picou claimed to have tutored Bechet, but the young clarinetist had little patience for standard lessons.[59] Bechet did appreciate, however, Nelson's "ratty" sound and the syncopated, rhythmic thrust of his playing, a style Bechet quickly incorporated into his own playing. A precocious player, Bechet evidently began playing with various local bands as early as 1908. These groups—which included an apparent stint with Bunk Johnson in Bolden's old band—performed a combination of ragtime and the blues, and Bechet continued his jazz apprenticeship in New Orleans until 1912 when he set out for Texas. Beginning with this trip, Bechet embarked on a travel-heavy career, rarely staying for long in any given city. Throughout the 1910s, Bechet visited New Orleans occasionally and eventually made his way to Chicago in 1917, where he acquired his first soprano saxophone. The soprano sax, now a fairly standard reed instrument in jazz, allowed Bechet to produce an even brasher tone than he had on the clarinet. Despite his admiration of improvised, blues-based music, Bechet accepted an invitation from Will Marion Cook, the director of the Southern Syncopated Orchestra, to play in Europe in 1919.[60] Bechet's constant travels modeled the lifestyle of other artists like Jelly Roll Morton and served as an important disseminating element in early jazz. In conjunction with his many recording dates in the 1920s, Bechet's touring career introduced jazz to a much wider audience than previous black or Creole musicians could have accessed.

As Sidney Bechet found remarkable success playing with a variety of bands, another group of local musicians helped set off a raucous revolution of sound that infected an entire generation of listeners. A five-piece band composed of native New Orleanians, the Original Dixieland Jazz Band represented the most important white jazz band active in the early years of the jazz age, and their success represents the beginning of the diffusion of early jazz from New Orleans to the rest of the country. Not the most technically proficient white band, nor the most original (despite what their name claims), the ODJB nevertheless brought New Orleans jazz to an audience that had never before heard this style of music: white, urban college kids. Undervalued routinely by many jazz scholars, the ODJB signifies in large measure the transition between the brass bands of late-nineteenth-century

New Orleans and the cabaret jazz bands popular in urban American during the 1920s. The band's combination of ragtime rhythms, brass band instrumentation, minstrel show antics, and youthful enthusiasm quickly won over young white Americans anxious for a music unique to their generation. Like rock 'n' roll in the 1950s, the Original Dixieland Jazz Band produced music larger than itself with a sound that had social implications at times more important than any specific musical contribution. Creating a noisy generational divide, the music of the ODJB "shocked, frightened, confused, and finally captivated the listener."[61] The Original Dixieland Jazz Band did not invent jazz (as has been claimed—mainly by members of the band), they did not perfect jazz, and within the evolution of jazz as a musical style, the ODJB remain a brief footnote. As the band that broke jazz to the American record-buying public in the late 1910s, however, the impact of the ODJB remains incalculable.

Cornetist Dominic "Nick" LaRocca established the Original Dixieland Jazz Band in New Orleans in the 1910s along with fellow local musicians Eddie Edwards (trombone), Larry Shields (clarinet), Henry Ragas (piano), and Tony Sbarbaro (drums). Each band member had certain strengths, but LaRocca led the group and, more than any other player, LaRocca's vision served as the template for ODJB performances. Born into an Italian immigrant family on Magazine Street in the Garden District neighborhood of the city, LaRocca began playing the cornet as a child despite his father's disapproval.[62] In the early 1910s, LaRocca encountered Edwards, a struggling local trombone player. The two young musicians practiced often, and eventually LaRocca and Edwards both began playing with one of Laine's Reliance bands. At some point around 1915, LaRocca, Edwards, Sbarbaro, Shields, and Ragas began performing separately from Laine's group under the name of "Stein's Dixie Jass Band." The origins of the word "jass" remain hidden, but most sources contend that it "was an obscene word" that had been "applied to almost anything and everything."[63] In early 1916, the group accepted an invitation to play a six-week engagement in Chicago, but within a year the band had relocated to New York City.[64] Early that year, the band, renamed as the Original Dixieland Jazz Band, began a stint at a new dance club in the Reisenweber Building, and the word "jazz" appeared for the first time in a major newspaper.[65] Proclaiming their originality, the ODJB combined a regional affiliation (Dixieland) with the promise of something that seemed intriguingly foreign (jazz). New York audiences immediately clamored for this oddly named band, and this intense popularity attracted New York–based Columbia Records, a company eager to cash in on a fad, even if the "Columbia people did not seem to grasp the idea of jazz."[66] Met with instant acclaim, the ODJB capitalized on this one performance by signing a contract with Columbia Records within one week. Columbia, however, balked at the recorded sound of the group and decided to shelve the project. At the end of February, the band recorded several songs for Victor Records, Columbia's rival, and finally saw the release of their "Livery Stable Blues" and "Dixieland One-Step." The record proved immensely popular, validated the Reisenweber performance, and persuaded Columbia to release two of the songs originally cut in January. Within weeks of moving to New York, the ODJB produced a record that would soon set off a mini jazz craze that prefigured the Jazz Age of the 1920s.

The Original Dixieland Jazz Band performed a style of New Orleans music that borrowed equally from the brass band tradition of Jack Laine as well as the minstrel show style of musical entertainment. Unlike later bands, the ODJB played a rather fast-paced, if stiff, form of jazz that featured the measured chaos of communal improvisation. The group, in other words, would decide on a certain chord sequence and then improvise individual melodies in the predetermined key. Like Laine's Reliance bands, the ODJB eschewed solos (save for a few instrumental breaks) for an emphasis on the ensemble. Their most famous song, "Livery Stable Blues," was an old LaRocca composition that developed out of an improvisation on the chords of a church hymn.[67] During the verses, each instrument would improvise various melodies, but the real attraction of the tune by the record-buying audience was the short breaks in the chorus where the band imitated barnyard animals. Featuring a trombone donkey, clarinet rooster, and cornet horse, "Livery Stable Blues" related to minstrel show corn instead of the blues tradition of the rural South. Still, although none of the members achieved any level of instrumental virtuosity, the band's combination of quick tempos, energized improvisation, and minstrel trickery signified something quite novel in New York City.[68]

Within seven years of their heyday, however, the ODJB had faded into obscurity. The group continued to have a strong influence on popular jazz in the 1920s as it influenced practically every major white jazz band active during that period, including the New Orleans Rhythm Kings, the Original Memphis Five, and Paul Whiteman's Orchestra. The Dixieland revival of the 1940s revisited some of the ODJB's music, but in general the most consistent supporter of the group remained Nick LaRocca, who later claimed his band as the clear originators of jazz music and that African Americans simply copied the ODJB.[69] The cornet player's declarations notwithstanding, scholars often argue that the ODJB only simplified a complex African American musical form and gained fame with a pale imitation of jazz music.[70] Although not an entirely incorrect assertion, the ODJB also emerged from a musical culture different from what black and Creole New Orleanians had experienced. Their blend of brass band instrumentation and minstrel show hokum, though short-lived, played itself out in a more commercial vein than folk music. Rather than a clattery aberration, the ODJB instead underscores the variances inherent in New Orleans jazz. Still, the primary influence imparted by the band concerned their discovery of the northern college-aged audience for their music and thus the commercial possibilities of jazz.

Whereas the Original Dixieland Jazz Band helped introduce jazz to white listeners and Sidney Bechet helped evolve the role of the iconoclastic soloist, the cornetist Joe "King" Oliver represented the most important and influential jazz musician of early jazz in New Orleans. Born into a similar socioeconomic environment as Buddy Bolden in 1885, Joe Oliver rose to fame and became the most important soloist and bandleader to leave the city and broadcast jazz throughout the Midwest.[71] Unlike Bolden, Oliver left behind a large body of recorded work that gives insight into the music played in New Orleans in the early twentieth century. Eclipsed early on by his protégé, Louis Armstrong, many of Oliver's innovations sound less startling due to their eventual commonplace nature in 1920s jazz. More than any other musician, however, Oliver represents the acme of the polyphonic, improvised jazz that came to characterize the New Orleans music scene. Oliver favored the ensemble style of jazz like that of the ODJB, but unlike LaRocca's band, Oliver emphasized a controlled and (somewhat paradoxically) arranged approach to improvisation. Instead of five instrumentalists wailing along in the same key, Oliver's groups maintained a collective polyphonic feel without devolving into chaotic braying. Short solo breaks punctuated the proceedings, producing a sonic blend of structured improvisation, syncopated rhythms, innovative soloing, and blues-influenced tonalities.[72] A leader above all, Oliver ably instituted a style of playing that preserved the delicate tension between the order of composition and the tumult of improvisation.

A relatively late start notwithstanding, Oliver became one of the strongest soloists in the city, boasting a brash, melodic style. Like Bechet, Oliver developed a distinctive and easily recognizable sound, and the cornetist combined a strong rhythmic pulse with a large number of dips, slurs, and growls. These coloring effects shared both minstrel show and rural blues antecedents, but Oliver also employed various mutes to achieve a different timbre as well as a unique "wah-wah" effect. His improvisations hewed rather closely to the melody but his technical flourishes turned many of his recorded solos of the 1920s into practice etudes for countless jazz followers. Unlike Bechet, Oliver combined brilliant solo playing with equally brilliant ensemble work, especially with his Creole Jazz Band.[73] Although the Original Dixieland Jazz Band found fame first, Oliver's Creole Jazz Band presented a clearer example of the New Orleans style. The ODJB tended toward a polyrhythmic, chaotic style of jazz that eschewed any real arrangement as each member improvised on a basic chord sequence. Oliver's band, in contrast, adhered to a more arranged sound with each instrumentalist performing a calculated role. In general, Oliver played the melody on cornet, the second cornetist supplied a basic harmony part, the trombone and clarinet provided counterpoint, and the rhythm section (bass, banjo, piano, and drums) propelled the entire endeavor. Not simply a creative instrumentalist, Oliver established the map that jazz music followed over the next decade.

Joe Oliver left New Orleans to seek fame elsewhere in 1917—a year that proved to be perhaps the most important in early jazz history. No one person or event brought jazz to the American people, but in 1917 a number of forces collided that helped transform jazz from a type of southern folk music into a mass-produced popular commodity in the 1920s. The nation's entrance that year in World War I spurred the creation of defense plants throughout the country. These plants, in turn, offered new employment opportunities for black southerners tired of low-wage agricultural work. Northern industrial opportunities coupled with the renewed racism of the turn-of-the-century South helped instigate a large pattern of black migration into the Midwest and North. Various black newspapers further fueled the Great Migration through the publication of enticing articles that described such cities as Chicago as the Promised Land. In New Orleans, the year 1917 also marked the end of Storyville as the United States Navy closed down the district of vice and illicit entertainment. Despite the work of many early jazz historians who tended to present the termination of Storyville as the final impetus for the propulsion of jazz out of the South, the larger pattern of emigration already existed and the closing of the district played no role in the process.[74] More important, the success in the Midwest and North of those first emigrating musicians hastened the travel plans of others. Jazz began to break out from the folk environs of New Orleans and enter the commercial world of American popular music, a transformation encouraged by one other event in 1917: the sudden acceptability of jazz by at least some Americans following the success of the Original Dixieland Jazz Band. A musical form barely two decades old (and only recently given a name), by 1917 "jazz" the southern folk music became "jazz" the profitable commodity.

The events of 1917 signaled the beginning of the end of the city's early jazz scene, and although bands would remain active locally throughout the 1920s, other cities—primarily Chicago and New York—would be the centers for musical innovation and transmission. Between 1908 and 1919, most of the leading jazz players left New Orleans for better opportunities elsewhere and signaled the first wave of jazz emigration from the city. Jelly Roll Morton left in 1908 as did bassist Bill Johnson; bandleader Freddie Keppard and trumpeter Bunk Johnson both left in 1914; members of the Original Dixieland Jazz Band left in 1915 and 1916; clarinetist "Big Eye" Louis Nelson and Sidney Bechet left in 1916; trombonist Honore Dutrey, clarinetist Jimmie Noone, and trumpeter Tommy Ladnier left in 1917; and trombonist Edward "Kid" Ory left in 1919.[75] Some of these players such as Ory headed out west to California, most spent at least some time in Chicago, but many simply drifted from job to job, city to city. Most of these players were born in the early 1890s—though some like Bill Johnson were much older, and some like Tommy Ladnier were still in their mid-teens—and came of age during the period of tremendous social and racial change in the city. This informal group foreshadowed a second wave of departing younger musicians including Louis Armstrong. New Orleans, "already a city in decline" in the 1890s, lost most of its jazz musicians by the early 1920s. Although New Orleanians would continue to have a tremendous impact on the jazz of the 1920s, the hometown jazz scene simply receded back into the shadows. Or as one writer contends, "one of the supreme ironies of the history of New Orleans jazz is that so much of it took place in Chicago."[76]

In the summer of 1923, Jelly Roll Morton joined the New Orleans Rhythm Kings (NORK), a group of white New Orleanians, for a series of recording sessions at the Gennett studios in Richmond, Indiana.[77] Signifying the first interracial jazz performance preserved on record, the Morton-NORK recordings also helped bring New Orleans music to a large audience.

Unlike the Original Dixieland Jazz Band records six years earlier, these sessions transcended novelty clichés and underscored certain defining elements of New Orleans jazz. The Morton tune "Milenberg Joys," in particular, represents a synthesis of early jazz music.[78] Featuring Paul Mares on cornet, Leon Ropollo on clarinet, Georg Brunis on trombone, and Jelly Roll Morton on piano, "Milenberg Joys" starts out as a straightforward mid-tempo dance piece.[79] Boasting a strong melody, the song maintains a steady rehearsed feel until the cornet solo breaks in with Mares providing a growling, Joe Oliver–inspired break.[80] Although not as improvisationally inventive as Oliver, Mares shares with his cornet hero a warm tone and a penchant for playing in the middle registers of the instrument. This section leads into a strong, vibrato-fueled clarinet solo by Ropollo supported by a rhythmic counterpoint figure performed by Morton. Tying the music to its roots, a glimpse of traditional New Orleans music appears near the end of "Milenberg Joys" as the band provides a rousing conclusion by launching into a short, blaring example of collective improvisation. Lacking the flaccid gimmickry of the ODJB, "Milenberg Joys" maintains a melodic and rhythmically forceful feel and serves as a summation of the various styles that helped distinguish early jazz. Although his piano playing on this piece relates little to the ragtime of Scott Joplin, Morton shares Joplin's concern for a moderate tempo and an emphasis on composition over improvisation. Paul Mares, in contrast, produces a blues-inflected solo that corresponds to the mannered blues of W. C. Handy, if not directly to the more innovative sounds of Oliver. The collective improvisation near the end references the sounds of their hometown, but without the sense of novelty instilled by earlier bands. A small-piece band performing a mixture of arranged and improvised jazz in a midwestern recording studio, the New Orleans Rhythm Kings with Jelly Roll Morton reiterated the past while constructing the context for jazz in the future.[81]

Fifteen years after these sessions, Morton sat in front of Alan Lomax's microphone and narrated his history of jazz. Despite the braggadocio, Morton's story hinted at some of the basic truths behind the creation of this new style of music. The Lomax interviews emphasized the importance of ragtime and the blues, the role Creole culture played in early jazz, and the variety of clubs that featured jazz performers in the early 1900s. Forgotten for most of the 1920s and 1930s, New Orleans fell into favor with historians and listeners interested in traditional jazz music and tired of swing's rather formulaic progression into popular music. This Dixieland revival of the 1940s helped create a rather picturesque take on early jazz history as colorful tales eclipsed documented fact. Congo Square and Storyville came to dominate these early narratives, and the rather complicated reduction of Creole culture or the upheaval of the 1890s simply faded into historical myopia. "A once admirable music," one scholar notes, "was reduced to the precincts of tourism, complete with moniker (Dixieland), costume (straw boater and garter belt), and snacks (peanuts and beer)."[82] Midcentury remembrances aside, the early jazz of New Orleans existed in the shadows—never recorded, preserved, or transmitted. Chicago (and expatriate New Orleanians) connected the dotted lines of early jazz history by placing the proto-commercial, quasi-folk music into the hands of record-buying midwesterners. Discovered only in retrospect, this early jazz scene found its identity a thousand miles away in Chicago as musicians entered recording studios and etched the weird pulse of New Orleans into wax.

PART TWO

DISPERSION

𝟹 Chicago and the Recording of Jazz in the 1920s

In the spring of 1923, Joe "King" Oliver and his Creole Jazz Band traveled from Chicago to Richmond, Indiana, for a two-day recording session for Gennett Records. Oliver's regular band, now augmented by Louis Armstrong on second cornet, recorded nearly thirty numbers for Gennett before retiring for the evening.[1] The sessions proved grueling as heat, humidity, and outside noise competed with the members of the band. Despite the supposed purpose of the recording building, the long, narrow studio stood close to railroad tracks and offered awkward acoustics for recording. The band would project their sound toward a large megaphone surrounded by heavy curtains with only sawdust-filled walls serving as sound dampeners. Although only a few feet away from each other, the musicians found it almost impossible to hear themselves or their counterparts. To further contribute to the uncomfortable situation, studio engineers kept the room humid to preserve the integrity of the wax used for recording. This notoriously volatile acoustic method of recording picked up only certain instruments and rendered low-frequency rhythm instruments, like the tuba, inaudible. Likewise, the recording method forced drummer Warren "Baby" Dodds to replace his trap sets with wood blocks to avoid disrupting the recording stylus. Only the clarinet, banjo, and trumpet could be recorded with any degree of consistency.[2] Claustrophobic conditions, humidity, and acoustic limitations notwithstanding, the Gennett sessions led to the next stage in young Armstrong's career. They served as the artist's initiation to the recording studio and cemented his position in a band that he had joined only two months earlier. These sessions, along with the Jelly Roll Morton and New Orleans Rhythm Kings recordings that same year, also ushered in the era of recorded jazz. The records they produced may not reflect the live sounds of the bands—the available recording format compromised the audible instrumentation—but they provide a useful account of the evolution of early jazz.

In the two days spent in Richmond, the band set down a number of recordings, but Gennett only saved a handful for release on their 1923 catalog, "Snappy Dance Hits on Gennett Records by Exclusive Gennett Colored Artists."[3] These 1923 records introduced the Chicago-style jazz that would dominate the jazz scene in the 1920s. Whereas New Orleans music proved ephemeral, Chicago jazz became connected with the recording industry, creating a tangible document of 1920s jazz. Over the span of five years, the elegant chaos of New Orleans jazz would evolve into a more arranged style, and Oliver's recordings provide a useful comparison for future developments. The Creole Jazz Band represented the transplanted nature of black Chicagoans, with each of the musicians (except Lil Hardin) hailing originally from New Orleans. This fusion of New Orleans and Chicago produced a unique style particularly evident in a song recorded by Oliver's band at the Gennett sessions. On the second day of recording, the Creole Jazz Band waxed a version of "Snake Rag," an improvised tune created specifically for the session.[4] "Snake Rag" features a traditional arrangement of ensemble improvisation along with several brief stop-time solos. Oliver joined Armstrong on harmonized cornet breaks throughout the song. When they performed for an audience, the horn players would expand and elaborate on these breaks, but in the studio, Oliver and Armstrong settled for more conservative solos in order to stay within the firm three-minute time limit imposed on songs by the recording process.[5] The improvised melodies and rhythmic propulsion of "Snake Rag" place it within the New Orleans style, but the song also borrows from various forms of African American music—work songs and the country blues, the sounds of Scott Joplin and Buddy Bolden.[6] Encapsulating New Orleans jazz with its insinuations of ragtime and blues, "Snake Rag" served as a snapshot of African American musical expression in the years immediately following World War I. Still, for all of its potency, the influence of "Snake Rag" proved fleeting. Within five years, musicians would build on Oliver's achievements and produce a new, more arranged, and more stylized form of jazz that would intrigue, shock, and entice black and white Americans alike.

The syncretic nature of "Snake Rag" underscores the importance of Chicago in the larger narrative of jazz evolution and diffusion throughout the 1920s as the city emerged as the foremost "jazz city" in the nation. Although the geographic diffusion of jazz followed no established map (musicians left the South in all directions during the late 1910s and 1920s), Chicago represented an important destination for many jazz performers pushed and pulled out of New Orleans during the years of the Great Migration. Between 1910 and 1920, Chicago's black population increased by almost 150 percent.[7] Much of this population transference had its roots in the transportation networks slowly integrating the South into the national marketplace, a process promised since the Civil War but not seen in large measure until the 1910s. Chicago's established rail lines—especially the Illinois Central line and its service to New Orleans—helped create much of this movement. Based on its expansive transportation networks, growing African American community, musical employment opportunities, and regional connections to recording studios, Chicago in the 1920s merged competing forces of urbanization, technological innovation, and the culture of modernity into a near-coherent representation of American life in the modern age.[8]

Much as myth defined the origins of jazz music in New Orleans—with narratives sensationalizing Storyville and Place Congo—early chroniclers of jazz routinely hyped the diffusion of the music to Chicago with the shadowed romanticism of riverboats and railroads. The tale of young cornetist Louis Armstrong, having recently been tapped by King Oliver to join him in Chicago, waiting on a train alone with a fish sandwich, has long been a central image of the music's reorientation from the South to the Midwest.[9] More than simply a quaint story, the introduction of jazz to Chicago signified a massive shift in the social, political, and cultural fabric of the nation as millions of African Americans left the South for better opportunities in the West, the Midwest, and the Northeast. Early jazz historians would often bank heavily on the symbolism of the northbound train and (despite geography) the Mississippi River as jazz conduits funneling southern musicians into Chicago. Modern transportation connections altered considerably the cultural mapping of the diffusion of the music emanating from New Orleans. Still, the train and the riverboat fueled much of the cultural exodus out of the South and into the Midwest either through transportation or musical diffusion. These differing modes of transportation helped define the New Orleans to Chicago relationship for musicians such as Louis Armstrong, who actually boarded trains and physically entered the city, as well as for musicians like Bix Beiderbecke, who first heard New Orleans–style jazz on the riverboats that operated near his hometown of Davenport, Iowa.

Arriving via the Illinois Central train in the late summer of 1922, Louis Armstrong traveled to Chicago at the request of his old mentor, Joe Oliver, who had moved north in the late 1910s. Missing his earlier connection due to playing at a last-minute performance for a funeral, Armstrong entered the Illinois Central terminal bewildered by the massive structure's multiple tracks and disoriented without a contact to direct his way to Joe Oliver. "I saw a million people," Armstrong noted in an interview in 1966, "but not Mister Joe, and I didn't give a damn who else was there. I never seen a city that big." In his autobiography first published in 1954, Armstrong writes of his introduction to Chicago in almost mythic terms, describing how a policeman gently helped usher the perplexed musician to a waiting cab. Despite this swagger, the chaos of Chicago made an impact on the young musician, and in the 1966 interview, Armstrong avowed, "I was fixing to take the next train back home—standing there in my box-back suit, padded shoulders, double-breasted wide-leg pants."[10] His immediate fears were displaced by the whirlwind of performance. Within hours of his arrival, Armstrong, who was to play second cornet in Oliver's band, stood inside Lincoln Gardens astonished by the crowd's response to his old friend's music.[11] This rushed orientation to Chicago prefaced some of the most creative years of Armstrong's career. The city served as the backdrop to a fundamental shift in the way jazz was performed, preserved, transmitted, and received. Armstrong's inspiration and the impetus for Chicago jazz in general were inextricably linked to the expansion of railroad accessibility to southern African Americans during the first decades of the twentieth century. The train, with its central position in both Afro-diasporic culture as well as jazz history, thus helped produce a dynamic transference of population and culture between the South and the Midwest.

Railroads signified an important mode of transference for jazz music, but riverboats, too, provided a crucial link between rural areas and the burgeoning urban culture of the modern era. Before leaving for Chicago, Louis Armstrong performed with bandleader Fate Marable on a host of riverboat excursions along the Mississippi River.[12] These excursion boats allowed younger musicians to cut their teeth by playing for long periods of time for diverse audiences, and the gigs also paid fairly well. In his autobiography, Armstrong relished the memory of receiving a bonus for finishing the season. "That was a nice taste of money," Armstrong recalled, "especially to a guy like me who was not used to loot that came in big numbers. I was heavily loaded with dough when I returned to New Orleans."[13] In addition to providing transportation and employment opportunities, riverboats also introduced jazz to areas outside of New Orleans. Born in Davenport, Iowa, in 1903, Leon "Bix" Beiderbecke first came into contact with jazz music through the riverboats that coursed up and down the Mississippi River. These traveling shows inspired Beiderbecke to seek out jazz phonograph records, which in turn inspired him to teach himself the cornet. This closed loop of traveling musicians inspired phonograph record purchases and illustrated the constellation of technological changes that eventually made jazz a national music.[14]

Although early histories tend to emphasize the uniformity of Chicago jazz, there were several distinct styles that emerged from different racial and musical influences. Three forms, in particular, discovered large audiences throughout the Chicago area: solo piano music, small bands playing improvised music, and larger bands performing arranged music. From the mid-1910s to the mid-1920s the most important black musicians playing in Chicago were Jelly Roll Morton, Joe Oliver, and Erskine Tate. The history of solo piano-playing that predated the 1890s resonated in Jelly Roll Morton's numbers. Morton, who had moved to Chicago in the 1910s, continued to play his amalgamation of ragtime, blues, and jazz in small clubs throughout Chicago. Joe Oliver's various bands represented the small band style of jazz that included between five and eight musicians who performed improvised jazz in the cabarets and smaller clubs in the city.[15] Erskine Tate's group, in contrast, exemplifies the larger (twenty-five- to thirty-piece) black bands that entered the theater circuit and provided music for silent films, ballroom dances, and various vaudeville acts. These jobs relied on written arrangements rather than improvised parts and thus required players to have strong music-reading skills. The stylistic divisions remained fairly evident for a large part of the 1920s, and although certain players— most notably Louis Armstrong—found success in various forms, most musicians worked primarily in one genre.

White musicians in Chicago had more employment opportunities and experimented with fewer styles. The New Orleans Rhythm Kings secured a place as the most important white band playing in Chicago in the early

1920s and adhered to a particular formula that cemented their popularity. Members of the group admired musicians like Joe Oliver and Louis Armstrong and regularly went to see them play in the South Side clubs. The band played a smooth style of improvised jazz, a sound that has been described as the "most powerful, most pervasive influence on Chicago's young, white, aspiring jazzmen."[16] Although their styles of jazz differed, the New Orleans Rhythm Kings shared at least two similarities with Oliver's Creole Jazz Band: both consisted of New Orleans musicians living in Chicago and both tremendously influenced a generation of jazz players through their recordings. These records reveal a band advancing a controlled agenda of sharp arrangements that still allowed spontaneity, and if the Rhythm Kings fell short of the transcendence of Oliver's best work, they still represented one of the few white bands of this period to produce music connected deeply to the black music of New Orleans. This biracial musical identity (further manifested in their performances with Jelly Roll Morton) made the group a popular part of the Chicago jazz landscape during this period. The success of bands like the New Orleans Rhythm Kings and individuals like Bix Beiderbecke inspired a number of white college-aged musicians to create their own bands and records.

The variety of musical and racial influences on jazz music in the city mirrored the geography of clubland in Chicago. To some degree the nature of the job and the demographics of the audience dictated the type of band, and ultimately racism played a substantial role in determining the hire of a white or black band. The sort of racism experienced by black musicians in Chicago reflected the larger social and racial realities facing African Americans living in the Midwest and North during the first half of the twentieth century, most notably the de facto segregation. Located primarily on the South Side of the city, Chicago's black neighborhoods contained a wide range of socioeconomic conditions. Separated from white neighborhoods, black Chicagoans often encountered housing shortages, high rents, and limited job opportunities. Still, Chicago's black community benefited from the presence of a supportive middle class, black-owned social clubs, and assertive black churches. In an attempt to counter white animosity with black self-sufficiency, Chicago's African American leadership created a vibrant African American social network that included a diverse and influential group of jazz musicians.[17]

For transplanted New Orleans natives, the virulent racism prevalent in the South dissolved into a more implicit form of racial prejudice. In particular, black Chicagoans faced certain limitations on employment opportunities as well as lower pay than their white counterparts. Black musicians found some support through the city's Local 208 of the musicians' union, an affiliate of the American Federation of Labor. During the mid-1920s, Verona Biggs served as union president and aimed to protect the issues confronting working black performers. His goal ran counter to that of James Petrillo, the aggressive leader of Local 10, the union for white musicians. Two particular geographic areas—the Loop and Bronzeville—encompassed most of Chicagoan nightlife and projected a noticeable racial divide. Located near the main commerce area of Chicago, the Loop housed the greatest concentration of white hotels, ballrooms, and theaters. White club owners occasionally hired black bands—especially the more famous groups—but the audience consisted solely of white patrons. On the South Side, Bronzeville clubs and cabarets employed only black bands that played to almost exclusively black audiences, although white jazz enthusiasts could be spotted in the clubs when Armstrong or Oliver played. The most important black clubs in Chicago—Dreamland, Elite #1, Elite #2, Plantation, and Royal Garden—could be found in Bronzeville on "The Stroll," the strip on State Street between 31st and 35th streets. Union regulations and racial prejudice trumped musical considerations in this environment. Under the auspices of Local 10, Petrillo forced out black bands from the Loop at various times during the 1920s. Biggs and Local 208 had little recourse against these actions, but Petrillo's arbitrary avoidance of standard hiring practices helped unite black musicians to some degree.[18]

In conjunction with the work of Local 208 and Verona Biggs, black musicians found support in the *Chicago Defender,* the most influential black newspaper at the time. Robert S. Abbott, the publisher of the *Defender,* endeavored to provide black Americans with a print media advocate. Operating on both local and national levels—the newspaper ran several different editions during this period—the *Defender* played a large role in enticing black southerners to travel northward as well as provided news on housing and employment. The newspaper also reported on various racially charged employment issues. On a national level, the *Defender* persistently supported anti-lynching laws and regularly covered racially motivated crimes throughout the country. Despite its activism, the *Defender* reflected the conservative values of the African American elite, and during this period the *Defender* combined a commitment to national civil rights with a local concern for social refinement. With this focus on the economic and social interests of the black middle and upper classes, the *Defender* received much of its advertising revenue from products that claimed to straighten black hair and offer a whiter skin tone. Thus, throughout the 1920s editorials blasting lynching abutted ads for "Bleacho," a skin-lightening cream that promised to "remove the greatest obstacle to your success."[19]

In terms of jazz, one of the most important contributions of the *Defender* was "The Musical Bunch," a weekly column written by Dave Peyton from 1925 to 1929.[20] In general, Peyton used his column to publicize concerts, deliver news from the jazz scene, and articulate his views on the expected responsibilities of musicians. Peyton's ubiquity in the music scene and his ardent, if slightly idiosyncratic, opinions on jazz made his column a popular entertainment source for black Chicago during the 1920s. Not simply a jazz scene gadfly, Peyton also contracted out musicians to other orchestras and occasionally performed himself. This multifaceted role influenced his writing, and Peyton routinely framed his columns around steely dictates of appropriate behavior for professional musicians to achieve success. Although he sometimes preached about the musical element of the trade, such as practicing scales and honing music-reading skills, many of these columns also laid out certain social values by which jazz musicians should abide. In this way, Peyton's social views complemented those of the *Defender,* and his numerous lectures on the proper behavior of musicians attest to his commitment to professionalism and respectability. Above all else, Peyton valued tactfulness, patience, selflessness, punctuality, sobriety, and cleanliness. The columnist respected a musician's shined shoes as much as any improvisational skills. "When the public learns that you are ratty and without culture," Peyton warned in 1928, "they learn to dislike your work."[21] Peyton believed that sobriety on the bandstand should accompany temperance in finances. In a 1926 column, for example, Peyton urged jazz musicians to invest in gold bonds or real estate rather than buying flashy new automobiles. Conservatism—in finances, in behavior, and even in performing— marked Peyton's columns in the newspaper. This commitment to respectability and responsibility mirrored the middle-class values of the *Defender* and governed his views on race.

Throughout the mid- to late 1920s Peyton's column served an important role in providing employment connections and concert advertisements for the Chicago jazz community. In his inaugural column in September 1925, for example, Peyton declared that "this new column will be devoted to the interest of our professional musicians endeavoring to give from week to week correct information concerning the gloom-chasing squad."[22] Despite such a stated commitment, his early columns expressed a marked ambivalence to the jazz music popular in the city during the mid- to late 1920s. From the outset, Peyton praised the larger, arrangement-centered jazz orchestras such as the bands led by Fletcher Henderson and Duke Ellington (both mentioned in his first column). In his third column, however, Peyton disparaged the New Orleans style of group improvisation as "clown jazz." "The day of clown jazz is over," Peyton argued, "and I would like to see the day come when our musicians realize this fact."[23] Peyton also encouraged musicians to focus on theory and private study to hone the skills necessary to play the written scores of current arrangers and to compete with white musicians in the area "who have had training and experience in the symphony orchestra and are well qualified on their respective instruments."[24] Even as Louis Armstrong was recording some of his most important pieces with the Hot Five (in the OKeh studios in Chicago), Peyton still pushed for "polite syncopation" and noted that "jazz seems to be on the wane nowadays in some of the most sedate places of amusement."[25] Peyton's tastes, as seen in his columns, consistently aligned more with the "sweet jazz" of Paul Whiteman and Guy Lombardo and the structured jazz of Fletcher Henderson and Duke Ellington, but he also showed a certain reevaluation in his writing, too, as he gradually and subtly broadened his view of legitimate music.

Peyton had strong opinions on the history of jazz, arguing that ragtime represented a more valuable precursor than the blues. In three columns—in December 1925, February 1927, and June 1928—Peyton explicitly traced the origins of jazz, and these articles provide an arc that represents his changing perspective on jazz music.[26] In 1925, in his first column on the origins of jazz, Peyton sketched out a jazz history that ignored both Jelly Roll Morton and the blues and instead drew a line straight from the ragtime of Scott Joplin to the music of composer Ernest Hogan (who wrote "All Coons Look Alike to Me") and from James Reese Europe to Johnnie Dunn, "the greatest jazz cornetist in America."[27] Peyton slowly shifted his jazz perspective over the course of 1927 and began dividing jazz into more precise categories to allow more jazz musicians into his purview.[28] His 1927 "Birth of Jazz" column signified this spirit of inclusion by incorporating W. C. Handy into his narrative. More important, this column reflected his growing defensiveness about white musicians claiming jazz as their own invention. "As usual," Peyton writes, "the white man has taken credit for the birth of jazz and its development. He has never considered the rights of our own

Race writers. He has taken the credit for everything in music."[29] By 1928, Peyton had finally written Louis Armstrong into his history and claimed that "today jazz music has developed into an institution."[30] In many ways, his view of jazz remains somewhat idiosyncratic.[31] Peyton preferred jazz that featured clean playing, good dynamics, limited improvisation, and strong arrangements. This perspective sometimes put Peyton on the defensive, as in a 1927 column where he asserted that "I am not against jazz music, but I do think it belongs in its place."[32] Peyton often commended Whiteman for his leadership skills, and in a column in 1928 Peyton summed up his high regard for Whiteman by proclaiming, "to know Paul Whiteman is to understand at last the phenomenon of American jazz."[33] These columns afford an incomplete perspective on Peyton's jazz evolution, but the tone of his writing did shift considerably by the late 1920s to incorporate a wider range of music under the jazz moniker than he had at first allowed.

Although Peyton's writing focused on music and business concerns, his columns also helped establish certain codes of conduct, both for musicians and for African Americans generally. The issue of race usually appeared in "The Musical Bunch" when Peyton discussed employment opportunities. Peyton understood that the livelihood of working musicians rested on the availability of jobs, and he used his column to promote black bands in the Chicago area and congratulate black bands when they obtained gigs in the Loop. Racial tensions certainly affected the work environment for African American musicians. "The rottenest kind of white orchestra," he wrote in 1927, "can get the best jobs when they in no way compare with our crack Race orchestras."[34] Still, Peyton rarely blamed racism for black bands losing jobs to white groups. With his constant admonitions to practice scales and learn theory, Peyton added that many white players had an edge due to their classical background. White players, Peyton believed, sometimes received better opportunities because of their talent and not necessarily their skin color. The atmosphere in Chicago, however, was not always conducive to pleasant racial interaction, and in 1925, Peyton wrote an extended piece on the maneuverings of white booking agencies that prevented black people from obtaining jobs in white venues. "The calls come to the booking agent's office," Peyton wrote, "and he replies that he is sorry, but he doesn't book Race orchestras because they are unreliable, barbaric and huge liquor indulgents."[35] Peyton then urged black musicians to use "advertising and propaganda to offset these untruths." "Opportunity," Peyton once wrote, "is all we want," and he argued that given a chance, black bands could be at least as successful as white bands. Once employed, however, the musicians needed to conduct their business professionally. "Now that we are getting our share of the work," Peyton concluded, "let us hold it by giving the service desired, and by all means watch your attire: have your shoes shining, collar white and clothes pressed." Peyton rarely strayed far from his core beliefs of ambition and thrift.[36]

At times, Peyton's allegiance to a particular style of jazz would intersect directly with his discussion of race. In 1929, for example, Peyton discussed two different recordings of W. C. Handy's "St. Louis Blues." He greatly admired Paul Whiteman and argued that a Whiteman recording of "St. Louis Blues" surpassed a recording of the tune by a band of African American musicians. "You can almost see four or five of our musicians blasting way," Peyton writes of the African American rendition of the song, "blowing any old kind of a note and getting all sorts of freakish, weird tones." Whiteman's record, in contrast, had sold millions, a sales achievement that indicated its popular worth to Peyton. This remark, however, directly followed Peyton's concern that black bands usually became "jim-crowed in some Race pamphlet."[37] Racial solidarity in business did not necessarily translate to supportiveness of the music being produced. Peyton would often praise white bands and use them to illustrate how black musicians should play. "There is a vast difference," he wrote in 1926, "between the two races when it comes to playing music. Our group seems to put more soul into the work, especially modern syncopation." "The white musician does everything mechanically," Peyton maintained; "he adheres to theory, while our musicians know how to improvise [and] add to the composer's ideas."[38] Although later writers would invert the values placed on these definitions by Peyton, the columnist provides a clear example of some of the African American responses to jazz music.

Overall, a social and cultural ambivalence coursed through Peyton's writing, and as much as he enjoyed jazz and urged musicians to be more prescient about the future, two issues—the social consequences of jazz and the effect of new technology—made him nervous. The social effects of jazz, or at least a less restrained variant of jazz, alarmed Peyton. Jazz could, Peyton believed, help uplift both the audience and the musician, but "dangerous jazz," he wrote in 1927, "is the barbaric, filthy, discordant, wild and shrieky music, that should be eliminated from the public dance halls and should be disqualified by the decent element."[39] Aware of its power but fearful of its consequences, Peyton argued that jazz music needed to be restrained. His columns relate to the larger, more virulent protest by critics who struggled to proscribe all forms of jazz, but they diverge sharply from many of the black writers active in Harlem during this period. Langston Hughes and others saw in jazz the unfulfilled promise of American life for black people. According to these writers of the Harlem Renaissance, jazz music exemplified African American creative expression and represented a key step in obtaining cultural equality. Peyton conceded elements of this argument but still fretted about the loosening of moral boundaries, which many in his cohort saw as the natural result of jazz music.

His protest against the impact of new technology on jazz music also underscores Peyton's hesitancy to embrace new ideas. During the silent film era, Peyton unequivocally supported the use of black bands in the theater, and he often argued that black bands needed to become a fixture in Chicago's movie houses. In a related attack, Peyton warned of technological advances in recorded music. An invention called the Vitaphone particularly worried Peyton, and in 1926 he wrote, "the greatest menace in the musician's future today is the Vitaphone."[40] Again, his concerns dealt with employment—Peyton resisted innovation because did not want to see bands replaced by machines. Even when he admired the results—as when he heard a Louis Armstrong record played on an Amplivox sound system— Peyton strongly urged theater owners to retain live music. In 1927, however, Peyton noted "there is too much jazz music played in the picture theater today."[41] Part of his criticism stemmed from his disapproval of wildly improvised hot jazz, the type that many of the bands played during movies. But Peyton also exhibits a larger concern for new technology taking the place of live musicians. In a column in 1928, he condemned canned music and its effect on the employment of jazz musicians. Although Peyton's aversion stemmed explicitly from technology's impact on employment opportunities, it also demonstrated his resistance to new concepts.[42]

Despite Peyton's reservations concerning the impact of new types of machinery on musical performance, new recording technology actually allowed for a more accurate preserving of sound. This improved fidelity lured larger audiences to jazz music and thus Chicago musicians achieved increased success. The theory behind the phonograph dated back to Thomas Edison's experiments in the 1870s with the etching of sound waves onto wax cylinders. By the 1890s, as Edison's company (later Columbia Records) patented and then mass-produced this wax-based system, Emile

Berliner was marketing a more practical machine that replaced Edison's cylinders with flat shellac discs. A court battle eventually erupted between Columbia and Berliner's Victor Talking Machine Company. During the protracted proceedings Columbia and Victor reached a compromise effectively monopolizing the production of phonograph records. Once the records proved popular to the buying public a number of smaller companies emerged and used (legally and illegally) patented technology to seize a share of the commerce. More legal battles ensued as Victor and Columbia attempted to maintain industry control. By the early 1920s, however, a number of court decisions ruled against the two major corporations and empowered a number of small companies to expand their manufacturing and distribution interests.

The burgeoning recording industry drastically altered the transmission of popular music. Sheet music—the traditional mainstay of popular musical distribution—conveyed neither the improvisational structure of jazz nor the emotional temper of the blues, the definitive attributes of the two genres. By presenting a new way of conveying music and by offering a musical product that could not be translated through printed music, record companies discovered a national market. In response to this changing economic culture, some sheet music companies shifted their focus away from the home piano player and began marketing to amateur and professional jazz musicians. In 1928, for example, Chicago-based Melrose Publishing discovered success with a collection of Louis Armstrong solos transcribed from his records. In this case, the sheet music followed the recordings.[43] Throughout the 1920s the primary mode of transmission was through the recording and distribution of records, and although New York City served as the business center for the music industry, several smaller labels in the Chicago area produced some of the most definitive records of early jazz. The most successful of these "independent" labels took advantage of the markets in the Midwest, where Chicago quickly became an important city in the recording of early jazz.[44]

Record companies had been recording jazz ensembles since the Original Dixieland Jazz Band (ODJB) introduced their sound to record buyers in 1917, with their sessions produced by Columbia and Victor Records in New York City. These early recordings, primarily "Livery Stable Blues" and "Dixie Jass Band One-Step," became quite popular, but overall, the major record companies followed up on the trend slowly.[45] The immediate response by consumers for the ODJB overshadowed the actual substance of their records. Though based in improvisation, the Original Dixieland Jazz Band relied less on spontaneity than on structured "improvised" breaks. Their stylized improvisations mirrored the clamorous vibe of New Orleans, but vaudeville entertainment, not musical innovation, served the band's purpose. Imitative barnyard whines served as the most prominent feature of "Livery Stable Blues," and "Dixieland One-Step" relates more to the dance music of the Castles than to the streets of New Orleans. Race has also obscured the band's role in jazz history. Since their introduction in 1917, the whiteness of the Original Dixieland Jazz Band has generated controversy and overstated opinions from both admirers and detractors. Supporters posit the ODJB as true originators of jazz music, while critics have dismissed the band as a novelty act producing only a vague representation of "authentic" jazz.[46] The importance of the band, though, exists less in the grooves of a shellac disc than in their influence on white Americans. The Original Dixieland Jazz Band introduced jazz music to a wide audience, and although their music related little to King Oliver or Jelly Roll Morton, their early success familiarized a generation of young white listeners with a music rooted in the experience of black Americans, however implicitly. LaRocca and company portended the careers of Paul Whiteman and Rudy Vallee, and the eventual national obsession with jazz in the 1930s fulfilled through happenstance the shadow promises of the Original Dixieland Jazz Band.

Despite the Original Dixieland Jazz Band's success, the major studios recorded little jazz in the late 1910s. In the early 1920s, OKeh and Paramount (a Wisconsin-based company) sparked a blues craze with their records featuring black female blues singers like Mamie Smith. Record companies promoted black blues singers and white jazz bands, but black jazz bands remained unrecorded. This trend began to change after Gennett recorded the New Orleans Rhythm Kings in 1922 and entered the developing jazz market in Chicago. The success of these first recordings of black jazz, along with the blues recordings of Mamie Smith, helped spawn a race records phenomenon as Chicago record companies began to pick up on this new sound.[47] In the 1920s, Brunswick, Paramount, and OKeh all recorded jazz music in Chicago, but somewhat perversely, Gennett Records—located several hundred miles away in Richmond, Indiana—emerged as the most important studio for Chicago jazz. Though not the most prolific or widely distributed record label, Gennett (along with its rival OKeh) epitomized the small, regionally based company that helped make jazz available on a larger scale. In the 1910s, as the phonograph began to be popular, the owners of

Star Piano Company created a rather inauspicious division called Gennett Records to tap the growing interest in sound recording. By the early 1920s, record sales for Gennett exceeded three million units, a figure lower than what the larger labels accumulated but still respectable competition.[48] After the major patent victory in 1921, Gennett expanded its sales catalog to include "classical, sacred, popular, and military band music, as well as specialty foreign-language and instructional discs."[49] These recordings took place in the back of the piano factory, in a building fifty yards away from the Chesapeake and Ohio railroad line. The studio's proximity to this noise and commotion, clamor, and reverberation interrupted not a few sessions and gave Gennett Records a certain mystique, both to contemporary musicians as well as later collectors and historians. External interruptions notwithstanding, studio engineers also had to contend with the acoustics of the room itself. Only marginal sound adjustments could be made, and usually these changes consisted solely of moving louder musicians a few steps away from the megaphone.

Apart from musical considerations, recording at Gennett forced African American musicians to experience rural midwestern race relations. Although far from problem-free, the large black community of Chicago provided some respite from outright racism, a situation soon recognized by black musicians traveling outside the city. Indiana, for instance, boasted the nation's largest number of Ku Klux Klan members during this period, and although nominally more anti-Catholic than anti-black, the Ku Klux Klan still embodied prejudice and bigotry. On recording trips to Gennett Studios, black musicians could not stay overnight in Richmond but had to arrange for safer accommodations outside of town. The racial temper of the city forced the New Orleans Rhythm Kings to assert somewhat facetiously that Jelly Roll Morton was Latin American rather than black.[50] In reality, Morton was neither, but his rather complex Creole ancestry would be a hard sell in an area rife with Klan activity. This Richmond-area Klan population, however, also purchased phonograph records, and the savvy business owners of Gennett Records took advantage of record buyers' prejudice by producing a number of Klan-themed recordings such as "Onward Christian Klansman" and "The Bright Fiery Cross." Thus, the studio responsible for the first integrated jazz-recording sessions and some of the most influential black music of the twentieth century stood in a town that denied services to African Americans and devoted much of its catalog to Ku Klux Klan recordings.[51]

Placing business before art certainly fails to distinguish Gennett from other record companies, large or small, and in fact, Gennett recorded jazz with little regard for posterity. The responsibility of selecting master recordings fell to the nearest employee at the time; thus, secretaries and day laborers determined which Bix performance transcended all others. But the company's proximity to Chicago and its emphatic willingness to produce records by local artists for a regional audience placed Gennett in an extraordinary position to preserve and transmit early jazz music. For most of the 1920s, Gennett—"the only record label based in the rural Midwest"—produced records independent from the larger corporate entanglements of New York City. As such, Gennett signifies the necessary link between jazz as an African American folk music prominent in New Orleans and jazz as a national commodity that resonated with black and white audiences. Aside from business concerns, this evolution depended on the diverse social structure and jazz scenes present in Chicago, where commerce and community mixed unambiguously as record companies discovered the available market in Bronzeville.[52]

Chicago represented the center of jazz recording in the 1920s, and Chicago bands released many of the most influential jazz records of the period. The city's active and diverse black community allowed for a dependable market for the music, and the coalition of record company and audience rewarded both parties. An example of this interaction occurred on June 12, 1926, when OKeh Records, in conjunction with the Consolidated Talking Machine Company and Local 208, the black musicians union, hosted the "OKeh Cabaret and Style Show."[53] Held at the Chicago Coliseum, the gala evening advertised a dance contest, festival booths, a style show, and a wide range of musical acts.[54] Promoters expected between 20,000 and 25,000 people. To support the bands the promoters installed "a specially built amplifying system consisting of a control board weighing three tons and requiring two operators' attention."[55] For $1.10 participants could dance to fifteen bands including Joe Oliver and his Plantation Serenaders, Sara Martin, Lonnie Johnson, and Louis Armstrong and his Hot Five.[56] The *Chicago Defender* enthusiastically supported the event and published a special music section the day of the gala to promote the various bands. One of the purposes of the event was to raise money for a new building for the black musicians union. Verona Biggs, president of Local 208, maintained a strong presence in the black community, and his support of black musicians garnered him some amount of influence. A considerable sum of money went into the program, and one of the main financial backers of the gala, the self-styled philanthropist E. A. Fearn of the Consolidated Talking Machine Company, noted that he had an "interest in ambitious and talented Race musicians."[57] OKeh Records and the other sponsors spared little expense to demonstrate their pride in black Chicago. Although no clear record exists documenting the demographics of the audience, the size of the crowd indicates that a reasonable cross-section of black Chicago attended the event. Black socialites, however, received most of the *Defender*'s attention, which noted, "At the Coliseum's box reservation office the box lists show that every man and woman on Chicago's South side who is important socially, politically or otherwise will be there."[58] Overall, Peyton pronounced the gala as "the greatest affair the Windy City has ever witnessed."[59]

As much as the 1926 gala presented the strength and diversity of Chicago's black community, it also attested to the popularity of Louis Armstrong. More than any other single musician, Armstrong personified the jazz scene in Chicago. Armstrong spent most of the decade in the city and played in a variety of bands—large and small—as well as produced the most influential recorded jazz of the period. Oliver and other Louisianans had introduced Chicago listeners to a New Orleans style, but Armstrong combined New Orleans rhythm with Chicago elegance and invented a new approach to jazz.[60] Armstrong quickly outgrew his Chicago surroundings, and in 1924, Armstrong moved to New York City to play with Fletcher Henderson's orchestra at the Roseland Ballroom. In the year that he lived in New York, Armstrong made three changes in his playing that would have a profound affect on Chicago jazz once he returned. First, Armstrong's tenure with Henderson's group introduced him to the power of a large band playing written arrangements. Although he continued to play and record with small units over the next few years, Armstrong began seeking out a more arranged style of playing during the later part of the decade. Second, he began singing regularly at gigs. His gravelly voice thrilled audiences, but it also helped to preserve his lip. Also, Armstrong switched from the harsh blare of the cornet to the more refined tone of the trumpet. He put these experiences to use once he returned to Chicago in 1925 to begin playing with a variety of bands. No longer connected to Oliver, Armstrong performed with Lil Hardin's band at the Dreamland, Erskine Tate's Vendome Orchestra, and Carroll Dickerson's large band at the Sunset.[61]

These bands brought Armstrong some money and celebrity (his name began appearing on promotional material during this time), but the trumpet player's real contributions to jazz occurred in the recording studio. In 1925, OKeh Records put together a five-piece recording unit—the Hot Five, as it came to be known—that existed only in the studio and included Armstrong on trumpet, his wife, Lil Hardin, on piano, Johnny Dodds on clarinet, Kid Ory on trombone, and Johnny St. Cyr on banjo.[62] They made several recordings between November and February, and on February 26, 1926, the Hot Five cut "Heebie Jeebies," a fairly unremarkable novelty tune connected with a popular dance. Armstrong, however, delighted in the playful lyrics, and punctuated the song with scat singing—the adlibbing of nonsense syllables rather than words. Armstrong did not invent scat, but "Heebie Jeebies" brought the singing style to the record-buying public. Funny, exhilarating, and utterly different from what had come before, Armstrong's "Heebie Jeebies" sold tens of thousands of copies, became the trumpet player's first hit record, and introduced Chicago-style jazz to the nation.[63] The song also generated considerable response in Chicago. Part-time clarinetist and full-time marijuana dealer Milton "Mezz" Mezzrow commented on the record's influence on white jazz musicians, especially Bix Beiderbecke. Armstrong's scat vocals served as key identifiers for the white jazz subculture, and Mezzrow noted that "for months after that you would hear cats greeting each other with Louis' riffs when they met around town—*I got the heebies*, one would yell out, and the other would answer *I got the jeebies*, and the next minute they were scatting in each other's face."[64]

Armstrong's popularity was at its peak during the years that Peyton wrote for the *Defender*, and the columnist regularly mentioned the jazz artist's activities. "Louis is in demand in the Windy City," Peyton wrote in 1927, "and there is a reason—he toots a wicked trumpet."[65] Despite his praise, Peyton also gently chastised Armstrong when the trumpet player veered from the columnist's canonical laws. In particular, Peyton criticized an Armstrong-led band that performed predominantly improvised hot jazz. "Louis will learn in time to come," Peyton maintained in 1927, "that noise isn't music."[66] Still, Peyton greatly respected Armstrong's talent, work ethic, and professionalism, and the trumpet player represented much of what Peyton desired in a musician. Armstrong, Peyton wrote, "is a fine example of ambition and thrift."[67] Considering Peyton's views on musicianship, Armstrong could receive no higher compliment. Armstrong, tired of the constraints of the New Orleans style, wanted to pursue a big band direction, and following the 1928 sessions he increasingly utilized larger band configurations and performed more popular tunes.[68]

In the summer of 1928, Louis Armstrong gathered an amended version of the Hot Five and scheduled a recording session at an OKeh studio in Chicago. Armstrong's tenure with Fletcher Henderson and Carroll Dickerson had piqued an interest in more arranged pieces so Armstrong began relying on more complicated charts and arrangements. He replaced his longtime trombonist Kid Ory, banjo player Johnny St. Cyr, and clarinetist Johnny Dodds with musicians who had more capable music-reading skills. For these recordings Armstrong also enlisted Arthur "Zutty" Singleton on drums and Earl Hines on piano.[69] The group's adoption of two additional musicians and Armstrong's insistence on clearer, more deliberate arrangements tightened the band's sound. Lil Hardin's steadfast, if unimaginative, piano work paled in comparison to Earl Hines who "unleashed broken chords and delicate improvisations with elegance."[70] To enhance the creative mood, Armstrong—a longtime advocate of marijuana—"insisted everyone smoke some of that good shuzzit before they began recording."[71] Supplementing Armstrong's creativity, tight band, and prodigious intake of marijuana, OKeh recorded the Hot Five electrically, contrasting the earlier acoustic sessions in 1923. Instead of a megaphone, microphones would pick up the sound waves, greatly increasing the power and vitality of the recordings. The larger studios had transferred over to electric as early as 1925, and Armstrong himself had recorded electrically in 1927, but the 1928 sessions marked the first time in which a modern approach to the music complemented modern recording methods.[72] Whereas "Snake Rag" symbolized a culmination of many of the preceding musical trends, the recordings produced by Armstrong in 1928 signified a break, a turn toward a new era of jazz music.

On June 28, 1928, Armstrong and the Hot Five recorded "West End Blues," a song by Joe Oliver.[73] Armstrong's version of the piece combines several elements of traditional New Orleans–style jazz, but overall, the tune inhabited a completely new context. Armstrong's opening trumpet cadenza—the most famous aspect of the song—relates back to the brass bands of his youth, and the song follows an established blues form. Armstrong reinvented and reconceived these elements, however, distilling them into a piece of music that marked the introduction of African American cultural modernism.[74] At once in and out of time, the opening blast prefaces a shift in tone as the Hot Five, completely in sync with one another, float along on a moderate pulse conveying both the constancy and mood of a traditional twelve-bar blues, but also allowing room for the soloists to drive the song forward. Near the middle of the tune, Armstrong puts his trumpet down and begins to scat melodies accompanied by Jimmy Strong's clarinet. No longer the vocal novelty as in the earlier "Heebie Jeebies," Armstrong's voice in "West End Blues" served as an extension of his horn with his scabrous syllables symbolizing a step forward in modern expression. The piece climaxes with another strong Armstrong solo in which he hits a piercing and prolonged high note that hangs in the air as a tease, a threat, a warning to what may lie ahead. Modern and mysterious, "West End Blues" stood apart from all preceding jazz tunes and bridged the gap between the shadowy prehistory of Buddy Bolden's jazz (the title itself referred to an area near Lake Pontchartrain) and the bold arrangements of Duke Ellington's swing.[75] With this composition, Armstrong, immersed in Chicago's technological and musical culture of innovation, had crafted a new sound manufactured specifically for mass consumption.[76] With the map redrawn, Armstrong thrust jazz toward something new with a performance more emotional, forceful, and immediate than earlier songs had intimated. A new age of modern expression was unleashed.

The 1928 Armstrong recordings attest to the changes that occurred in jazz in the 1920s, and Chicago served as the backdrop for much of this evolution. By the late 1920s, however, the jazz scene in the city was completely altered. A number of national and local forces acted on Chicago's jazz scene forcing many musicians to leave the city for brighter prospects elsewhere. In 1927, the advent of talking pictures compelled occupational changes for musicians as sound systems replaced live bands, and a number of the largest area theaters disbanded their pit orchestras.[77] During this same period, local moral reformers succeeded in closing down a number of clubs on liquor violations, a move that further impacted employment opportunities for the city's musicians.[78] Furthermore, economic despair eroded the once-thriving recording industry in and around Chicago, limiting the ability of musicians to record. At its peak in 1927 the national recording industry averaged sales of over 104 million records. Five years later, during the Great Depression, sales dropped to barely six million records. The economic depression and resultant drop-off in record sales helped accelerate an emerging pattern of industrial consolidation as the major record companies bought out smaller rivals. Less than a decade after producing many of the most influential jazz records of the 1920s, Gennett Records could afford only to market budget-priced recordings of novelty sound effects.[79] In 1929, in a reflection of Chicago's changing musical temper, the *Defender* removed Dave Peyton from his column. Most important, a large number of musicians, including Jelly Roll Morton and Louis Armstrong, left for the East Coast. For all of his promise, Bix Beiderbecke ended the decade in an alcoholic haze and would be dead by the age of twenty-eight. Despite this depressing end, for five years, Chicago stood at the center of a major transformation in both jazz music (with Armstrong defining a new vocabulary for jazz musicians) as well as the emergence of a new entertainment economy (with record companies directing new lines of consumption). By the end of the decade, however, New York City began to supplant Chicago as the foremost center of jazz transmission. Radio, not the phonograph, served most consumers of music during the Great Depression, and the broadcasting towers of New York City soon eclipsed the recording studios of Chicago as the primary purveyors of American popular culture in the 1930s.[80]

4 New York City and the Broadcasting of Jazz in the 1920s

Despite the innovative sounds produced by musicians in the Midwest, New York City—not Chicago—stood at the center of the jazz world during the 1920s. East Coast jazz would come to characterize the nation's popular music for the next two decades. Records made in and around Chicago emitted an original sound but acquired a narrow audience greatly limited by both region and race. Connected to Chicago in spirit, New York jazz differed considerably from its midwestern counterpoint in style. In contrast to the Chicago scene, New York City featured large bands that played arranged pieces for an increasingly white audience. Many of the best musicians from Chicago—most notably Bix Beiderbecke and Louis Armstrong—collaborated with various New York bands throughout this period, but New York jazz maintained a distinctive form that would eventually appeal to a mass audience. During the 1920s, New York introduced jazz to a national audience through the city's unique combination of jazz music, a thriving black intellectual community, and the presence of major radio corporations. The jazz scene in Manhattan incorporated both the polished dance music of Fletcher Henderson and the ambitious art music of Duke Ellington. The Harlem Renaissance facilitated the acceptance of jazz music as an African American cultural art form equal to poetry and literature, a new cultural context that attracted white elites who sought a connection to the "New Negro." The increased exposure to jazz by white listeners and dancers coincided with the emergence of radio broadcasting. Unlike the more regionally based companies operating out of Chicago, New York City hosted national music publishing and recording industries as well as the most powerful radio corporations. By the early 1930s, jazz had emerged as the predominant popular music of the United States, and the jazz scene in New York City during the 1920s generated much of this success.

On May 29, 1925, Fletcher Henderson's Orchestra piled into a New York studio to record "Sugarfoot Stomp."[1] At the time, Henderson's group represented the epitome of big band dance music, and although the band had made earlier recordings, the recent addition of Louis Armstrong provided the 1925 sessions with an even stronger sense of swing. In addition to his talent, Armstrong also contributed a new repertoire of material. "Sugarfoot Stomp," for example, was a rearranged version of King Oliver's "Dippermouth Blues." Don Redman, Henderson's arranger, reworked the piece into a song only tangentially related to Chicago jazz. Recorded two years after Oliver's "Snake Rag," "Sugarfoot Stomp" sounds nothing like the music of the South Side, presaging instead future stylistic developments in jazz. More significantly, the song establishes the pattern for big band swing music of the 1930s with a band divided into sections, a dynamic riff-based structure, and a swinging rhythm section—a model that would come to define popular music into the 1940s.[2] By dividing the band into different sections—brass, reeds, and rhythm—the arranger could have each section perform short, melodic lines (known as riffs) to produce a dense, warm sound. This arrangement allowed for a more complex harmonic structure (a larger band generates more instrumental voices) as well as provided a thick undercurrent for the various soloists. Redman's arrangements transcended earlier styles of jazz playing by incorporating a more complex use of timbre, harmony, and melody; polyphony, not monophony, became the new template.[3] A key component of this intricate style concerned the written chart. Chicago bands removed some of the New Orleans spontaneity and cacophony from their music, but most of the smaller bands, such as King Oliver's Creole Jazz Band, still employed unwritten (or "head") arrangements. Henderson's band, in contrast, used charts for all of their songs, and only the soloists were able to improvise material, and then only occasionally. Larger dance bands did exist in Chicago, most notably Erskine Tate's Vendome Orchestra, but ten- to twenty-piece orchestras playing an arranged style of music constituted the fundamental units of New York jazz. This larger arrangement signified the general connection of the New York jazz scene to more traditional structures. Thus if King Oliver's Creole Jazz Band or Louis Armstrong's Hot Five typified the Chicago scene, then Fletcher Henderson's Orchestra or Duke Ellington's Cotton Club Band characterized the jazz produced in New York.

Perhaps the clearest example of the newly discovered power of this arrangement is Don Redman's work on "Sugarfoot Stomp," a staple of Henderson's repertoire.[4] The basic melody, of course, relates back to King Oliver's band, but the instrumentation and rhythmic pulse of the band connect the piece to New York. Beginning with a short, standard trumpet introduction, Redman's version then leads into the melodic theme played reasonably straight. The tuba, banjo, and drums follow a careful dance band pulse, with the accents falling on the first and third beats. A brief clarinet and saxophone section precedes a quick trombone solo by Charlie Green. The first half of the tune thus follows a somewhat standard dance band arrangement. The second half of "Sugarfoot Stomp," however, diverges into a more interesting combination of Chicago and New York styles. After Green's solo, Louis Armstrong enters with a blaring, swinging trumpet solo that invigorates the entire song. Redman counterbalances Armstrong's solo with a subtle underpinning of saxophones, trumpets, and trombones, and Kaiser Marshall, Henderson's drummer, provides an animated counterpoint to all of the brass action.[5] After the two solos, Redman alternates sweet sections of the band, including a banjo maintaining the tempo, playing a rather drawn-out melody, with the more raucous, Chicago-style jazz. Although not fully improvised, the boisterous sections at the end of the piece clearly prefigure swing music, with the organized cacophony of different sections playing contrasting melodies supported by a driving tuba part emphasizing all four beats. This subtle bass shift from an emphasis on the first and third beats to playing on all four beats directly foreshadows the basic rhythmic element crucial to swing music.[6] Between Armstrong's solo and the proto-swing of the rhythm section, "Sugarfoot Stomp" marks a clear transition from Chicago jazz to the uniformity of New York dance music.

Born within two years of each other in the late 1890s, Fletcher Henderson (born in Georgia) and Don Redman (from West Virginia) came to represent a new type of jazz musician.[7] If Louis Armstrong's childhood in New Orleans indicated one aspect of black life, then the relatively comfortable middle-class upbringings of Fletcher Henderson and Don Redman reflected the degrees of variance experienced by African Americans during this period. The son of a school principal and a music instructor, Henderson developed a dual passion for tinkering with chemistry and playing the piano. Classical music, not jazz, filled the Henderson home, a musical cadence interrupted by the jazz scene Henderson encountered after he moved to New York City. A child prodigy from a similar background, by the time Redman graduated high school he could play proficiently the cornet, piano, trombone, and violin. Both Henderson and Redman attended college, and both men had eventually made their way to New York by the early 1920s—Henderson intent on a career in chemistry and Redman focused on playing the alto saxophone for a traveling band. Differing considerably from many of the players in New Orleans and Chicago in terms of economic background, educational opportunities, and musical interests, Henderson and Redman spearheaded a new, if related, style of jazz. The music of Henderson and Redman—who began playing together in 1923—emerged from a different array of social and musical influences than did earlier jazz. Instead of building upon a dynamic folk tradition as had musicians from New Orleans, Henderson's jazz found its direct antecedents in ragtime, vaudeville, and popular dance music. In essence, Henderson and Redman (as well as their friend, saxophonist Coleman Hawkins) crafted the archetype of the educated musician who actively sought out new sounds, and though anomalous to the 1920s jazz scene, their background and attitude prefigured the quintessential bebop musician of the 1940s.[8]

New York allowed this new style of jazz to prosper within the city's diverse network of nightclubs, music publishing companies, recording studios, and radio stations. Though important similarities link the three cities, in general, the developmental pattern of New York jazz deviated in important ways from what had occurred in New Orleans and Chicago. In New Orleans and Chicago, jazz maintained a strong identity as African American folk music. Musicians in these cities, for example, came from essentially the same racial, social, cultural, and economic backgrounds as their audiences. The New York jazz scene, however, lacked this folk music dimension. Instead, New York jazz bands from the beginning generally associated—both implicitly and explicitly—with the music business. This sociomusical distinction impacted the way that jazz music found white adherents. The jazz styles present in New Orleans and Chicago percolated out of the black communities of each city and only gradually attracted large groups of white listeners over the course of the 1910s and 1920s. In contrast, much of the jazz played in New York developed from musical trends already popular with a white audience. Ragtime rhythms and vaudeville songs, in particular, defined the repertoire of the dominant bands in New York during the 1920s. Thus, despite certain developmental similarities, New York jazz differed greatly from jazz with midwestern or southern origins. This style of jazz, with its diluted folk influence and strong relationship to commercial culture, helped generate mainstream white acceptance of jazz more rapidly than in any other city during this period.

During the first two decades of the twentieth century, the music scene of New York City incorporated several genres that would eventually give rise to a rather unique form of jazz. Notwithstanding certain stylistic differences, two general types of jazz music came to dominate the city. One musical trend centered on the bands that provided music for dances, vaudeville performances, and Broadway shows. Unlike the brass band tradition of New Orleans, these New York bands used primarily written arrangements, maintained larger configurations, and played songs predominantly made popular through the sheet music industry. More than any other individual, James Reese Europe personified this style of band performance. Europe, who became an icon for many African Americans, achieved much of his fame through his work with Irene and Vernon Castle as well as with his military band, the 369th Infantry Hell Fighters. Europe directed the Society Orchestra to accompany the Castles, a noted dance team that helped popularize the foxtrot in the 1910s. The band (originally a rather large string-based ensemble) maintained a working core of about seven members and played lightly syncopated dance music infused with a ragtime spirit. In 1913, Europe recorded several numbers with the Society Orchestra, and, although stiff compared to later bands, the rhythmic drive of Europe's group struck a chord with dancers.[9] Europe's work with the Castles ended with the eruption of World War I and the bandleader's induction into the military. Stationed in France, he directed the 369th Infantry Hell Fighters, an all-black ensemble that introduced ragtime rhythms overseas. Wildly popular, Europe successfully grafted ragtime syncopation onto the military brass band tradition. At least one scholar has posited the Hell Fighters as an absolute precursor to big band jazz. Though connections exist, Europe represented only a whispered foretelling of something more complex.[10] Knifed to death by a fellow musician, Europe failed to witness the ways in which his music would inspire a new direction of black artistic expression.

Whereas ragtime coursed through the brass band music of James Europe, the other trend popular in New York during this period centered on a type of ragtime-influenced piano playing. Although classic ragtime originated in the Midwest, ragtime song emerged from Tin Pan Alley, and the casual syncopation of popular ragtime emanated from the East Coast. Furthermore, the ragtime craze of the 1910s occurred in large measure because the sheet music industry was housed in Manhattan. Also cementing the ragtime influence in the East, Scott Joplin moved to New York and near the end of his life staged *Treemonisha,* his failed rag opera, in the city.[11] The ragtime craze lasted only a few years, but its syncopated spirit enkindled a dynamic culture of solo piano playing. These piano players performed a mix of ragtime, blues, and Tin Pan Alley music that reverberated throughout New York City. Whereas New York bands played in black cabarets, white dance halls, or in theaters, solo piano players performed in more informal venues. Predominantly black, these pianists mainly played for neighborhood events such as parlor socials and "rent parties." A trend in lower-income areas of the city, rent parties were usually hosted by a group of neighbors to raise enough money to placate the monthly demands of the landlord. The hosts would often hire a piano player and charge admission to acquire that month's rent. These frequent parties made the better piano players quite popular throughout much of the city. Between the late 1910s and the 1930s three piano players, James P. Johnson, Willie "The Lion" Smith, and Fats Waller, came to prominence in New York City, and each player represented a key link between ragtime, the blues, Tin Pan Alley, and improvised jazz music.

Born in New Jersey in the early 1890s, James P. Johnson helped conceive a new style of piano playing known as stride in the 1910s. With its complex syncopation and ragtime origins, stride piano emanated from innumerable cafes, bars, and house parties throughout New York City. "The most sophisticated of all popular piano playing," stride invigorated the somewhat stilted and controlled ragtime style with a looser and more relaxed feel.[12] Unlike most piano ragtime, which maintained only a syncopated melody, stride piano added a strong syncopated rhythm to the song. Stride pianists, in other words, fused the traditional duties of each hand, creating a style replete with syncopated forcefulness.[13] One of Johnson's rivals, Willie "The Lion" Smith, added a more pronounced blues harmonic structure to stride piano and combined a syncopated ragtime-stride style with a blues feel and a strong sense of vaudeville showmanship.[14] In a sense, the stride piano of Johnson and Smith combined elements of the most popular music forms in the 1910s and bridged the stylistic divide between ragtime and jazz. Jelly

Roll Morton produced a similar type of music, but the stride piano players of New York maintained stronger interests in popular music, allowing for a more marketable style of playing. Both Johnson and Smith found degrees of commercial success—Johnson through the production of piano rolls and records, and Smith through his tenure with various bands including Mamie Smith's Jazz Hounds. More than any other piano player of this period, however, Fats Waller exemplified the combination of musical innovation, exuberant showmanship, and commercial appeal.[15]

Born in 1904 in the Greenwich Village neighborhood of Manhattan, Thomas "Fats" Waller perfected a syncopated blend of ragtime, the blues, popular song, and vaudeville on the piano, and eventually surpassed his mentor, James P. Johnson, to become "the most popular black entertainer of the 1930s."[16] His father, an active deacon, and mother, a church pianist, instilled in Waller an appreciation for hymns as well as for the pipe organ, a rather uncharacteristic jazz instrument. Waller perfected the rolling stride style of Johnson and Smith and combined piano prowess with vaudeville clowning.[17] The musician, however, mixed successful entertaining with unsuccessful business planning, and eventually he took on too many jobs in an ultimately futile attempt to remain solvent.[18] Despite his business failures—financial problems plagued the pianist throughout his life—Waller wrote some of the most vibrant jazz of the late 1920s. In the mid-1920s, Waller began playing engagements at various theaters, and in 1929 he composed his most famous piece, "Ain't Misbehavin'," for the popular musical revue *Hot Chocolates*. A somewhat distinctive character (few musicians rivaled his clowning and fewer still attempted jazz on a pipe organ), Waller still epitomized New York piano culture at its peak. His popularity throughout the early 1930s "did more than any of these players to bring the Harlem style to the attention of the broader American public."[19]

Though stride piano players discovered some success outside of New York City during this period, other jazz performers found a much wider national audience. In particular, a five-piece band of white New Yorkers garnered acclaim with their flurry of (slightly stilted) syncopation and noise. Conforming to the era's fetish for adjectivally hyperbolic, regionally specific, and numerically appropriate names, the Original Memphis Five exemplified the small band style of New York jazz.[20] Taking their moniker from W. C. Handy's "The Memphis Blues," the Original Memphis Five initially included five white musicians from the Northeast: Phil Napoleon (cornet), Miff Mole (trombone), Jimmy Lytell (clarinet), Frank Signorelli (piano), and Jack Roth (drums). Formed in 1917 when the Original Dixieland Jazz Band began to gain popularity, the Memphis Five began its career by accompanying dancers at a club on Coney Island. The Original Memphis Five shared certain similarities with the ODJB, namely a rather inflexible style of improvisation as well as a stiff, mundane rhythmic feel. The Original Memphis Five, however, overcame a jerky ragtime beat through the talents of its two main soloists—Miff Mole and Phil Napoleon—who combined technical ability with a graceful jazz energy entirely absent from the ODJB recordings.[21] Whereas the Original Dixieland Jazz Band looked to the past with its stilted form of New Orleans folk music, the Original Memphis Five projected instead the eventual emergence of jazz as a commodity. Borrowing their name from the blues, utilizing a ragtime beat, prolific in the recording studio, and popular on the road, the Original Memphis Five touched upon the defining elements of jazz in the early 1920s. Moreover, the success of the band relates in part to its adherence to one of the hallmark historical trends of this period. In 1922, the Original Memphis Five officially became the Original Memphis Five, Incorporated. Unusual for a jazz band—though large brass bands followed a similar business route—this registration created a corporate arrangement of stockholders, rules of accountability, and a system of fines to enforce these rules. A band savvy in business that also incorporated popular songs in their sets, the Original Memphis Five presented formidable competition in New York and their achievement helped bring jazz music into the homes of white America.[22]

Although issues of race delineated elements of the New York jazz scene—the stride pianists were black, the small bands tended to be white, and the large bands were of both races (though segregated)—racism proved less of an obstacle musically than it was occupationally. In other words, despite certain stylistic differences between black and white musicians, race constricted the venues available to and the resultant audiences for these bands. White bands performed for a predominantly white audience in clubs that barred the admission of African Americans. Black bands, in contrast, performed for segregated audiences of both races and for moderately mixed audiences in black clubs that tolerated white patrons. Geography provided defining limitations as the jazz scene cleaved New York City into two distinct areas: downtown (mid-Manhattan), and uptown (Harlem). White bands played primarily in such downtown clubs as the Casanova, Trocadero, and Hollywood, clubs that featured floorshows. Larger bands found gigs at Le Perroquet, the Midnight Frolic, and the Little

Club.[23] Black bands generally lacked downtown club opportunities, but both Fletcher Henderson and Duke Ellington had acquired enough fame to gain entry to the most popular ballrooms in the city: the Arcadia and Roseland. Most black bands performed in Harlem at such venues as the Cotton Club, Small's Paradise, and Connie's Inn.[24] Several of these clubs catered to white patrons, though this arrangement primarily existed due to the cost-prohibitive nature of the venues rather than outright constriction.[25] White Manhattan knew of these clubs, but a host of other Harlem nightspots maintained a predominantly black clientele. The most famous of these clubs was the Savoy Ballroom, the black equivalent of the Roseland. A large, block-long structure on Lenox Avenue, the Savoy could accommodate 1,500 dancers. White customers "were tolerated," but the majority of the Savoy's crowd came from the surrounding black neighborhoods.[26] Boasting strong dance bands and a low admission fee (less than one dollar), the Savoy Ballroom provided black entertainment for a black audience. Throughout this period, a white New Yorker (with money) had the opportunity to see any white jazz band and most black jazz bands he or she desired. A black jazz fan, however, faced certain racial and financial obstacles that limited the available music. By the late 1920s, the popularity of radio helped erase some of these racial constraints on the city's jazz scene, and, though not completely colorblind, the broadcasting medium provided new opportunities (and a certain degree of anonymity) for black jazz bands. As audiences increased and diversified, jazz music challenged and changed American culture, and New York City stood at the center of this transformation.

During the mid- to late 1920s, two major developments greatly impacted the transmission, reception, and style of jazz music. The writers of the Harlem Renaissance created a broad cultural context for jazz as an example of African American creative expression, and radio broadcasting allowed for wider dissemination of jazz, especially as the Great Depression eroded record sales in the 1930s. The radio industry and the Harlem Renaissance shared few similarities, but together this combination of art and technology removed jazz from its folk music moorings and helped transform jazz into the preeminent musical art form of modern America. In addition, these two forces deepened the connection between jazz and modernism. As many Americans drifted away from nineteenth-century Victorianism, a new spirit of moral, cultural discontent framed intellectual debate. Writers directed much of this discourse, but jazz illustrated their prose assertions with its combination of folk tradition, African primitivism, and a musical potency detached from the previous century. As radio produced a larger national audience for a new music, and the writers of the Harlem Renaissance crafted a new language of modernity, jazz came to define a decade, a generation, and a nation. New York City served as the backdrop for most of this change as African American artists and writers inundated uptown and the largest radio corporations established offices downtown.[27]

The history of jazz often overemphasizes the importance of the Harlem Renaissance, but the movement underscores two themes that would dramatically impact jazz: the importance of a powerful and creative black population and the creation of a culture that valued jazz as art. Optimistic and progressive, the Harlem Renaissance maintained a primary focus on literary and intellectual achievements and failed to embrace jazz music as immediately as other artistic forms.[28] Poets such as Langston Hughes experimented with jazz rhythms in their work, but the leaders of the Harlem Renaissance focused much more on the "respectable" arts of literature, art, and classical music. Age explains part of this indifference, as the intellectual leaders—such as W. E. B. Du Bois and James Weldon Johnson—tended to be older than many of the writers. Like Dave Peyton and the *Chicago Defender,* the leaders of Harlem maintained certain middle-class affectations precluding an immediate embracing of the music. Jazz, though perhaps enjoyable, was certainly not scholarly. "And while many Harlem intellectuals enjoyed the music of the cabarets," Nathan Irvin Huggins notes, "none were prepared to give someone like Jelly Roll Morton the serious attention he deserved."[29] Immediate acceptance of jazz by black intellectuals failed to materialize, but a newfound respect for black art and a growing attachment to modernism provided a base for the future legitimization of jazz music as an art form.

Although black leaders in the 1920s promoted Harlem as a spirit, a mood, and an intellectualism, Harlem was also a place. Occupying the northern end of the island of Manhattan, Harlem and its cultural manifestation, like Chicago's South Side, were a direct product of the Great Migration. In the 1890s, predominantly white Harlem exploded into a series of real estate deals and developments. This housing boom soon became a bust, and the ensuing depressed housing market created a tenuous situation for a large number of Harlem residents.[30] Black Harlem continued to grow throughout the early twentieth century, and by 1930 over 100,000 people lived in the area bordered by 126th Street on the south, 159th Street on the north, the Harlem River to the east, and Eighth Avenue to the west. Of this population, over 95 percent were African American.[31] Not the largest black community in terms of numbers—Washington, D.C., held that distinction—Harlem served as the spiritual center of black life in the 1920s. Significantly, despite the middle-class ideals espoused by many of the writers and intellectuals of the Harlem Renaissance, Harlem never obtained a strong middle-class social structure. This lack of a business class prevented continual regeneration, a condition that when combined with the effects of the economic crisis of the 1930s resulted in the gradual ghettoization of Harlem. During the 1920s, however, Harlem served as the center for creative black thought in the nation.[32]

This flowering of African American cultural talent notwithstanding, black musicians still faced many obstacles in terms of obtaining jobs outside of Harlem, especially in clubs catering to an all-white clientele. Exceptions existed, however, and in 1924, Fletcher Henderson, fresh from his tour with Ethel Waters, acquired a job directing an orchestra at Club Alabam.[33] The club furnished Henderson with somewhat steady income, but more important, a New York radio station, WHN, set up regular broadcasts of the bands featured at the Alabam. These remote broadcasts brought live dance music to a listening audience, and WHN (through the impulsiveness of a jazz-loving station director) made Henderson a star.[34] Stemming directly from the exposure gained from these broadcasts, Henderson's band received an invitation to play at the Roseland, one of the most prestigious white ballrooms in the city. Station WHN continued to broadcast Henderson's music, and during this period his band included some of the finest players in jazz, including Louis Armstrong, who moved to New York specifically to work with Henderson. His career at Club Alabam and the Roseland attests to the power and influence of radio, but the reserved Henderson would reap few other rewards from this new medium. Henderson, in fact, barely survived the decade at all. Other musicians would follow the vague template established by Henderson and would discover much greater success, but Henderson's early broadcasts proved that black culture could find a voice in the burgeoning radio industry.

In the late 1920s and 1930s, the radio industry united Americans through national broadcasts that crossed regional, economic, and, to some degree, racial lines. A young medium, radio came to symbolize much of the technological progress that arose from the corporate mentality driving business in the United States in the first part of the twentieth century. Between the early 1890s and the late 1910s, a number of individuals struggled to create a viable broadcast medium capable of sending code, then voice and music, across long distances. Guglielmo Marconi, a young Italian, succeeded in sending Morse code along radio waves by way of an antenna. Soon after, Alexander Popov, a Russian who had visited the 1893 World's Fair in Chicago, developed a theory of electromagnetism. Both Marconi and Popov obtained various patents for their discoveries as well as received naval sponsorships (Marconi with Britain and Italy, Popov with France and Russia), and early radio technology became closely entwined with maritime exploits. Lee DeForest, an isolated and idiosyncratic Iowan, and Reginald Fessenden, an enterprising Canadian, built upon both Marconi's and Popov's work by independently experimenting with transmitting music and voice (not simply Morse code) across radio waves. By the 1910s, the technology behind simple radio receivers became accessible enough to allow for a growing number of radio hobbyists in the United States. These amateurs, predominantly young men, read various technology journals, built elementary receivers and transmitters, and marveled at the great distances covered by their creations. A 1912 law made clear that these amateurs could be shut down in times of national crisis—a threat acted upon five years later with the declaration of war on Germany—but in general, amateurs directed much of this early stage of radio development as "experimenters in bedrooms, attics, shacks, and rooftop laboratories" created the foundation for the radio broadcasting industry.[35]

Between the early 1890s and the mid-1910s, radio amateurs and hobbyists formed a base for the radio industry. By the 1920s, however, large corporations called the shots, and radio broadcasting quickly became embroiled in a sea of patent lawsuits, copyright confusion, corporate entanglements, and questions of governmental control. Chaotic as it seemed, the radio industry continued to grow, and in 1924 sales of radio equipment topped $358 million. The potential wealth promised by radio lured even more licensed and unlicensed stations into the field. Corporate consolidation allowed for a small number of people to exert their authority over the industry. By 1921, General Electric (GE), the Radio Corporation of America (RCA), American Telephone and Telegraph (ATT), and Westinghouse controlled over 2,000 patents and effectively directed the broadcasting industry. For most of this period the industry operated under the rather vague guidelines of the 1912 law, but by the mid-1920s the rampant confusion forced the federal government to reevaluate the situation. In 1927, Congress passed a new radio law creating an independent commission with licensing authority to oversee the industry. The Radio Act of 1927—based on the premise of my-riad independent stations—failed to account for advertising or broadcast networks, two issues that had already begun to influence the industry. In 1926, RCA created the National Broadcasting Company (NBC), allowing for one station to "speak at once to east and west, city and country, rich and poor."36 Within months, NBC established two national networks, desig-nated red and blue, setting the pattern for regional affiliates' broadcasting programs emanating from a central studio. These radio programs gener-ated revenue through corporate sponsorship and reached people through-out the country. The Radio Act of 1927, however, neglected both the idea of networks and advertising, an inherent flaw that weakened its legislative power, and the act thus failed to regulate the industry as it entered its peak of popularity.37

As with the music industry, New York City dominated radio broadcast-ing. The largest companies established Manhattan offices, and the city quickly exerted control over the burgeoning network system. The power of New York was made clear early on with the controversy surrounding "silent nights." Due to the large number of stations competing for a limited amount of broadcast frequencies, many cities established proscribed peri-ods of inactivity. These self-imposed "silent nights" allowed for listeners to tune in to stations at a great distance. New York stations, however, fre-quently balked at this somewhat casual arrangement. "One cannot help but suspect that," one radio commentator noted, "when there is so strong a de-mand from listeners to hear programs from other localities, there are seri-ous lacks in the local programs. There has never been, in the New York area, for example, any similar widespread desire for a silent night."38 Stations began to phase out silent nights in 1927, but the impact of New York City remained strong. In general, New York City broadcast stations represented some of "the most technologically advanced in the nation," and the owners resented semirural transmissions impinging on their freedom.39 During the prenetwork period, local studio owners (much like local record produc-ers) would put just about anything on the air that would attract an audi-ence. The larger stations usually maintained a regular performance sched-ule of "potted palm music," a genre that included light classical selections and parlor pieces. "It was the music played at tea time," one scholar writes, "it was recital music."40 Jazz rarely made it to the airwaves. Chicago's WBBM was the first station to specialize in jazz, Henderson had success lo-cally on WHN, and certain stations picked up conductors such as Paul

Whiteman or Vincent Lopez, but jazz remained rather elusive on the national level until the mid-1920s.[41]

As a new medium derived from the work of Americans and Europeans, instantly popular with young people (especially the greatly increasing college-age crowd), and maintaining a certain aura of the exotic, the emergence of radio mirrored the cultural evolution of jazz. The radio industry, rather unsurprisingly, thus served as the primary instrument in the creation of jazz as a national music, and the growing popularity of national broadcasts in 1926 coincided with the appearance of more jazz music on the air. By 1927, jazz had finally discovered a truly national audience, and radio surpassed earlier media as the primary transmitter of jazz music. The sudden popularity of radio drastically impacted the music business as attested by the rapid drop-off in sales of sheet music and phonograph records. In 1921, for example, record sales peaked at over 105 million units. Four years later, sales had dropped to fewer than 60 million records per year. Radio had a similar effect on piano sales, an industry already sluggish because of the emergence of phonograph records.[42] Radio, however, also produced jobs, and a number of musicians found employment in radio-sponsored bands once broadcast networks began to flourish. The NBC orchestra, in particular, provided tenure for many of the most popular white swing musicians of the 1930s, including the Dorsey Brothers, Red Nichols, and Benny Goodman.[43] Radio and its reverberations reconfigured the music business, completing the transformation of jazz into a popular commercial music. Sheet music failed to denote the improvisational qualities of jazz, and phonograph records could not connect groups of people simultaneously over long distances, but radio succeeded in combining the immediacy of live performance with a broadcast radius of thousands of miles. As network broadcasting blossomed in the late 1920s, one of the premier artists to take advantage of its possibilities was a stylish twenty-eight-year-old bandleader from Washington, D.C.

On December 4, 1927, Edward "Duke" Ellington's ten-piece orchestra began its tenure at the Cotton Club, the most famous nightclub in Harlem. Built in 1923, located on 142nd Street, and featuring a rather eccentric blending of African "jungle" images and a fake log cabin exterior, the Cotton Club earned its designation as "the aristocrat of Harlem."[44] Accommodating nearly seven hundred dancers and carousers, the club featured black entertainers in highly choreographed and risqué floorshows performing for a white audience. The Cotton Club also serves as an example of the uneasy racial context of jazz in the 1920s as wealthy white New Yorkers traveled north to Harlem to enter a club masked as a sham log cabin and decorated as a southern plantation with jungle accoutrements. This jumbled set of visual metaphors complemented the service arrangement of black staff (many dressed as plantation butlers) and entertainers serving illegal booze to white customers.[45] By the late 1920s, Ellington's orchestra itself became the prominent draw for the club, a band that featured black, Creole, and, in the case of trombonist Juan Tizol, Puerto Rican musicians. Along with its mob-based management and radio antenna connection, the Cotton Club illustrates the peculiar synergy that defined Jazz Age America. At the center of this barrage of explicit and implicit tropes stood Duke Ellington, the heir apparent to Fletcher Henderson.[46]

Born in Washington, D.C., in 1899, Edward Kennedy Ellington experienced a comfortable, middle-class childhood in a city that boasted the nation's largest African American community. In 1900, for example, the nation's capital maintained a black population of 87,000 people, or roughly 37 percent of its total population. In many ways, Ellington's early life paralleled the lives of men such as Fletcher Henderson and Don Redman. The three musicians emerged from similar socioeconomic backgrounds, and ragtime provided the soundtrack for much of their formative years. An attentive student, Ellington began playing the piano at a young age, and as a teenager he started frequenting a neighborhood pool hall. Frank Holliday's poolroom served as the noted place of respite for local musicians (particularly piano players), and Ellington received his informal training in this bar.[47] Because of its central location and large African American population, Washington, D.C., attracted many of the most talented ragtime, blues, and early jazz performers, and Ellington had the chance to hear James P. Johnson and Mamie Smith (apparently on tour with Fletcher Henderson) among others. By 1923, Ellington had outgrown the Washington scene and sought an opportunity to relocate to New York.[48] His chance arrived on the vaudeville circuit in 1922 when Wilbur Sweatman performed in Ellington's hometown. Ellington may or may not have seen him play, but Sonny Greer, Ellington's drummer, was in the audience, and in 1923, Sweatman invited Greer to play for his band in New York. Greer agreed with the condition that Ellington and saxophonist Otto Hardwick could come along as well. Sweatman acquiesced, and Duke Ellington moved to New York City that spring.[49]

After a brief stint with Sweatman, Ellington began making contacts of his own, especially with the Harlem piano players. Both Willie "The Lion"

Smith and J. P. Johnson opened doors for Ellington, and throughout 1923, his band, the Washingtonians, played in and around Harlem's circuit of small clubs and cabarets. Unlike many of his contemporaries, Ellington also endeavored to bring his music to the white-dominated areas south of Harlem.[50] A few months after moving to the city, Ellington made several songwriting contacts with publishers in Tin Pan Alley and found some initial success on Broadway at "a cramped cellar" called the Hollywood.[51] Ellington's early career encapsulated the history of jazz as well as set the stage for the future development of the music in the 1930s and 1940s. A heady combination of ragtime, rent party piano, vaudeville, Broadway showpieces, Tin Pan Alley popular song, and Chicago jazz growl, Ellington explicitly blurred African, European, and American motifs into an engaging and complex form of music that appealed to audiences of both races. This musical alchemy effectively reconceptualized the New Orleans/Chicago jazz style as something altogether modern. Although antecedents existed in Don Redman's work with Fletcher Henderson, this transformation of early jazz is seen most clearly in Ellington's prodigious output during the late 1920s. On the surface, Ellington's band related directly back to the music made by Fletcher Henderson a few years earlier. Both bandleaders utilized similar dance band formations and arrangements, and both Henderson and Ellington took advantage of the recording studio and radio broadcasts. Henderson, however, lacked a managerial personality, a deficit that debilitated his position as bandleader.[52] Despite his roster of incredibly talented musicians and the original arrangements of Don Redman, Henderson never transcended his early success, a career flaw that only worsened after an automobile accident in 1928 severely affected his demeanor and disposition. In contrast, Ellington's personality—a combination of affability and resolution—fostered a creative work environment, and his active pursuit of critical appointments such as the Cotton Club coincided propitiously with the broadcast boom of the late 1920s.[53]

In the decade between 1925 and 1935, several musical changes significantly impacted the sound of big band jazz. In the early 1920s, Don Redman's arrangements helped to divide the band into sections allowing for a more complex, warmer sound. The appearance of the saxophone gave a new tone to the band as well. A relatively new instrument, the saxophone was used mainly as a novelty in Chicago jazz. By the 1920s, however, the saxophone found a new home in large jazz orchestras and would eventually eclipse the clarinet as the predominant jazz reed. The sax altered the tone palette available to composers, but developments in the rhythm section would change the overall feel of jazz music. In the mid-1920s, the guitar began to replace the banjo as the driving rhythmic instrument. This shift caused both a change in timbre as well as a further distancing from the minstrel trappings of a black banjo-picker, allowing jazz to develop an even stronger urban identity. Also, guitarists usually played chords using all downstrokes, instead of the banjo style of alternating up- and down-strokes. This altered strum pattern brought a more propulsive rhythmic feel. Perhaps more audibly explicit, the string bass replaced the tuba as primary bass voice in the rhythm section, a shift that allowed for greater definition as the plucked string bass had more presence and attack. Furthermore, bass players began playing on all four beats, rather than only two as in New Orleans and Chicago jazz. This four-beat style of "walking" bass— playing a different note of a particular chord on each beat—created a sense of forward movement with the rhythm, as seen in Henderson's "Sugarfoot Stomp." Finally, drummers began emphasizing beats one and three with a slight kick, a subtle anticipation of the beat that helped to give big band jazz a momentum and drive that earlier jazz had achieved only intermittently.[54]

These various changes in the rhythm section transformed the role of the big band soloist. As the rhythm developed from accenting two beats to all four, the soloist had less space to define his melodies; although the number of beats per measure had not changed, the rhythmic feel had been altered. In New Orleans jazz, many songs transcribed in 4/4 time (four beats per measure) would actually maintain the feel of music in 2/4 time (two beats per measure).[55] This shift in the metered feel of the music obliged soloists to impart more subtlety in less space than had earlier jazz musicians. Furthermore, these musical nuances became nearly impossible to transcribe and created a gulf between the sound made by large bands and what the written chart actually signified. These changes would not be widespread until the mid-1930s with the appearance of the Count Basie and Benny Goodman bands, but in New York City in the late 1920s, Duke Ellington incorporated many of these elements and produced some of the most nuanced and creative jazz of the twentieth century.

Although Ellington's recording career began in 1924, most of his recordings prior to late 1926 lack the overtures of creative distinctiveness.[56] During that period Ellington gained compositional proficiency, discovered a successful working arrangement with his band, and, perhaps equally important, acquired a manager. Irving Mills signed on as Ellington's manager in late 1926, and Ellington remained under his controversial leadership (the musician's contract stipulated that 55 percent of his earnings would go to Mills and his lawyer, both white men) until the late 1930s. One of the first recording sessions during the Mills era produced a subtly transitional piece composed by Ellington entitled "The Creeper."[57] Recorded for Vocalion on December 29, 1926, "The Creeper" borrowed from King Oliver and Fletcher Henderson, but Ellington's arrangement, and the solos by his band, formulated a newer sound. A fairly straightforward, up-tempo dance number, "The Creeper" combined melodic "short, fragmented phrases" with a number of hot solos (especially the muted trombone solo by Joe Nanton), and a "close, three-part voicing resembles Don Redman's writing for Fletcher Henderson."[58] More explicitly, Ellington's arrangement quotes directly a break from Oliver's "Snake Rag" in the final chorus. Echoing the preeminent sounds of Chicago and New Orleans, the "freewheeling solos" of Ellington's band declared a conceit equaled only by Louis Armstrong's Hot Five.[59]

Four years after "The Creeper," Ellington recorded one of his most important and popular songs of this period. With a deceptively simple arrangement, "Mood Indigo" undercut traditional jazz with a sense of modernism.[60] In particular, Ellington employed an inverted form of the New Orleans front line. Instead of a strong trumpet framed by a high-voiced clarinet and low-voiced trombone—the mainstay of New Orleans jazz—Ellington arranged the melody for a muted trumpet, a trombone played an octave higher than usual, and a clarinet played an octave lower.[61] The resultant warm sound, with all three instruments playing within a similar range, gave "Mood Indigo" a distinctive harmonic structure that quietly upended the jazz tradition. Originally entitled "Dreamy Blues," the piece fits into a category of Ellington's compositions known as the "moods." Throughout his career Ellington revived this style as seen in "Misty Mornin'," "Awful Sad," "Melancholia," "Solitude," and "Prelude to a Kiss." Each of these songs emphasized emotion and mood over distinct melodies, and in this way, Ellington's mood pieces relate directly to the emotional energy of the blues. Also, Art Whetsol's thick, warm tone proved exceedingly apt for these mood pieces, and along with the close harmonies, the "melancholic, sentimental" strain affected by Whetsol gives "Mood Indigo" its feel.[62] With its tight harmonic construction, lilting but not cloying melody, and attention to tone, "Mood Indigo," like Armstrong's "West End Blues" two years prior, borrowed from the past while pushing jazz forward. Between 1928 and 1931, Ellington recorded over 160 songs, a set of compositions staggering in its "wide-ranging experimentation and intuitive probing."[63] With "Mood In-digo" and "West End Blues," Ellington and Armstrong had effectively created a new jazz language of minimal cool. Stripping New Orleans jazz down to its essential syncopated and harmonic forms, these two artists suc-ceeded in reconfiguring nineteenth-century black folk music into some-thing peculiar to the modern age of the United States. No longer simply music for dancing, jazz, through the experimentation and creativity of Duke Ellington, had become art music. "It is very simple," Ellington later recalled, "it is just one of those very simple little things that you throw to-gether. Of course, the arrangement makes it. But it really isn't anything; the melody isn't. It's funny, I threw ["Mood Indigo"] together, and it has caught on." "Isn't it queer," he continued, "not to have anything for a great deal of work, and something for no work at all?"[64]

The new electrical methods of recording, which replaced acoustic horns, gave a crisper sound and greater fidelity. They also brought drums and bass into the recordings, allowing record buyers to hear a sound much more faithful to the live performances. These new methods also provided Elling-ton with inspiration as the hum of the microphone provided him with a new musical device—one that connected with his newfound interest in tone poems, putting sound to color. Thus, as Ellington began experiment-ing with a more modern compositional sensibility—connected directly to Marshall Berman's concept of the "attempt by modern men and women to become subjects as well as objects of modernization, to get a grip on the modern world and make themselves at home in it"—he was also incorpo-rating new sounds and new technologies.[65] A musical experiment at once modern in inception and reception, Ellington ably defined the newness of the 1920s as well as the modernist capabilities of jazz and black artistic ex-pression. This innovative sound helped provide Ellington with fresh com-positions, as the song "Dreamy Blues" attests, but it also intersected directly with the broadcasting abilities of radio. The performance of "Mood In-digo" underscores the commercial power of radio broadcasts, as a national audience demanded (and received) a recorded version of the song soon after the performance. Heightening the emotional, historical, and ideologi-cal significance of the song were the technological innovations that helped give Ellington the inspiration to experiment with original sounds and the vehicle to connect to listeners. Throughout the late 1920s and early 1930s, Duke Ellington harnessed the power of radio to transmit modern jazz to America. Phonograph records allowed consumers to obtain a wax imprint of a performance, but little relationship existed between artist and audience (aside from an occasional royalty check). Radio shortened the gap between performer and audience—a song aired, mail followed—as well as widened the pool of listeners.[66]

What made "Mood Indigo" truly different, however, was its modern reception by a radio audience. "The next day," Ellington writes, "wads of mail came in raving about the new tune, so Irving Mills put a lyric on it."[67] This comment speaks both to the newfound power of radio as well as to the input of Ellington's manager. Large corporate radio networks carried Ellington's Cotton Club broadcasts throughout the United States, which allowed a national audience to tap into a single source. The New York–based radio industry tied the performer to their audience, and the city to the farm, effectively creating a national music. Ellington, however, rooted the more modern elements of his music in the traditional context of African American folk music. The emotional tenor of the blues, in other words, undercut even the most modern of Ellington's compositions, and this combination of rural and urban musical forms helped generate Ellington's unique jazz sound. Thus the urban and rural combined with an immediacy that did not exist a few years prior. By a subtle inversion of a traditional jazz form, Ellington produced a stunning example of modern African American musical expression. In so doing, he prefigured not only commercial jazz of the 1930s—including his own performances, such as his take on Billy Strayhorn's "Take the 'A' Train," and so forth—but also the various manifestations of jazz in postwar America. A muted hum, with its warm echoes of electricity, a simple melody, and historical and cross-cultural resonance, "Mood Indigo" serves as a key example of black modernist expression. At once self-aware and reflective of a mechanical process that inspired its creation, the song cut across musical boundaries and (via the radio) slashed through space as well. Modernist in creation, modernist in expression, modernist in reception, Duke Ellington's "Mood Indigo" redefined both the commercial potential of jazz music as well as the capacity of mass media to bring disparate groups of Americans into a national culture.

As he created a new jazz vocabulary, Ellington also used his success at the Cotton Club to create new opportunities for black musicians. In 1929 Duke Ellington and his Cotton Club Orchestra starred in a short film produced by RKO at Gramercy Studios in New York. Written and directed by Dudley Murphy—an American filmmaker living in Paris—*Black and Tan* features Ellington playing himself as the bandleader of the Cotton Club orchestra.[68]

The rather melodramatic story centers on Ferdi Washington, a featured dancer at the Cotton Club (and Ellington's girlfriend), and her decision to disregard medical advice and continue dancing even after learning of a potentially serious heart condition. The first part of the short involves two stereotypically ignorant movers attempting to repossess Ellington's piano. The movers interrupt Ellington as he is rehearsing a new tune with Whetsol. "Brother, remove your anatomy from that mahogany," one of the movers says to Ellington, who appears reasonably unaffected by the events. Washington enters the room and proceeds to bribe the movers with a bottle of gin to leave the piano for another day. The second half of the film is set in a mockup of the Cotton Club's interior as Ellington's band performs two numbers in support of the Five Hot Shots, a black dance troupe. Washington watches from the wings, but she begins to feel faint. Nevertheless, she enters the stage and launches into a wild dance performance before collapsing onto the stage. The film ends with Ellington's band, augmented by the Hall Johnson choir, surrounding Washington's deathbed as she drifts off to sleep.

The melodramatic story notwithstanding, *Black and Tan* remains a remarkable film for 1929. Featuring an all-black cast, the film uses racial stereotypes sparingly (especially in contrast to other jazz-themed movies from this period). The two piano movers (played by Alec Lovejoy and Edgar Common) represent the only real clowning. Even though their job regularly involves addresses and the clock, neither man apparently can distinguish numbers, nor can one mover tell time. The men also fall too easily for the siren call of booze, as Fredi Washington quickly bribes them with a bottle of gin. Still, these images lack the racism behind the satirical blackface comedy of Amos and Andy, and in general, these characters represent the only overt racist imagery in the short. Murphy and Carl Van Vechten (who had a major, if uncredited, role in the development of the film) endeavored to produce a positive picture of black life, and this subtle connection to the values of the Harlem Renaissance helps to elevate this early jazz film. Other elements do appear—a vague jungle setting at the club, Ellington is in hock—yet, the overall image of the film presents Ellington in a flattering light. In fact, Ellington's first movie role would be his most substantial, and although he would continue to appear in films over the next three decades, he rarely had the speaking roles that he had in *Black and Tan.*[69]

Stripping New Orleans jazz down to its essential syncopated and harmonic forms, Duke Ellington succeeded in reconfiguring nineteenth-century black folk music into something peculiar to the modern age of the

United States. His "Mood Indigo" also points to the power of technological change as new ways of transmitting sound led to a successful artistic experiment and product. The film *Black and Tan* illustrates a similar convergence as new technologies allowed for a larger reception. This film also speaks to the complexities inherent in modern artistic expression especially in terms of the projection of race. Whereas technology heightened the experimental elements of "Mood Indigo," the power of film helped make clear the bizarre negotiation of racial images on screen as blackface is used not only to distinguish a white performer as "black" but also to maintain the expectation of segregation. Together, Ellington's "Mood Indigo" and his appearance in *Black and Tan* underscore the promise and power of modern entertainment technology as a black composer found artistic acceptance within a nation struggling to discover its own racial identity in the first decades of the twentieth century. Film added a new dimension to the transmission of jazz, and although radio maintained its dominance throughout the next decade, Hollywood and its culture of celebrity greatly affected jazz music. Jazz musicians became movie stars, but racial prejudice corrupted the accolades thrust upon these highly visible entertainers. Motion pictures removed the theoretical colorblindness of radio broadcasts, forcing many black artists to accept demeaning stereotypical roles in order to pursue a career in film. Many more African Americans were barred from the film industry altogether. New York City continued to serve as the epicenter for the music industry, but Los Angeles projected a new visual identity for jazz, one that would inherently alter the way Americans experienced jazz music. The jazz that flickered and crackled in movie houses across the nation, however, differed greatly from the music of Armstrong, Henderson, and Ellington as Hollywood cast jazz with a predominantly white face.

5 Los Angeles and the Diffusion of Early Jazz

In the summer of 1930, Duke Ellington and his orchestra left New York City and traveled to California to appear in their first feature film, *Check and Double Check*.[1] Directed by Melville Brown, *Check and Double Check* served as the film debut of Amos and Andy, one of the most popular comedy duos on radio. With such a high-profile film, Irving Mills hoped to involve Ellington in order to expand the band's audience and profitability. Unlike the eighteen-minute short *Black and Tan*, *Check and Double Check* was a full-length film, though the band only appears in an early scene performing for a society dance. This scene represented the first appearance of a black band in a predominantly white film, but this distinction fell under the burnt cork umbrage of the stars of the film, Freeman Gosden and Charles Correll, who performed in blackface as Amos and Andy. Gosden and Correll, both white actors, had developed their comedy team a decade earlier on the vaudeville circuit, but discovered a wider audience with their radio program *Amos 'n' Andy* in the late 1920s. By 1928, Gosden and Correll had one of the most popular radio shows in the nation. Their show, set in an urban ghetto, attracted a large, racially mixed audience. Despite the show's demeaning caricatures, both white and black listeners enjoyed the program, in large measure because the radio hid the obvious whiteness of the two actors.[2] Combining the immense radio popularity of Amos and Andy with the appeal of Duke Ellington's orchestra, *Check and Double Check* revealed the potential of the adolescent motion picture industry and the opportunity presented to musicians by this widely disseminated form of mass media. As this media revolution bridged moviegoers across the nation, a complex negotiation of race emerged, with racial stereotypes openly combined with legitimate expressions of African American artistic achievement. Los Angeles transmitted jazz to a national audience, but it did so within the convoluted context of race and racism in America in the twentieth century.

Filmed on the RKO studio lot in Los Angeles, *Check and Double Check*'s convoluted plot focuses on Amos and Andy, the operators of the "Fresh Air Taxicab Company of America Incorpulated," and their attempts to bring a young couple together in marriage, a union that is subsequently complicated by a haunted house. Ellington and his band only appear in an early scene set in a mansion as they perform for an extravagant dance. Neither Ellington nor any of his band members had speaking roles, but the orchestra performed two complete songs and sections of three others. Despite their brief onscreen appearance, the band's rendition of "Old Man Blues" represents some of the finest jazz of the period preserved on film. An original Ellington composition, "Old Man Blues" showcases the solo talents of Harry Carney and Johnny Hodges—on baritone and alto sax respectively—as well as the band's powerful trumpet lineup of Freddie Jenkins, Cootie Williams, and Art Whetsol. An exciting up-tempo performance, this piece captures the band at an early high point. Anticipating the swing era, the song combines improvised solos and organized riffs all propelled by Wellman Braud's driving, four-beat bass line and Sonny Greer's cymbal-focused drumming. The band also emphasizes its theatrics with the flashy muted work by Jenkins, Williams, and Whetsol, and "Old Man Blues" climaxes with a blaring clarinet rising above the muted trumpet and trombone riffs. In just over three minutes, Ellington and his band brought the excitement and artistry of their limited live shows to a broad, moviegoing audience.

The musical triumph of "Old Man Blues" notwithstanding, a complicated combination of on- and off-screen racially themed behavior overshadows the other elements of the film, and this arrangement underscores the peculiar presentation of race in early film. Unlike radio, motion pictures showcased the overt whiteness (and conspicuous blackface) of Amos and Andy in ways that highlighted the racial buffoonery of Gosden and Correll. Disembodied voices on the radio gave way to painted faces on the screen, and these blackface performances trumped the comedic elements of the duo for black audiences. A significant change of scenery also affected black audiences, as "most of the action had been moved from the radio program's black urban ghetto into white suburbia."[3] The film's racism forced changes in the band's appearance, as the filmmaker directed New Orleans Creole Barney Bigard and Puerto Rican Juan Tizol to wear burnt cork makeup in order to reinforce the image of a segregated band.[4] Despite these decisions, the inclusion of a black band in an otherwise all-white movie denoted a considerable breach of racial barriers even with the imposed conspicuous stereotypes. In addition to these confused racial messages, the film also included a more subtle moment of racial complexity when the band performed their other full-length number, "Three Little Words." This piece ostensibly features the voices of Ellington's trumpet section, who are shown somewhat fuzzily in the background crooning into megaphones. The trumpeters, however, only pretended to sing, as the soundtrack actually featured the voices of the Rhythm Boys.[5] An all-white trio that included a young Bing Crosby, the Rhythm Boys discovered early success as the vocalists for Paul Whiteman's orchestra. Thus, apparently unknown to the audience, three black men received the singing credit for three white men, an example of the racial ambiguity generated by the uneasy amalgam of technological advancement and social prejudices. Racial representations were challenged even as they were being upheld, and this confusion made its way to a broader audience because of the mass market for film. Movies such as *Check and Double Check* show that Americans began to accept jazz as well as the racial complexities inherent in this modern form of music.

If "Mood Indigo" illustrates the positive side of modernist art and mechanical reproduction, then *Check and Double Check* underscores the bizarre. The film failed on most levels with the large black audience, who reacted with anger to the obvious blackface buffoonery of the actors—something, of course, hidden by radio—and the flaccid plot removed all of the elements that made the radio show work. Ellington and his band, however, had produced an excellent example of late 1920s jazz music and provided a filmic glimpse into the stage show performed by the band during this period. The modern technology that inspired an authentic example of African American modernism also illustrated the limits to which this art would be accepted by an audience. Ellington's fans were thrilled with his performance, and there exists the idea in some contemporary press accounts that Ellington was a role model of sorts in breaking down certain racially constructed walls. And yet, the corniness of the movie (and the overt secondary status of the band's performance) attests to many of the obstacles that confined black entertainers during the late 1920s and early 1930s. If Ellington reached a wider audience because of the synergy of radio broadcasting and phonograph recording, the new technology of film created an odd mixture of opportunity and constriction as blackface-enforced artificial segregation abutted an authentic jazz performance. These two performances—"Mood Indigo" and his scene in *Check and Double Check*—helped Ellington's career immensely, but that does not obscure the strangeness created by the intersection of musical performance and audience reception, technological innovation and modern black art.

This combination of musical innovation and ambiguous racial imagery illustrates the role Los Angeles played in the diffusion of jazz in the late 1920s and early 1930s. Los Angeles produced a new representation of jazz music and then broadcast images to accompany the sounds to the nation through the medium of film. Although not as widespread as phonograph records or as immediate as radio broadcasts, motion pictures redefined the commercial power of jazz, and Los Angeles facilitated greatly the transformation of jazz from regional folk music to a dominant form of American popular music. Unlike New Orleans, Chicago, or New York City, the jazz scene of Los Angeles during this period provided commercial viability and national distribution rather than deliberate musical innovation. This variation in emphasis reflects the way the city's black community set Los Angeles apart from other jazz cities. Compared to Chicago or New Orleans, which maintained black populations of at least 20 percent throughout the 1920s, Los Angeles sustained an African American community of just over 15,500 people, or just under 3 percent.[6] This disparity in the size of the Los Angeles black community points to one of the major distinctions between that city's jazz scene and the jazz culture seen in other areas. Technologically driven diffusion—not musical originality—delineated the city's contribution to early jazz history, and though a rather anomalous jazz city, Los Angeles succeeded in bringing jazz music to the nation.

The history of jazz in Los Angeles corresponds generally with the growth and development of the city's black community. Although a few black people lived in Los Angeles at the time of the city's founding in the late eighteenth century, migration to the city occurred at such a slow rate that there were only twelve black residents in 1850. Between 1885 and 1905, however, the city witnessed three distinct periods of increase in its black population. In 1887, a local land boom brought large numbers of African Americans to

Los Angeles from neighboring Pacific-area states as well as from the South Atlantic area. In one year, the city's black population had increased to over 1,200 residents.[7] A second wave of black immigration occurred five years later when a group composed mainly of rural transplants moved to the city to escape some of the ravages of the 1893 economic depression. Another period of growth followed in 1903 as railroad companies offered incentives for black laborers to migrate west to replace striking Asian and Hispanic workers.[8] Despite these frequent increases, African Americans still represented less than 3 percent of the total population of Los Angeles throughout the 1920s.

The small size and geographic dispersion of the black population throughout the city tempered race relations between black and white residents. Asians and Hispanics bore the brunt of racial and ethnic animosity, and throughout the 1920s black Angelenos largely avoided racially motivated attacks. The black community of Los Angeles, unlike that in other jazz cities, lacked a large working-class identity.[9] As most of the city's black residents adhered to middle-class values, elements of shared bourgeois culture thwarted more overt animosity between white and black Angelenos. African Americans endured the degradation of segregation, especially in terms of employment and transportation opportunities, but the city's black community fared much better than other minority groups living in Los Angeles.[10] This relatively peaceful Jim Crow existence began to crumble once the city's aggregate population increased during the 1920s and placed greater strain on the local housing market. The resultant widespread housing shortage prompted the white community to institute residential restrictions to maintain their all-white neighborhoods. By 1930, the comparatively harmonic race relations of Los Angeles gave way to a more aggressively segregated system of racial bias and tension, especially in terms of the housing market as growing congestion and demand exacerbated overt discrimination.[11] Despite these restrictions, over 30 percent of black Angelenos owned their own home, an extraordinary figure in comparison to Chicago (with 10 percent ownership) and New York City (with 5.6 percent ownership). Thus, despite an increase in racial discrimination, many local black residents escaped dependence on white landlords, a situation practically impossible for African Americans across the nation.[12]

Although small, the black community of Los Angeles offered employment opportunities and economic stability that appealed to southern blacks who had the means to travel out west. In particular, the city's well-defined connection to show business also made it an attractive vaudeville and minstrel show stop. Throughout the 1910s, a number of jazz musicians made the trip to Los Angeles as members of touring shows, and some stayed behind to contribute to the creation of the jazz scene of the 1920s. As early as 1908, New Orleans bassist Bill Johnson ventured to Los Angeles with the Creole Band, a group that included cornetist Ernest Coycault, who remained in California.[13] Johnson returned to Los Angeles in 1912, this time with an amended Creole Band including famed New Orleans musicians George Baquet on clarinet and Freddie Keppard on cornet. Two of the most prominent individual musicians to travel west from New Orleans were Jelly Roll Morton and trombonist Edward "Kid" Ory. These two musicians embedded themselves in the Los Angeles scene, made crucial connections to important local players, and drew other skilled New Orleans musicians to the area. Morton, during his period of musical wandering, journeyed to southern California in the early 1910s and by 1917 considered Los Angeles home.[14] Between 1917 and 1922, Morton played in a variety of clubs throughout the Los Angeles area and began recruiting musician acquaintances from New Orleans to fill out his band. In 1919, Kid Ory left for Los Angeles where his band recorded several jazz compositions with a local entrepreneur in 1921.[15] Ory performed in the same circles as Morton, and like the piano player, Ory brought out other New Orleans musicians such as bassist Pops Foster.[16] Both Morton and Ory had strong music-reading abilities, but many of their recently transplanted sidemen from New Orleans almost exclusively performed improvised jazz. This musical distinction mattered little in New Orleans, where both reading and nonreading musicians could often find ample employment. In contrast, a certain conservatism marked the music scene (and black community in general) in Los Angeles, where jobs rewarded readers far more than improvisers.[17] This dichotomy continued to mark the city's jazz scene for the next two decades, especially as the motion picture industry began using jazz music as soundtrack material. By the late 1920s—only a few years removed from the early travels of Morton and Ory—Hollywood emerged as the dominant mechanism for jazz commodification, an evolution wholly unique to Los Angeles.

The sketchy prehistory of itinerant musicians floating in and out of the area during the 1910s gave way to a more stable and established jazz scene in the 1920s. This western music community, however, contained a hodgepodge of talent, with New Orleanians merging with other musicians from the Mid-Atlantic and Southwest.[18] In general, the bands of this period combined the larger band arrangements of Fletcher Henderson with occasional New Orleans and Chicago-style instrumental breaks. Between 1913 and 1916 the Wood Wilson Band achieved the status of premier ragtime dance band in the city, and throughout the period this group provided an early ragtime apprenticeship for most of the important bandleaders and musicians of the 1920s. Another major Los Angeles–based jazz band of the 1910s, the Black and Tan Orchestra, underwent a musical transformation that mirrored that of other groups across the nation as they adopted the more popular style of syncopated music. A ten-piece ragtime band from Texas, the Black and Tan Orchestra began to play more and more syncopated dance tunes featuring at least some improvisation, especially after the addition of Coycault and trombonist Harry Southard.[19] By 1918, in fact, the group amended its name to reflect these changes, and the Black and Tan Jazz Orchestra emerged as one of the most prominent bands in the area.[20] These bands produced relatively few records during the 1920s, but the recordings that exist point toward a controlled, arranged sound suitable for dancing (and later for instrumental film scores). Overall, no unified style came to dominate Los Angeles jazz, and with only a few exceptions, instrumental virtuosity remained limited to short breaks.[21] Together, the music and careers of Reb Spikes, Sonny Clay, and Paul Howard underscore the inherent qualities of Los Angeles jazz as they each created music indicative of the West Coast jazz scene of the 1920s.

Perhaps the most important figure in the early jazz scene of Los Angeles was Benjamin "Reb" Spikes, a music teacher, an arranger, a bandleader, a music publisher, a booking agent, a record label owner, a music store proprietor, and, for a short time, a restaurateur. Many of these ventures included Spikes's brother, Johnny, and together these two musicians defined in large measure the early jazz scene of Los Angeles. Born in the late 1880s in Dallas, Texas, Reb Spikes moved with his family to Los Angeles in 1897. The journey west—apparently due to a "racist-inspired campaign of arson"—coincided with Spikes's introduction to music through the purchase of a set of drums.[22] In 1907, Reb and Johnny Spikes (who played piano) developed a musical act and began touring the Southwest with various minstrel shows.[23] During the mid-1910s, Reb Spikes moved to San Francisco and played saxophone in Sid LeProtti's So Different Orchestra, a job that brought him back to Los Angeles on tours.[24] These early musical experiences provided Spikes with performance skills as well as a developing business sense as to how jazz could be marketed to a larger (or at least paying) audience. In 1919, Reb Spikes applied these acquired skills and opened a music store on Central Avenue, an area that featured black-owned businesses and integrated jazz clubs and served as the de facto heart of the black community. His stock included everything from musical instruments and sheet music to radios and phonograph records.[25] This foray developed into a race record business, and Spikes soon scheduled recording sessions for local and traveling musicians.[26] Between producing and selling records, Spikes maintained intimate connections with the city's jazz scene and served as the unofficial organizer of jazz talent in Los Angeles. Spikes eventually entered the recording studio himself, and in October 1927 he recorded "My Mammy's Blues" released under the billing of Reb Spikes' Majors and Minors.[27] The song combines a straightforward ragtime arrangement and a standard dance tempo with several hot jazz elements, especially in terms of the violin and trumpet solos. A nice recording—if barely a footnote in even Spikes's own career—"My Mammy's Blues" hinted at the blurred lines between popular dance music and jazz, an ambiguity that tended to define Los Angeles jazz during this period. Not unlike Jack Laine in New Orleans or Dave Peyton in Chicago, Reb Spikes affected greatly the Los Angeles jazz culture even if his fame remained almost nonexistent outside of the California area.

The near ubiquity of Reb Spikes in the jazz scene of 1920s Los Angeles guaranteed that most black jazz musicians of the period performed in one of Spikes's bands.[28] The incestuousness of Los Angeles bands during the 1920s provided a small group of players a considerable amount of experience as well as ensured a degree of uniformity to the city's jazz music. One important musician in this Spikes-centered coterie was William "Sonny" Clay, who hailed originally from Chapel Hill, Texas (though as a child his family moved to Arizona). Clay began playing the drums and piano (among other instruments) and spent most of the late 1910s playing ragtime and dance music throughout the Southwest. At some point during his travels, Clay met up with Jelly Roll Morton in Tijuana, but eventually he made his way to Los Angeles by the early 1920s. In 1921, Clay played with Reb Spikes and his Famous Syncopated Orchestra, and the next year he performed with Kid Ory. After these sideman forays, Clay started his own band, the Eccentric Harmony Six, which performed a mixture of ragtime, jazz, and syncopated dance music. In 1925, under the name Plantation Orchestra, Clay recorded "Jambled Blues," an original piece representative of his jazz style.[29] The first half of the song features Clay on the piano unaccompanied except for short breaks. Clay plays in a lightly syncopated, ragtime style not far removed from the music of Scott Joplin. Though not quite the stride piano of the Harlemites, Clay provides a strong bass figure, partly to make up for the lack of tuba or string bass on the record. Still, New Orleanian Ernest Coycault's trumpet work constitutes the only real example of instrumental virtuosity, and his playing elevates the final "Dixieland" section of collective improvisation at the end of the song. This controlled dance number had compelling echoes of Jelly Roll Morton (specifically, his "Jambled Blues") and Sonny Clay's recordings, underscoring the orderly and arranged style prevalent in Los Angeles during the 1920s.[30]

If Reb Spikes exemplified the jazz community in Los Angeles and Sonny Clay personified an efficient, workmanlike attitude, then Paul Howard served as the architect of a big band style of California jazz. Analogous to Fletcher Henderson and Duke Ellington's tinkering with large band arrangements, Howard began infusing the early California jazz model with a stylistic verve not seen consistently in the work of Spikes or Clay.[31] Between 1918 and 1923, Howard played with the Black and Tan Orchestra and other smaller bands throughout the area. After this period of apprenticeship, Howard gathered a strong lineup of musicians under the Quality Serenaders moniker. During 1927 and 1928, the Quality Serenaders boasted a residency at the New Cotton Club, a venue inspired by Ellington's headquarters in New York City. The club attracted wealthy Hollywood celebrities with its floorshows and jazz music, and Howard's band became one of the most popular jazz ensembles in the city. The Quality Serenaders' performances peaked over the next two years, reflected in their recordings that indicate the skill of the tight band with strong soloists and ensemble players fully comfortable with unique arrangements.

In 1930, Howard's band recorded several numbers in Culver City including "Cuttin' Up," a number arranged by Charlie Lawrence, Howard's clarinet and alto saxophone player.[32] Along with trombonist Lawrence Brown, Charlie Lawrence wrote a large number of Howard's arrangements, and his unique instrumentation and riff-based arrangements presaged clearly the big band jazz of the Swing Era.[33] By 1930, Howard's band had evolved into a strong unit featuring harmonized riffs and powerful, swinging solos, a pattern clearly in place by the "Cuttin' Up" session. After a rather distinctive saxophone and trumpet introduction, "Cuttin' Up" launches into a spirited chorus featuring muted trumpet and trombone contrasted by a warm reeds section.[34] Most of Lawrence and Brown's arrangements included almost iconoclastic introductions. Eschewing formulaic and rote figures, Howard's arrangers usually began each of their songs with either a call and response type of riffing or a rhythmically complex section of contrasting instruments. This opening part sets the mood for the song as subdivisions of unison riffs alternate with solos. After a rousing trombone solo near the middle of the piece, the band commences a section of short, two-measure solo breaks from each of the lead instruments. In the second half of the song, Howard's drummer, Lionel Hampton, sings a short scat melody before the sax section performs an arranged segment of harmonized riffs.[35] Following a piano solo that relates more to the sophistication of Earl Hines than the ragtime of Scott Joplin, the song concludes with a strong trumpet solo by George Orendorff, the band's true virtuoso.[36] An often-overlooked band, Paul Howard's Quality Serenaders thus helped bridge the gap between the ragtime-influenced music of the early Los Angeles jazz scene and the swing music of the 1930s.

The Quality Serenaders remained a popular live band throughout the Los Angeles area, and in 1930, the band took up residency at the Montmartre, an exclusive Hollywood club that catered to the film industry.[37] Like New York City, Los Angeles fostered this relationship between wealthy white patrons and black jazz bands, but unlike Harlem, the moneyed interests of Hollywood generated film opportunities for jazz music. Howard's associations with the Hollywood elite landed him in an advantageous occupational situation, but this relationship between wealthy film stars and jazz musicians also spoke to the broader trend of the emergent synergy of the two burgeoning forms of mass culture. Both jazz and motion pictures materialized around the same time, and both cultural forms elicited as much derision as excitement. Jazz music also directly accompanied the film industry as various stride pianists and small jazz ensembles found employment performing the live soundtracks to silent movies. With the advent of motion picture sound, filmmakers had the ability to incorporate jazz music seamlessly into their movies, and many directors used local talent (in conjunction with nationally recognized celebrities such as Duke Ellington) to fill out the soundtrack. The unconventional jazz scene in Los Angeles, however, predicated the inclusion of a type of jazz somewhat different from the music heard on the records coming out of Chicago or the radio stations centered in New York. Despite the lack of a singular style defining jazz in the city, the regularity of employment opportunities for musicians allowed for some sense of consistency, at least with the larger bands. Few distinctive or innovative soloists emerged from this group, but a number of these players performed for long periods of time with popular ensembles in the area. As Los Angeles musicians matured, several of them formed their own bands and continued the pattern of mentor-apprentice relationships somewhat unique (at least in scope) to the city. Constancy and consistency, not innovation or inventiveness, thus provided the defining element of Los Angeles jazz, and the relatively conservative nature of the city's black middle-class culture only served to heighten these factors.[38] Throughout the late 1920s, the American public encountered jazz on the big screen, and in many instances the sounds related only tangentially to the music developed over the previous decade in New Orleans, Chicago, and New York City.

Similar to the development of the recording and broadcasting industries, the film industry combined technological innovation, quickly contracted patents, complicated lawsuits, burgeoning consumerism, and (last and usually least) an occasional sense of artistry and aesthetics. Although not in widespread use until the late 1920s, inventors had discussed or designed plans for talking pictures since the 1880s. As early as 1877, for example, Thomas Edison saw motion pictures as a potential complement to his phonograph system.[39] Fifty years would pass, however, before technology allowed for the completion of this fantasy. Once Edison began focusing full-time on motion picture technology in the 1880s, he tended to view it as a particular type of working-class entertainment, not unlike vaudeville shows.[40] In fact, the vast majority of early subjects for this invention, termed the "kinetoscope," came from the vaudeville and minstrel show stage as the cameras focused on contortionists, magicians, and pantomimes.[41] An immediate middle-class fascination notwithstanding, the machines were marketed as a novelty for mostly working-class vaudeville and saloon patrons. This class distinction marked the motion picture industry for the next two decades.[42] None of these early movie attempts involved integrated sound, though some filmmakers experimented with phonograph records crudely synchronized by the theater projectionist. Despite drawing from a similar pool of talent (and catering to a similar audience) as jazz music, the lack of sound obviously delayed the inclusion of musical acts in early motion pictures.

Two developments—one corporate, one spatial—redefined the film industry during the 1910s, and the move toward middle-class approval coupled with the move out to Hollywood had a massive impact on the eventual inclusion of (and reception of) jazz music. Like the radio and to some extent the record industry, the evolution of projected film involved a set of corporate demands unique to the business model of early-twentieth-century America. Through the creation (and sometimes misappropriation) of various technical patents, Edison dominated his competition.[43] This monopoly of film resources—known as "The Trust"—defined the motion picture industry in the early 1910s but came under attack from a host of independent companies that capitalized on an informal network of unlicensed theaters. This tension between the Edison establishment and these primarily immigrant independents allowed for a change in subject matter, and somewhat ironically the independents (drawn from the original working-class audience for film) spearheaded the move toward middle-class acceptance.[44] The director David Wark Griffith epitomized this shift in tone as he almost single-handedly brought motion pictures to a new audience. To attract this new group of viewers, Griffith and his fellow independents endeavored to incorporate both larger spectacles as well as middle-class values into their films.[45] Historical epics and stage plays thus became the new model for film subject matter—a model exemplified by Griffith's 1915 film on Reconstruction, *The Birth of a Nation*.[46] The film, despite its explicit and implicit racism, appealed to a large new audience, a group attracted to the spectacle of the film if not its political and social message.

In addition to the shift in audience following the success of *The Birth of a Nation*, the film's location also foreshadowed a larger development in the evolution of the motion picture industry. Unlike his East Coast counterparts, Griffith chose to shoot the picture in southern California.[47] The Los Angeles area appealed to filmmakers for a number of reasons, including temperate weather, a diverse selection of scenery, and an assemblage of low-wage workers. The West Coast also (and almost as importantly) offered an alternative to the Trust-driven business practices of New York City. The conservative population of Los Angeles received Hollywood with suspicion, if not outright antipathy, and many Angelenos saw Hollywood as culturally disconnected from their city.[48] The reform-mindedness of local officials paradoxically contributed to the growth of young Hollywood, however, as various antitrust laws were enacted that provided the industry with a constant labor supply.[49] Also, despite the concerns of local residents, Hollywood helped to redefine the subject matter and audience of the motion picture industry.[50] This mixture of social conservatism and political progressivism set Los Angeles apart from New York City. Hollywood, too, self-consciously promoted its distinctly new type of entertainment as a new frontier in the entertainment industry. Within a few years of its creation, Hollywood had developed into the national center for abundance, consumption, and a progressive vision of individualism. By the 1920s, the motion picture industry had reformulated and reopened the western frontier of opportunity and promise, and Los Angeles threatened to eclipse New York's hold on mass culture.[51]

On October 6, 1927, *The Jazz Singer*, the first full-length talking picture, debuted in New York City, ushering in the age of sound film fifty years after Edison's original proposal.[52] Based on a series of short stories and a stage play, *The Jazz Singer* conveys the tale of a Jewish singer conflicted by his faith (and his father's demands) and his desire to sing jazz music. The film starred Al Jolson, the actual inspiration for the short story, who immediately related to his role as Jakie Rabinowitz/Jack Robin. At its heart, *The Jazz Singer* serves as a study in immigrant assimilation, a tension expressed through Jolson's vacillation between his Jewish heritage and popular American music. The plot hinges on the disapproval by Jack Robin's father (the cantor at a synagogue) of his son's decision to make a career of jazz singing. His father urges him to train as a cantor to carry on the family tradition, but Robin refuses to leave show business. In the film's climactic scene, the father, on his deathbed, forgives his son's rebelliousness, and Robin delays his Broadway opening to serve as cantor at the Yom Kippur service. The film's finale, however, allows Robin to satisfy both desires by performing "Mammy" in blackface at the Winter Garden for an ecstatic audience.[53] The film quickly garnered wide acclaim as audiences flocked to see *The Jazz Singer* if only to witness the novelty of a talking picture.[54] By the end of 1927, the film had opened in New York, Chicago, and Philadelphia, and by February of the next year the film attracted over one million viewers a week.[55] Not everyone, however, offered the movie a warm reception. Warner Brothers, for example, invited the author of the original short story, Samson Raphaelson, to the movie's premiere. Completely unimpressed by the film, Raphaelson later categorized *The Jazz Singer* as "a dreadful picture."[56]

Film historians routinely echo Raphaelson's sentiments and dismiss *The Jazz Singer* as a lackluster film that fails even to deserve its standing as the first talking picture.[57] "It is absolutely no secret," one writer argues, "that *The Jazz Singer* is, to all intents and purposes, a lousy movie. Many knew it in 1927, and anyone who sees it today expecting a masterpiece will be rudely awakened."[58] Although the film focused on Jewish assimilation and the lure of show business (as well as Robin's rather odd fixation with his mother), the more implicit elements of race and jazz as seen in Jolson's blackface performances illustrate the importance of the film in terms of jazz diffusion. Despite Jolson's overreaching and emotive performance, the main criticism of the film tends to focus on its title and the fact that no jazz actually appears in the movie. "The blackface jazz singer," one writer notes, "is neither a jazz singer nor black."[59] Despite the prejudices of many of the critics of the movie, the lightly syncopated music of the film fits clearly into the broad definition of jazz in the 1920s.[60] In some cursory ways, of course, the music featured in *The Jazz Singer* relates to the Los Angeles style of jazz. Jolson's performances associate more with vaudeville than jazz, and in this sense, "the film condensed into a single feature film the entire history of American popular entertainment, from minstrelsy through vaudeville to silent films to talking pictures."[61] Besides the title, jazz appears throughout the movie as various characters (particularly Robin's father and Moisha Yudelson) refer unequivocally to the music.[62] More important, this film underscored the growing acceptance of jazz as the movie industry began to see the marketing power of this type of music.[63]

Coupled directly with the film's portrayal of jazz music is the complex use of blackface and racial stereotypes by the actors and filmmakers in an attempt to represent racial identity. In *The Jazz Singer*, Jolson's application of greasepaint serves more as a minstrel signifier of his show business roots rather than a spoof of African Americans. The specific issue of race crops up only briefly in the film as the director takes care to keep the main focus on the tensions surrounding Robin's Jewish identity. The shooting script of the film contains more racially pointed language than in the final version, with the phrase "nigger songs" and "he looks like a nigger" ultimately not used in the film. The script includes a description of another scene (involving Robin in blackface talking with his girlfriend in his dressing room) with a note explaining that "playing a romantic scene in blackface may be something of an experiment and very likely an unsuccessful one."[64] Instead of simply highlighting his whiteness, the blackface makeup connects Jolson to the stage, and in those scenes Jolson uses blackface as a reference to his participation in the vaudeville tradition.[65] Unable to articulate his desires to his family, Robin only realizes his inner yearnings and aspirations through makeup and song.[66] A comparison of Robin's conversations with his father (without makeup) and his actions (with makeup) emphasizes the inherent transformation allowed by the application of blackface. Only through the visual conjuring of race in terms of face paint and the aural adoption of black music in terms of jazz can Robin rise above his familial and occupational restrictions. In addition, in blackface and through jazz, Robin invokes the emotional elements of African American music, particularly the blues. This "positive" (and I use that word guardedly) use of blackface starkly contrasts with Gosden and Correll's use of makeup in *Check and Double Check* to reinforce the racial differences between white and black people. Unlike Jolson—who actually sang jazz-based songs—Gosden and Correll affect crude dialects and caricatured actions to parody black Americans. No longer merely a prop, in *Check and Double Check* blackface works as a key method of denigration and humiliation. That film also included the compulsory use of blackface by two members of Ellington's band in order to impose an unambiguous visual sense of racial segregation. This use of blackface, however, differs considerably from the other two as the makeup disguises (rather than emphasizes) racial identity. Seemingly unbeknownst to most of the audience, the filmmakers employed blackface surreptitiously to prevent race from becoming an issue.[67] This racial ambiguity and complexity only deepens once African Americans began accepting more prominent roles in mainstream films.

Within this multifaceted construction of race in early film, Hollywood offered African Americans new roles in entertainment, especially as Hollywood began to realize the commercial possibilities of jazz music. The bands active in the Los Angeles area discovered a number of opportunities in Hollywood, and many of the more popular bands eventually found employment in the elite clubs north of the city that catered to film celebrities. The Les Hite band, in particular, took advantage of the business generated by Hollywood and successfully combined studio work with regular live performances to create a steady career. By the early 1930s as the Depression increasingly affected the entertainment industry, Hite's band remained somewhat financially secure through the extra income produced by performing on film soundtracks. This movie-based windfall allowed Hite's group to continue operating throughout this period, thus producing one of the most consistent band rosters of the era.[68] Other musicians also pieced together Hollywood livelihoods, and Sonny Clay began selling his arrangements to other performers, adapting Fletcher Henderson's business model to the film industry. Overall, both black and white musicians found new opportunities in Hollywood during this period, and although old stereotypes persisted, this new platform of exposure generated a new audience for jazz music.

In the five years after *The Jazz Singer*, Hollywood inundated American moviegoers with a number of shorts and feature films that attempted to capitalize on the emergent jazz craze of the late 1920s.[69] Many of these films maintained only tangential connections to jazz music, but as promotional tools, these short movies demonstrate the growing marketability of jazz music. These films shared an array of positive and negative racial images as implicit black stereotypes abutted dazzling examples of jazz music. White musicians also discovered some success with this film format, and by the early 1930s, a number of white singers and instrumentalists appeared in short films to promote their records. Few of these films contained noteworthy acting, but the better ones transcended their advertising potential and combined a brief story arc with two or three musical numbers. Usually preceding the main attraction, these short films helped introduce jazz to a larger audience and signified a growing acceptance of the music. Four films in particular highlight the various ways the motion picture industry incorporated jazz in the late 1920s and early 1930s. In 1932, Paramount Studios produced a short film based around Louis Armstrong's recording "I'll Be Glad When You're Dead, You Rascal You." In 1931, the Boswell Sisters appeared in a short, nonacting clip to showcase their version of Armstrong's "Heebie Jeebies." In 1933, Cab Calloway played himself in *Hi-De-Ho,* and finally, popular white crooner Rudy Vallee starred in *The Musical Doctor* (1932), a short film featuring Vallee as a physician who prescribes various musical selections to heal patients.

Together, these four films provide an examination of the arc of acceptance as mainstream white America emerged as a viable audience for jazz music—and in return, the way Hollywood began marketing films directly to middle-class white consumers. Furthermore, these films illustrate some of the complexity surrounding the portrayal of women in connection to jazz during this period. Each of these films includes either central female roles or (in the case of the Boswell Sisters) the entire clip is one of female performance, but within these films there exists a variety of ways in which filmmakers featured women within the jazz context. From the abrasive and abusive, to the cloying and sexualized, Hollywood offered strict parameters to the image of women on film. In contrast to studies of blues women, such as Hazel Carby's important essay, "It Jus Be's Dat Way Sometime: The Sexual Politics of Women's Blues," jazz films offer more diffuse images and roles than the representations articulated within the blues genre.[70] To be sure, the social and sexual conflict underscored by Carby courses through many of these performances, especially within the context of African American–centered films. Yet, within these films a striking combination of race, class, and gender percolates beneath the jazz-themed surface. Thus, within the larger narrative of white America's acceptance of jazz is situated a filmic dialogue of the various roles allowed for women during the early years of Hollywood's infatuation with musical shorts.

In the early 1930s, having lived in New York City for a few years, Louis Armstrong headed out west to perform with Les Hite's band in Los Angeles. While living in southern California, Armstrong made several movie appearances including *A Rhapsody in Black and Blue,* a ten-minute short based on his recording of "I'll Be Glad When You're Dead, You Rascal You."[71] The film—its title an apparent play on the music of George Gershwin—begins with a black man (played by Sidney Easton) drumming along with an Armstrong record as his wife incessantly commands him to clean the apartment. The man agrees only if he can listen to his new Armstrong record of "I'll Be Glad When You're Dead, You Rascal You." His wife (played by Victoria Spivey) knocks him unconscious, and he awakens to Armstrong singing the song dressed in animal skins (as is his band) on a stage covered in bubbles. The husband, now known as the king of "Jazzmania," decrees Armstrong to perform "Shine."[72] Enjoying the song, the man is jolted awake as his wife smashes the record over his head. A strikingly different image of African Americans than the one seen in *Black and Tan,* the black couple at the center of the action represents a lower-class lifestyle with the husband apparently unemployed. The beleaguered and underprivileged husband fantasizes of a life characterized by power and opulence, but once given authority he can only ask for an Armstrong performance. Armstrong complicates matters further by playing both a legitimate jazz star as well as an entertaining (and harmless) clown. The jazz music in this film receives a considerable amount of attention due to Armstrong's stature in jazz culture. Still, his musical performances in these early film roles display less of his innovative trumpet work with the Hot Five and instead presage his future career as a vocalist.[73] Both of the featured songs highlight Armstrong's gravelly voice and not his trumpet playing (though flashes of his virtuosity remain in the brief solo sections), and he clearly enjoys playing up the commercial popular culture imagery and sexual innuendo of the lyrics, such as "you bought my wife a bottle of Coca-Cola so that you can play on her Victrola."

Despite the presence of "authentic" jazz, Armstrong's performance in animal skins offers a much more visible correlation to blackface posturing.

Both Armstrong and the husband genially mug for the camera, grinning and making faces throughout the film. Done for comedic effect, these actions also serve to present black Americans either as powerless husbands; severe, sexless women; or court-appointed jesters. Not simply a racist gesture, these stereotypes expose the constraints placed on black entertainers. In order to benefit from the new form of mass communication, social conventions forced many black actors and musicians into racially confined roles. Some African Americans ably escaped these trappings—Ellington in *Black and Tan,* for instance—but most black entertainers participated in depicting these stereotypes in exchange for a larger public forum. "The shenanigans," Krin Gabbard argues, "might even be tolerated as a sop to the less sophisticated members of the audience, an interlude between the moments of improvisatory art."[74] Instead of conveying a savage or dangerous persona, Armstrong wears the skins simply to denote a cartoonish image of Africa, and his costume parallels visually the husband's ostentatious marching band regalia. Armstrong also dilutes the sexual energy of the recording by delivering the sexual innuendo of the lyrics with humor rather than vulgarity. Furthermore, the film presents the gender role reversal of a powerful wife and out-of-work husband—a situation generated by the economic crisis of the early 1930s—as a farce. The most striking element of the film remains the usurpation of traditional gender roles as the wife dominates her browbeaten husband. Rather than a proto-feminist take on engendered roles, the film serves as an inherent dismissal of black families by parodying the inverted power structure of the black home.[75]

Singer and bandleader Cab Calloway presented a completely different interpretation of black life in *Cab Calloway's Hi-De-Ho,* a short film produced in 1932.[76] Like Armstrong, Calloway (who replaced Ellington at the Cotton Club) had a flamboyant performance style, but unlike the trumpeter, Calloway avoided most of the jungle accouterments that surrounded Armstrong. Unlike the unemployed and impoverished couple in *Rhapsody in Black and Blue, Hi-De-Ho* features a black couple that maintains a more comfortable (if not upper-class) lifestyle. In this film, the husband—who works as a train porter—purchases a radio for his wife to entertain her while he is away at work. Calloway, playing himself as a flashy bandleader, charms the wife through his performances on the radio. Her husband's gift, in other words, grants the wife the opportunity (through film magic) to have an affair with Calloway—and his whole band, apparently, as at the end of the film, the entire group marches out of the bedroom playing a song.

Calloway still clowns, but the portrait of black life in *Hi-De-Ho* eschews most of the obvious caricatures and stereotypes present in *A Rhapsody in Black and Blue*. Sexually independent, the wife relates little to the sexless wife in Armstrong's film and lacks both the frumpy dress and oppressive demeanor apparent in the earlier film. In addition, the husband in *Hi-De-Ho*, with his regular employment as a train porter, presents a more positive image of black masculinity than the fantasy king of "Jazzmania." Still, if *Hi-De-Ho* lacks the coarse generalizations of *A Rhapsody in Black and Blue*, Calloway's film forces the stereotypes of a licentious black woman and a controlled husband (who is ultimately made a cuckold).

During this same period, the Boswell Sisters, a popular vocal trio composed of three white sisters, appeared in a brief clip promoting their version of Armstrong's "Heebie Jeebies."[77] The sisters—Connee, Martha, and Helvetia—grew up in New Orleans and experienced the cosmopolitan musical culture of the city.[78] Connee, the oldest and most talented sister, played saxophone, trombone, and piano among other instruments; Martha played the piano; and Helvetia could play a number of stringed instruments including guitar, banjo, and violin. Raised in a middle-class environment in New Orleans, the sisters developed a tight singing style showcasing their close-harmony singing. Familiar with jazz and blues records—if not local firsthand experience—the sisters maintained a strong rhythmic pulse in their vocalizing, and light syncopation infused most of their work. One hallmark of their singing style relates to the precise harmonic arrangement of much of their material. "Instead of the on-the-beat barbershop style of close harmony that was then current," Linda Dahl writes, "the Boswells established a swinging, jazz-influenced vocal sound."[79] This sound, in conjunction with their creative use of microphones, made the group exceptionally compatible with radio audiences, and the sisters discovered a wide audience while singing with the Dorsey Brothers in the 1930s.[80] To capitalize on their fame, a short film was made for their version of Louis Armstrong's "Heebie Jeebies." This short features a close-cropped, stationary shot of the sisters arranged behind a piano performing the song with a bluesy feel. This first section—especially with Connee's rather dramatic mannerisms—tends toward an affected approximation of the blues played almost as a vaudeville-style joke. The second half of the song, however, erupts in a boisterous scat section performed in three-part harmony by the sisters. By the end of the piece, the Boswell Sisters ably transcend the arrangement's novelty elements. Not simply a reduction of "real" jazz, the carefully arranged harmonies and rhythmic structure of the song articulate the growing acceptance of jazz music by national listeners.

The filmic arc of the white acceptance of jazz begun by Al Jolson culminated in 1932 when Paramount Studios produced *The Musical Doctor*. The elaborate eleven-minute film starred Rudy Vallee, the popular radio crooner, and Mae Questel, the voice for Betty Boop.[81] The rather stiff and seemingly uncomfortable Vallee presides over a musical hospital where he prescribes different styles of music to cure his patients' various ailments. Vallee, who speaks in odd rhyming phrases, presents his philosophy to fellow doctors in "Keep a Little Song Handy," a song that instructs them to use music as a medical remedy. This song leads into a scene in which a patient requires immediate attention. The other doctors debate the man's condition—possibly indigestion, the gout, or hammertoes—before Vallee enters and gives the diagnosis of "musical starvation." He then orders the patient to follow a strict musical diet (which includes a "salad made from a very light ballad," "a sandwich of two standard blues," and "a little hot song for dessert"), and the other doctors then perform the recommended music at the patient's bedside. The doctor in charge of the blues (on a muted trumpet) plays the music for laughs, but the inclusion of blues and jazz along with classical and popular music illustrates the emerging tolerance for jazz music. This acceptance, however, fails to affect the included black actor as he performs in a broad style reminiscent of the husband in *A Rhapsody in Black and Blue*. With bugged-out eyes and singing a dialect-drenched "Missin' All the Kissin'," the black actor is relegated to a clownish minstrel performance. Despite the stereotypes inherent to the performance, the subtle inclusion of a black patient in an otherwise all-white hospital also speaks to a certain inclusionary spirit in the film. Vallee deepens this complex combination of inclusion and caricature through his treatment of the black patient. Asking for his favorite instrument, a megaphone, Vallee proceeds to croon a version of "Mammy" to the patient.[82] By deliberately echoing Al Jolson's blackface performance in *The Jazz Singer*, this film attempts to connect Vallee to the popularity of *The Jazz Singer* and in doing so heightens the underlying racial stereotypes of the song.

Born Hubert Prior Vallee in Vermont, Rudy (the singer adopted his stage name from a saxophone player) constructed a successful singing career on the radio in the 1930s. His northeastern ancestry coupled with an Ivy League education separated Vallee from most other singers of the period, but his smooth voice enabled him to perform vaudeville, and eventually

Vallee challenged Bing Crosby's reign on the radio. The singer's elite pretensions—and average looks—prevented Vallee from obtaining lasting fame, but during the 1930s he strung together a number of popular hit songs.[83] Paramount spared little expense in promoting Vallee, and *The Musical Doctor* signified one of the more elaborate short films produced during this period. The film, for example, includes two brief scenes of animation as well as an exterior shot of an ambulance barreling down a crowded city street.[84] These expensive touches speak to Vallee's marketability, and overall, *The Musical Doctor* exhibits the major themes underlying the eventual acceptance of jazz music through the medium of film. The film presents jazz as merely one element in a normal diet, and by placing it alongside classical music, the film includes jazz with the more traditionally accepted genres of music. The short also combines a popular radio singer with a popular film actress (or at least her famous voice) and illustrates the synergy involved in cross-promoting two forms of mass media. The filmmakers counter these attributes, however, with the casual stereotyping of black American life, a move that relates the movie to most other filmic images of African Americans during this early period of motion pictures.

Together, implicit and explicit racial stereotypes offered in *A Rhapsody in Black and Blue,* the pointed disruption of gender as well as racial constructions in *Hi-De-Ho,* the appropriation of jazz music by three middle-class white women, and the inclusion of jazz in a balanced musical diet trace the peculiar ways in which the motion picture industry recast jazz music during the early 1930s. In each of these films, despite the obvious issues of stereotyping, jazz was posited as a legitimate cultural form worthy of a national audience. Furthermore, because of the relatively inexpensive and transitory nature of these projects, black entertainers discovered more opportunities in these shorts than in full-length motion pictures.[85] Though their popularity remains difficult to judge, these films underscore the growing acceptability of jazz music as well as the continued stereotyping of black life. Los Angeles played a unique and central role in dispersing jazz to a national audience. On one level, mainstream films included white actors and musicians (Al Jolson, Rudy Vallee, Paul Whiteman, Bing Crosby) that submitted a particular style of jazz to white moviegoers. Widespread endorsement of racial discrimination contributed to the neglect of black performers, but the preponderance of white musicians (as well as a simplified form of jazz music) helped produce a larger audience for jazz during this period. For black musicians, Los Angeles provided artistic opportunities to a degree unknown in other cities. Still, these jobs came with the ugly constraints of racial stereotyping, creating a hard choice for black artists (play along with convention and push through black artistry). Much of these positive and negative consequences emerged the way they did because of the particular social setup of Los Angeles. A relatively small black community provided a different social context for the jazz played in Los Angeles, and as Hollywood gravitated to the local jazz community the early film industry quickly adapted jazz music to their artistic goals. Although jazz had its origins elsewhere, the jazz produced in Los Angeles had a profound impact on the national popularity of the music through its incorporation in a number of films during this period. Los Angeles provided a necessary seedbed for this transformation. The unconventional jazz scene in the city predicated the popularization of a type of jazz somewhat distinct from the music heard elsewhere in the nation. Still, for jazz to make the transition from black folk music to mainstream popular music it needed the acceptance and consumption of middle-class audiences. The symbiosis of the Los Angeles jazz community and the film industry created the cultural nexus necessary to introduce jazz to America during the late 1920s and early 1930s.

PART THREE

ACCEPTANCE

In 1943, Gordon Parks photographed Duke Ellington's band in New York City as they recorded a radio broadcast. In this photo—featuring (from left to right) Joe "Tricky Sam" Nanton, Harry Carney, and Harold "Shorty" Baker—Parks captured the musicians performing Ellington's 1930 hit, "Mood Indigo." This image, taken over a decade after the record's original release, attests to the enduring power and popularity of the "Mood Indigo" sound. (Library of Congress, Prints & Photographs Division, FSA-OWI Collection, LC-USW3–023926-C)

An American Music

On February 12, 1924, Paul Whiteman and his orchestra performed a program of modern American music at the Aeolian Hall in New York City.[1] This highly promoted performance proved to be the most anticipated and publicized (if not actually the first) instance of jazz featured in the respectable setting of a concert hall.[2] In general, Whiteman's concert bore little resemblance to the live performances in ramshackle halls in New Orleans, clubs on Chicago's South Side, extravagant ballrooms in New York, or theaters in Los Angeles. Musicians in those venues performed a functional form of jazz; the music served as the backdrop for dancing, socializing, or selling records. Whiteman's concert, in contrast, eschewed a functional jazz performance for a show explicitly designed to redefine jazz music as respectable entertainment. In the press release for the concert, Whiteman announced that he intended

> to sketch, musically, from the beginning of American history, the development of our emotional resources which have led us to the characteristic American music of today; most of which, by the way, is not jazz. . . . I intend to point out, with the assistance of my orchestra, the tremendous strides which have been made in popular music from the day of discordant jazz, which sprang into existence about ten years ago from nowhere in particular, to the really melodious music of to-day, which—for no good reason—is still called jazz.[3]

To illustrate this point, Whiteman opened the program with a musical section entitled "A History of Jazz." A whitewashed narrative of early jazz, this section of the concert demonstrated both Whiteman's commitment to enrich jazz with an aura of genteel decency and his specific and dogmatic interpretation of jazz history.[4] Paying backhanded homage to the Original Dixieland Jazz Band with a cheeky version of "Livery Stable Blues," Whiteman played the song for laughs. His band exaggerated many of the discordant elements of Dixieland-style jazz in order to distinguish that music from the less raucous orchestrations to follow.[5] Caricaturing the barnyard sounds of a song that already served as an inaccurate representation of black music, Whiteman's history lesson upended a narrative less than a decade old. Throughout the concert Whiteman contrasted performances of his own "respectable" music with examples of raw, unseemly jazz frequently performed in nightclubs. The band illustrated this point by performing one of their more popular recordings, "Whispering," twice—once as a heavily syncopated example of discordant jazz, and again as a lightly syncopated orchestral dance tune.[6] On the surface, Whiteman's goal was to devalue earlier jazz and show off the strengths of his own music. In the context of the racial attitudes of his time, however, Whiteman's interpretation of jazz history symbolized a much larger trend: the dismissal of African Americans from the jazz story. With their rendition of "Livery Stable Blues," Whiteman's white band perverted the music of another, earlier white band that won popularity through an approximate abstraction of black music. As a presentation of Whiteman (and by extension the white mainstream coterie of newspaper reviewers and concertgoers), the concert reduced the contributions of African Americans to a vague combination of syncopated rhythm and aural clichés.

Aside from proclaiming his interpretive history of jazz, this concert underscored Whiteman's resolve to place jazz into a more acceptable context. The concert therefore showcased the public premiere of *Rhapsody in Blue*, a long-form symphonic jazz piece written specifically for the event by the young composer George Gershwin. A symphonic jazz hybrid, *Rhapsody in Blue* proved both the talent of Gershwin as well as the compositional genius of Ferde Grofe, Whiteman's arranger who wrote the orchestral parts from Gershwin's piano score.[7] Though billed as modern dance music, *Rhapsody in Blue* relates little to the contemporary jazz being performed by Jelly Roll Morton or Louis Armstrong. An arranged, symphonic stylization of jazz music, Gershwin's piece featured jazz instrumentation (plus strings) and an underlying jazz-influenced rhythmic pulse. The composition's various tempo changes and shifts in dynamics resulted in a piece more directly defined as a concert fixture rather than as dance music. Olin Downes, the classical music writer for the *New York Times,* was impressed with elements of the performance but noted that "this composition shows extraordinary talent, just as it also shows a young composer . . . struggling with a form of which he is far from being a master."[8] Still, Whiteman (and to some extent Gershwin) set out to lend respectability and credibility to jazz music—to blend jazz and classical music rather than create simply another jazz composition.[9] Whiteman designed the evening to lend jazz a more reputable platform for white listeners and allow jazz into the canon of respectable music. Discussing the concert later, Whiteman commented that "it proved one thing, they can't go on questioning jazz forever. . . . I proved, and it was conceded as such, that the popular highbrow conception of jazz was wrong."[10]

Paul Whiteman was born in Denver in 1890, and his early life related little to the biographies of most other contemporary jazz musicians. A western violinist contracted with large symphony orchestras, Whiteman developed a style unique to his period. His comfortable middle-class upbringing in Colorado provided him with a set of environmental and musical circumstances far removed from those of most other jazz artists. A privileged home life and domineering father characterized Whiteman's early years and help explain his eventual interest in the regimented training of classical music. A talented—if not a virtuoso—violinist and viola player, Whiteman squelched a jazz-hued rebelliousness in pursuit of a career in symphony orchestras. A move to California defeated Whiteman's jazz defiance, however, when he discovered West Coast nightclubs. His experiences in San Francisco and Los Angeles inspired Whiteman to combine the rhythm and spirit of jazz with classical music forms. By 1920, Whiteman and his band relocated to the East Coast and established themselves in Atlantic City, where he continued tinkering with a style of music that integrated jazz rhythms into classical music.[11]

Whiteman's early career climaxed with the 1924 Aeolian Hall performance, but musically he hit his stride with the numerous recordings he made during the mid- to late 1920s. The music produced during this period illustrates his nascent talents of burnishing the sounds of earlier jazz and bringing an innovative style of jazz to a mainstream audience. In August 1920, Whiteman began recording for Victor Records, which produced a number of popular recordings for the band. In 1928, however, Whiteman switched to Columbia Records in a media-invented spectacle that included a short film showing Whiteman tearing up his Victor contract. Whiteman still owed an array of recordings to Victor Records, and over a four-month period he fulfilled his earlier contract by recording over sixty records for his former company. To compete with this new trove of unreleased records, Columbia also forced Whiteman into the studio, haranguing the band to record two dozen songs over a brief two-week session.[12] The music during this period embodied the high point in Whiteman's recording career, as his band included some of the finest white jazz musicians active during the 1920s. In 1927, alone, Whiteman hired a number of musicians from Jean Goldkette's Detroit-based band, including trumpeter Bix Beiderbecke, saxophonist Frankie Trumbauer, reedman Jimmy Dorsey, and trombonist Tommy Dorsey.[13] In addition to these musicians, Whiteman hired the Rhythm Boys, a three-piece singing group featuring Bing Crosby, an increasingly popular singer who had developed a voice uniquely tailored for radio microphones. These musicians provided Whiteman's orchestra with the jazz integrity that his earlier bands lacked, and Ferde Grofe adapted his arrangements to accommodate the talented new soloists. Though primarily composed and formally structured, Grofe's arrangements still remained somewhat flexible to accommodate the improvisational talents of these artists.[14]

The 1924 concert helped formulate Whiteman's character as the "King of Jazz," a title that defined the bandleader for most of his career. The concert, however, fell short of convincing all critics that jazz represented a viable (and harmless) form of American music. Still, Whiteman's career, and in a limited sense the 1924 Aeolian Hall concert, indicates the rapidly rising undercurrent of mass acceptance. The eventual acceptance of jazz stemmed from many of the same sources that fueled jazz criticism, namely the emergence of a modern, interconnected nation. This process served to underscore the cultural ambivalence that marked the 1920s as jazz critics and proponents used the music to highlight their respective positions concerning the impact of modernity.[15] Whereas critics of jazz loosely shared a distrust and fear of the effects of modernity, the movement toward jazz acceptance served less as a reaction against cultural change than a casual approval of modern values. The music originally existed outside of mainstream culture, and white college students in particular sought out black music as a rebellion against the cultural confinement of traditional values. Americans removed from mainstream society through their particular race, class, or ethnic status also listened to jazz music as an alternative to the more inaccessible dominant culture.[16] Not until commercial jazz (a music generally disconnected from black art forms) increased in popularity, however, did jazz begin to impact American culture in the mainstream. The widespread acceptance of jazz therefore depended on the eventual acquiescence of highbrow critics and middle-class white audiences. The shift from Victorianism to modernism formed the context in which Americans reacted to jazz music.[17] In general, Victorianism created a dichotomy separating controlled human instincts from natural impulses, and modernism strove to reunite these two forces. The refashioning of traditional musical forms into something more modern—both rhythmically and harmonically—characterized the larger cultural role jazz performance played during this period. Modernists, in other words, accepted the complex and ambivalent nature of modern American life, and artists, writers, and philosophers endeavored to create a fusion of all elements of society. Jazz signified one method of merging the disparate cultural forces rent asunder by Victorian culture.[18]

The modernist cultural revolution resulted not in an immediate victory for the new order—though mainstream America eventually signaled this shift—but rather a period of deep ambivalence as Americans vacillated between two competing images of American life. Jazz, for both detractors and proponents alike, represented the evolving modern social order as a challenging new culture entered the national conscience accompanied by a novel soundtrack. Throughout the 1920s jazz fell under attack by a variety of critics representing all segments of American society. Various community leaders from across the nation labeled the music as dangerous, pastors regardless of denomination posited jazz as immoral, art critics dismissed jazz as a vulgar approximation of traditional musical forms, and a number of African Americans agonized that the popularity of jazz would only further debase the image of the black community. Overall, the array of anti-jazz rhetoric that appeared during this decade reflected a larger pattern of action and reaction to the evolving modern nation. These critics—urban and rural, secular and religious, black and white—shared similarities with the groups of jazz adherents that explicitly advocated the acceptance of the music, a comparison that underscores the profound ambivalence of the period. The jazz debate paralleled a larger discussion over the nature of American society as articles on dancing and syncopation implicitly related to broader deliberations occurring across the nation. The overt quickening of industrial life, for instance, stimulated much of the concern over the general direction of American society. Jazz, with its upbeat tempos, served as a useful tool to examine the supposed declension of cultural values.[19] "We are living," one musician wrote in the 1920s, "in a state of unrest, of social evolution, of transition from a condition of established order to a new objective as yet but dimly visualized. This is reflected in the jazz fad."[20] Cultural historian Warren Susman argued that this "great fear" concerned "whether any great industrial and democratic mass society can maintain a significant level of civilization, and whether mass education and mass communication will allow any civilization to survive."[21] As a mass-produced music with clear associations to the groups that characterized a changing modern culture (African Americans and young men and women, in particular), jazz epitomized the growing tensions and divisions created by the ambivalence embedded in the introduction of new standards of productivity, morality, and consumption.

The new industrial order and World War I—the global articulation of this new industrialism—helped define the parameters of much of the discussion surrounding the role of jazz music. The jazz debate focused on fears of a rapidly growing industrial network as machines skulked into factories and automated repetition came to define the monotony of the workday. [22] To some critics, the clatter and clang of jazz echoed this new factory floor reverberating with the metallic cacophony of "efficiency." Jazz usurped traditional music much as machines had replaced older methods of industrial production. Other critics also associated jazz with the workplace, but in a further illustration of the ambivalence that framed much of the developments of the 1920s, these commentators did not see raw, brutal efficiency as a soul-destroying element of modern life. Instead, these commentators argued that jazz introduced pure inefficiency into the workplace as the music instilled laziness and shiftlessness in workers. "In almost every big industry where music has been instituted," Anne Shaw Faulkner argued in the *Ladies Home Journal*, "it has been found necessary to discontinue jazz because of its demoralizing effects upon the workers." "This was noticed," she continued, "in an unsteadiness and lack of evenness in the workmanship of the product after a period when the workmen had indulged in jazz music."[23] Furthermore, some writers connected these fears of industrialization to the increased visibility of network radio in society, and a standard line of reasoning concluded that simply because a radio could pick up jazz, no reason existed as to "why it should be allowed to do so."[24] This writer also related the story of the planned deportation of forty American jazz bands from Germany. "That is bad news," the writer argued, "for the effect may succeed, and then there will be forty more jazz bands in the United States than there are now, and already we are much more than adequately supplied with these baleful groups of conscienceless noisemakers."[25] World War I stood as the definitive symbol of this "frenetic era," and a number of writers posited jazz as a music emblematic of this cultural change.[26] One commentator, for example, connected the war with a "revolt against conventions of all sorts—artistic, religious, moral, social, political."[27] In general, critics of jazz argued that the music "represented the manifold paradoxes of modern life: hedonism and urban mechanism, the components of consumption capitalism," and they applied this cultural apprehension to most areas of changing American life.[28]

Outside of the factory gates, critics most often warned of the way jazz threatened to demean and degrade all forms of national culture during this period. "For years past," composer Robert M. Stults wrote, "I have watched the gradual deterioration of the so-called popular music of the day." "This jazz epidemic," he continued "has also had its degenerating effect on the popular songs of the day."[29] The diffusion (and methods of diffusion) constituted as great a threat to mainstream culture, critics argued, as the music itself. "Nothing," one *New York Times* article maintained, "is safe from [jazz's] devastating touch."[30] Still, a number of commentators disparaged the potential social effects of jazz while maintaining a guarded optimism concerning the eventual expiration of the noise. "It will disappear," music director Will Earhart contended, "like all things that are not sound and fundamental always have disappeared."[31] "If America did not think jazz, feel jazz and dream jazz," Rabbi Stephen Wise declared, "jazz would not have taken a dominant place in the music of America." "When America regains its soul," he maintained, "jazz will go."[32]

The perceived destruction of culture by jazz reverberated throughout the musical community as a number of music professionals began to express concern over the potential effects of jazz on classical music. Throughout the 1920s newspapers and magazines routinely invited nationally recognized composers to offer their thoughts on jazz music and to express their contempt for jazz and the larger social changes that it reflected. Most of these composers deplored the notion that jazz might have the power to alter more traditional (and accepted) forms of music. One of the leading critics on the supposed effects of jazz on classical music, Frank Damrosch, served as the director of the institute that would become the Juilliard School of Music and argued that jazz only debased respectable music. "Attempts have been made," Damrosch wrote, "to 'elevate' jazz by stealing phrases from the classic composers and vulgarizing them by the rhythms and devices used in jazz."[33] Much of Damrosch's displeasure stemmed from the syncopated rhythm of jazz: "Jazz is a monotony of rhythm, it is rhythm without music and without soul."[34] Other music directors agreed with Damrosch. "I don't like 'Jazz,' and don't approve of it," Pittsburgh conductor Will Earhart asserted. "My reason for not liking it is that it does not come pleasingly to my ears."[35] Again, the rhythmic pulse of jazz lay at the center of the debate as the director cataloged his displeasure. "I do not approve of 'jazz,'" he contended, "because it represents, in its convulsive, twitching, hiccoughing rhythms, the abdication of control by the central nervous system—the brain."[36] The critics of jazz often attempted to prove a physiological argument to bolster their anti-syncopation attitudes.

Rhythm signified only one of the issues confronting music professionals, and other critics within the music business feared the improvisational elements of jazz. "Is it possible," one writer asked in a 1922 *New York Times* article, "to protect from jazzing by anything but moral suasion?" This particular article focused on the problems confronted by sheet music publishers as improvised jazz began to take precedence over written arrangements. "How can you legally prevent a man," the writer asked, "from playing a piece the way his fancy or his interest dictates?" Only through moral persuasion, or "by being present at every performance," the writer concluded, can critics contain improvisation.[37] Encompassing an odd combination of democratic apprehension, progressive reform, and capitalistic fervor, the writer despaired that improvisation would abrogate sheet music production. Although more complementary of and sympathetic toward jazz, the National Federation of Music Clubs still believed that "they were fighting the 'jazzing of the noble compositions of the great composers.'" Improvised modern music, according to the organization, "has its own place," but society must first preserve the sanctity of classical music.[38] Many professional musicians simply did not know what to do in the absence of a musical score and could not make the transition into the extemporaneous Jazz Age. One classically trained cellist, despondent of the jazz revolution, resolved not to play jazz even if that meant his occupational options dwindled. Without the flexibility of a jazz resume, the article implies, the musician's concert assignments evaporated. The cellist eventually took his life rather than "insult his cello."[39] Most music professionals did not resort to such dramatic displays of opposition but still related the influence of jazz to larger social concerns of a more moral nature. "Jazz is to real music," Frank Damrosch argued, "what the caricature is to the portrait. The caricature may be clever, but it aims at distortion of line and feature in order to make its point; similarly, jazz may be clever but its effects are made by exaggeration, distortion, and vulgarisms."[40] Jazz signified an assault on respectable music and tastes, a number of composers and music directors argued, a moral crisis indicative of the impact of modernity on American life in the 1920s.

New definitions of femininity and sexuality born in the 1920s exacerbated the fear of vulgarity that critics associated with jazz. In fact, antimodernists pointed to jazz music as the most prominent representation of the loosening of inhibitions they perceived as degrading to American culture. Much of their criticism derived from the cultural shift away from the traditional values of emotional repression and aggressive morality that they regarded as the necessary ingredients of social stability. Women constituted a particular concern as they shed some of the more inhibiting standards of Victorian dress and behavior to reveal a new, more modern femininity. This led to the creation of two opposing symbols of female life—the daft, uninhibited flapper confronting the dour, corseted Victorian—that battled for dominance in the 1920s. Modern women adopted new clothing designs and hairstyles, and in many ways, these outward expressions of style reflected an inward change in attitude.[41] As the "boyish and single" modern mode of expression replaced the "maternal and wifely" Victorian ideal, women's fashion provided a conspicuous way for young women to distance themselves from traditional roles.[42] Designers produced lighter clothing "better suited for busy, athletic women" to complement the modern feminine ideal centered on activity and movement.[43] Short bob haircuts also accommodated a more active lifestyle, with young women across the nation clamoring for the style first popularized by the dancer Irene Castle.[44] More conservative social patrons associated this collapse of traditional gender roles with jazz music and feared, in particular, the vulgar image of uninhibited women dancing to jazz tunes in public.[45] Jazz, in other words, loosened the corset and led directly to unredeemed activity. "That jazz," Anne Shaw Faulkner argued in an article for Ladies Home Journal, "is an influence for evil is also felt by a number of the biggest country clubs, which have forbidden the corset check room, the leaving of the hall between dances, and the jazz orchestra—three evils which have also been eliminated from many municipal dance halls."[46] Listening to a jazz performance, Faulkner not so subtly implies, led directly to unsupervised relationships between young people and sexual experimentation. "It is somewhat of a rude awakening for many of these parents," Faulkner admonishes, "to find that America is facing a most serious situation regarding its popular music."[47]

As Faulkner alludes, the fear of debauched young women cavorting with shameful young men aroused perhaps the most explicit attacks on jazz music as a source of moral degradation. Newspapers latched onto this new-found anxiety in the 1920s and published sermons composed by religious leaders decrying the rampant wantonness of America's youth and their musical preferences. "Jazz music," one writer argued in 1926, "is just as much a revolt against the standards of modesty and decency as is the jazz tendency in dress."[48] Most of these sermonizers condemned the sensual closeness of jazz dancing, arguing that it enhanced the popularity of the music, which hastened the demise of traditional values of decency and in-nocence. "Dancing in itself is a substitute for sex contact," one pastor noted, "but when it becomes an instrument for a gratification then the whole psychological process is turned about, and instead you have an injury."[49] An Episcopal minister made a similar judgment, contending that jazz music and dancing "lead to jazz manners and jazz morals among the younger members of the Church."[50] Jazz music, he reasoned, led to dancing, which then encouraged young people to leave the dance floor to pursue other, more immoral acts.[51] Sparing much sympathy, the pastor defined the jazz musician as "an outlaw and a musical bandit. Like the gunman he is running amuck and should be relentlessly put down."[52] Modern America, as symbolized by the liberating pleasures of parked automobiles and jazz records, created in the minds of pastors across the nation the specter of an amoral wasteland for young people.

The menacing appeal of jazz had global implications, and many religious leaders saw in jazz a worldwide conspiracy to destroy the Christian way of life. "Jazz," one reverend argued, "was borrowed from Central Africa by a gang of wealthy international Bolshevists from America, their aim being to strike at Christian civilization throughout the world."[53] The introduction of jazz, in other words, with its roots in Africa (and, apparently, communism), sounded the death knell for western civilization and Christianity. "Jazz," an-other minister claimed, "is a picture of the world fiddling, for the leisure of the few, while the rest of the world burns up like Rome under Nero." "The church," he added, "is the best remedy for jazz."[54] Throughout this period, religious commentators attempted to associate jazz music with hedonism and cultural savagery, using references to Africa—either in terms of an international conspiracy or musical origins—to underscore the crude and uncivilized aspects of the music. "Jazz," an Episcopal rector explained, "goes back to the African jungle and is one of the crying evils of today." The emphasis on Africa in this critic's sermon pointed to the perceived devolution of American society and the role of jazz in this supposed unraveling of culture. "Jazz is retrogression," he continued, "it is going to the African jungle for our music."[55] Although direct references to black Americans remained slightly veiled within this commentary, this sermon from 1922 established an early pattern of presenting jazz as foreign, generally, and African, specifically, and therefore detrimental to American society. Taking the racial criticism further, other jazz critics throughout the period elaborated on the African elements inherent in jazz music and worried about the cultural and social impact generated by the mainstream acceptance of the "savage crash and bang" of jazz.[56]

Issues of race and racism framed much of the debate concerning jazz music as many observers warned of the social implications of accepting black cultural forms into white American society. "Symbol of the surface of American life," one writer notes, "jazz was perceived primarily as a carrier of dangerous romantic blackness, of undisciplined sensuousness."[57] Most of the commentary tended to agree that jazz represented a valid expression of black culture in the black community. Problems arose only as this African American folk music seeped into the white community. As a subculture of musical expression, in other words, jazz served as a unique cultural indicator. "If jazz originated in the dance rhythms of the negro," composer Frank Damrosch argued, "it was at least interesting as the self-expression of a primitive race." Problems arose only once "jazz was adopted by the 'highly civilized' white race," he continued, and jazz then "tended to denigrate" white society "towards primitivity." Once jazz began to bleed out of the black community and into mainstream culture, criticism of the music increased dramatically. Black people playing jazz for other black people did not significantly threaten white culture. It was not until white people began performing and listening to jazz that the larger white community regarded the black musical form as a direct attack on their traditional music and values. "When a savage distorts his features and paints his face so as to produce startling effects," the writer concluded, "we smile at his childishness; but when a civilized man imitates him, not as a joke but in all seriousness, we turn away in disgust."[58]

Between the 1890s and 1920s, waves of southern black migrants moved to urban communities in the North. The black neighborhoods in cities such as Chicago and Detroit doubled and tripled in size over the course of a decade, leading to increased racial fears in these areas. As a central mechanism of relocating jazz out of the South, black migration was thus connected inherently to a rapidly changing culture.[59] Anti-modern commentators connected this increased black population to a growing acceptance and believed both to be serious threats to traditional values. The music critic for the *New York Herald Tribune,* for example, associated jazz with the alleged immorality of black Americans, massive black migration to the urban North, and the effect that these issues would have on white culture. Jazz, he fretted, would "soon emanate from the Negro brothels of the South."[60] Anti-jazz critics consistently pointed to interracial sex—at least implicitly—as the real danger of jazz acceptance. Jazz music "was made to stand for the devolutionary forces of sensual blackness" that would desecrate white society as well as black. [61] Many of these racial fears found superficial rationalization with a rash of social science literature that appeared in the 1910s and 1920s that sought to prove the biological inferiority of African Americans. In 1916, for example, Madison Grant published his theories of racial determinism (all based on assumptions) in *The Passing of the Great Race.* Grant provided the supposed biological evidence to bolster segregation and racism, and his work connected with the larger pattern of Nativism that reemerged as a cultural phenomenon focused on the elimination of foreign influences from American society throughout the early twentieth century.[62] Many critics of modern culture thus fused the emergence of large black communities in the North with a growing literature supporting biological racism and created a multifaceted condemnation of jazz and African American culture.

One of the most explicit condemnations of jazz appeared in an article printed in the *New York Times* in 1927 with a musician's racial polemic against jazz music. "Jazz must be banned by the white races," he argued, "if they wish to maintain their prestige."[63] Recapitulating the main racial arguments of the jazz debate, this article indicts modern culture as the harbinger of diluted morality and the corruption of American society. The article stresses the importance of cultural continuity and positions jazz as a threat to the stability of white culture. He suggested that in order to maintain cultural permanence, modernist values and their expression through jazz music had to be resisted. "Jazz was largely responsible for lowering pre-war standards," he contended, "and it must be taboo in every shape and form until its baneful influence is gone." Although the musician fails to define clearly the social standards in danger of degradation, he outlines the musical flaws of jazz, culminating in the comment that the music "cannot be made anything but the essence of vulgarity." Jazz, he argued, "is a low type of primitive music founded on crude rhythms suggested by stamping feet and clapping hands." "The popularization of jazz," the writer concluded, "and the attendant immodest dances are lowering the prestige of the white races."[64] Relating the fears of the encroachment of jazz to the corruption of traditional values and the supposed implications of white people accepting black forms of music, this article illustrates the constellation of issues that fueled critics of jazz music.

As many white Americans fretted over the changing course of main-stream culture, they found some allies in black jazz critics, and a sizable number of black Americans worried that the increased exposure of jazz music would further distort white perceptions of the black community. Whereas most white critics tended to assail jazz as detrimental to the moral fiber of the nation, black critics of jazz worried that a focus on the more salacious elements of jazz would only augment already held white stereotypes of African Americans. This perspective tended to emphasize ragtime rather than the blues, and many black writers deemphasized any African connections in an attempt to escape some of the racial connotations and stereotypes associated with the music.[65] J. A. Rogers, for example, in his chapter on jazz in Alain Locke's *The New Negro,* declared ragtime as "the direct predecessor of jazz."[66] For Rogers, jazz signified a fundamental element of African American culture, especially in terms of an emotional expression within the modern context.[67] Primitivism also played a large role in Rogers's fascination (and ultimate misunderstanding) of jazz music, and throughout his article, Rogers simply connects jazz performance to an earlier period of civilization that stood in marked contrast to the industrial, modern age. This emphasis on the "primitive" elements of jazz music underscores the importance of modernist thought behind the Harlem Renaissance, especially in terms of demonstrating the supposed superiority of the preindustrial past.[68] Overall, the jazz debate as articulated by many black Americans echoed the concerns of white critics in terms of the general ramifications of jazz music. Black intellectuals, however, also had to contend with prospects of white America defining the black community exclusively through jazz music.[69]

The writers of the Harlem Renaissance treated jazz with wary neglect. The general elitism of the intellectual movement, uncomfortable with the coarser elements of jazz culture, disallowed an extensive discussion of the music.[70] Few writers outright condemned jazz, but jazz failed to fit into the larger arguments made by Alain Locke and W. E. B. Du Bois. [71] Both Locke and Du Bois focused more intently on the cultural importance of black spirituals and gave only a passing nod to jazz music.[72] Although jazz represented one of the greatest achievements of black culture in the twentieth century, most leaders of the Harlem Renaissance simply dismissed the music as lowbrow noise.[73] Put simply, jazz proved problematic for black intellectuals in the 1920s. The centrality and agency of African Americans in the creation of jazz represented a key asset to the music, but the increasing attention on the supposed immorality of jazz (both in mainstream opinion and the black press) made the absolute acceptance of jazz music somewhat challenging. For black intellectuals concerned about the identity of the black community, African American poetry, spirituals, plays, and novels represented more comfortable areas of study than did jazz with its associations to lowbrow pursuits. Black writers and scholars relegated jazz music to a lower level of discourse and devoted most of their academic energies to cultural forms of a more highbrow nature.[74]

The racial, musical, and moral confusion that defined the jazz debate during this period continued to concern critics (both black and white) into the early 1930s. Swing music, for example, produced a similar spasm of anti-jazz sentiment as it came to dominate American culture in the years before World War II. Despite their prevalence in mainstream newspapers and magazines, jazz critics did not determine all of the debate during the 1920s, and the overt fearful nature of the commentary diminished as the popularity of the music crested. By the late 1920s, for example, newspaper articles began to incorporate a more balanced examination of jazz. In 1926, the *New York Times* published an article that labeled jazz as the "agency of the devil." At first glance, the piece resembled any number of contemporary anti-jazz articles with an emphasis on ministerial complaints. At the end of the article, however, the writer noted that not everyone agreed with this negative assessment. Marguerite d'Alvarez, a celebrated opera singer, enthusiastically endorsed jazz music. "Jazz is my reason for living in New York City," d'Alvarez claimed, "I prefer to live in New York because here I can best find the inspiration of good jazz music." "To me [jazz] is truly great music," she continued, "and certainly it is the music that best expresses us moderns." Although not quite an editorial acceptance of the music, these types of endorsements became more common as jazz entered the mainstream. [75]

The larger forces that created modern America—urbanization, industrialization, accelerated black migration, increased ethnic diversity, technological expansion—also helped frame the jazz debate. Americans therefore responded to jazz in ways similar to their reaction to the emergence of a modern state. During the shift away from traditional values, the distinctions between highbrow and lowbrow cultural forms began to dissolve. At no point did the jazz controversy disappear completely, but the loudest, most virulent criticisms of the 1920s gave way to a begrudging acceptance. This growing approval materialized on two different levels: several eminent bandleaders actively sought to combine jazz and classical forms, and the music press (in conjunction with the mainstream press) began publishing positive articles on jazz.[76] This combined set of circumstances—gradual acceptance reflected in the press and the concerted quest for respectability by certain jazz musicians—allowed for a growing tolerance for jazz music. By the mid-1930s, the cultural transformation of the nation produced a new, nationally recognized expression of modern America as swing music (the first cousin to the jazz music performed in the 1920s) came to prominence. Much of this musical development stemmed from the music of Paul Whiteman, the premier articulation of respectable jazz during the 1920s.

In the summer of 1929, the Whiteman orchestra traveled to Los Angeles to commence filming *The King of Jazz,* an extravagant motion picture set to canonize Whiteman's contributions to jazz.[77] After spending a large sum of money to house the band, the studio could not agree on a script and had to delay filming.[78] Warner Brothers finally decided on a revue-style show, but the band had to leave California to fulfill other engagements. In between the original meetings and the revised date of shooting, however, trumpeter Bix Beiderbecke left the band and moved back to Iowa in order to try to curb his growing alcohol addiction. That fall, the band (without Beiderbecke) reconvened in Los Angeles to record the music for the soundtrack as well as commence primary filming of the band numbers.[79] The first full-length Technicolor motion picture produced by Warner Brothers, *The King of Jazz* combined modern filmmaking techniques with a standard vaudevillian framework. Elaborate production numbers appeared between short skits, individual musical performances, and dance sequences.[80] The sets included ornate ballrooms; giant, divided bandstands; optical illusions; and camera techniques that presented a forty-piece band in miniature. An elaborate spectacle, *The King of Jazz* rewrote the narrative of American music in an attempt to place Paul Whiteman at the center of all jazz history and innovation. Black musicians may have played a role in the creation of jazz, the film suggests, but they needed Whiteman's talents and abilities to provide the music with compositional integrity. By surrounding jazz performances with humorous sketches and popular ballads, Whiteman effectively placed jazz into the larger context of vaudeville entertainment. Rather than an aberration, Whiteman urged his audience to relate jazz music (or at least his symphonic form of jazz) with popular currents of modern American culture. The first segment of the film was a short cartoon by Walter Lantz, more famously known later as the creator of Woody Woodpecker. In an attempt to justify Whiteman's title as the "King of Jazz," the narrator explains that the conductor, "tiring of his life in the great city," went on a big game hunting excursion in "darkest Africa." In Africa, Whiteman is crowned the "King of Jazz" simply by his ability to bring out the inherent musicality of Africans.[81] In support of this animated claim of Whiteman as the "King of Jazz," the film segues directly to one of the only segments featuring legitimate jazz in the film, as Whiteman introduces the entire band over a banjo-driven dance piece. Although the song eventually devolves into a lightly syncopated classical piece, this segment features several distinguished moments including a strong violin and guitar duet by Joe Venutti and Eddie Lang.

Whiteman's *The King of Jazz*, essentially a mainstream white film about the fictional career of a mainstream white bandleader, provides a substantive account of the way a number of white Americans viewed the role of race within the jazz narrative. Balancing the manifest purpose of the film in proclaiming Whiteman the "King of Jazz" is a second theme involving the subtle exclusion of African Americans from the creation and diffusion of jazz music. Black characters (or at least characters presumed to be black) appear sporadically throughout the film and usually in the guise of cartoon animals, as children, or as dancers. In the Lantz cartoon, for example, Africans are included only through the use of animated animals that interact with Whiteman in the segment. At the beginning of the cartoon, as Whiteman shoots at a lion, the animal rips open his skin and the musket balls bounce harmlessly (but musically) off his ribs like a xylophone. Later, hearing Whiteman's violin, the lion falls to his knees in an Al Jolson pose and sings "Mammy." Although the film makes no direct reference to race, the overt minstrel elements of this scene provide a subtle questioning of African American agency in the creation of jazz music.[82] "Jazz," Whiteman argues in the one scene featuring a black adult, "was born in the African jungle to the beating of the voodoo drum." A dancer in silver paint then proceeds to jump around on a large African drum as an introduction to Gershwin's *Rhapsody in Blue*. Throughout the film, African Americans are reduced to stereotypes, children, and heavily costumed dancers—racial inclusion, to be sure, but only within the parameters of stereotype and debasement. Overall, *The King of Jazz* thoroughly redefines jazz history, replacing any concept of African American agency with the supposed musical innovation of Paul Whiteman.[83]

The interconnected themes of racial myopia and the primacy of Whiteman in the creation of jazz coalesce in the final segment of the film. Entitled "Melting Pot of Music," this section serves as Whiteman's attempt to illustrate the "diversity" of American music. "America," the title card proclaims, "is a melting pot of music wherein the melodies of all Nations are fused into one great New Rhythm—JAZZ!" The orchestra then presents in brief musical vignettes the various nationalities that supposedly coalesced to create jazz. A British foxhunt song thus segues into an accordion-based Italian melody followed by a Spanish dance song, a Highland bagpipe tune, a French minuet, and finally a Russian melody played on balalaikas.[84] These diverse instruments and songs then blur together in a lightly syncopated classical style. Standing over this musical stew, Whiteman pretends to stir together each of these genres into something new, something uniquely American. The segment ends with a collision of visual and aural images. As dancers clad in Western-style fringe emerge from behind the cauldron, the band opens with "Stars and Stripes Forever" before launching into a rousing upbeat jazz song. Africa disappears completely as Whiteman imagines jazz as an American art form with definite European musical forbearers. The Western iconography connects jazz unambiguously to the American themes of democracy and expansion, and the inclusion of "Stars and Stripes Forever" signifies the adoption of a new jazz-themed national anthem for America.

The film premiered in Los Angeles in April 1930 and received a noticeably mixed reaction. "Hot jazz fans," Whiteman's biographer notes, "were disappointed and disgruntled by the preponderance of jazzless entertainment, but they forgot that they were not picking up the tab." "For true connoisseurs of jazz," the writer continues, "the unforgivable flaw was the absence of Bix from the soundtrack, a conspicuous void occasioned by Universal's failure to begin filming on the band's first trip to Hollywood."[85] In the years following *The King of Jazz*, Whiteman remained committed to symphonic jazz, but he never recaptured the musical triumphs of the 1920s. Whiteman's music reflected a growing acceptance of jazz, but his attempts at reconfiguring jazz into a classical framework all ended in disappointment. Gershwin's *Rhapsody in Blue* ably mixed syncopation into an orchestral setting and featured strong instrumental work from Beiderbecke and Trumbauer. Still, Whiteman's music experiment, though well received, failed to inspire an entire musical trend. Jazz connoisseurs may have admired the inclusion of Bix, for instance, but the long-form orchestral facets of the composition were not the same as an improvised blast of hot jazz. Mainstream jazz progressed along a different path from the one forged by Whiteman, the jazz of the 1930s relating more to the New York sounds of Fletcher Henderson and Duke Ellington than to the King of Jazz. Whiteman's music, however, served as the catalyst for the conception of jazz criticism as jazz-friendly writers looked to Whiteman as the primary arbiter of jazz taste. Thus, although Whiteman had little impact on the musical direction of mainstream jazz, his music played an exaggerated role in the burgeoning jazz narrative constructed by writers heavily influenced by symphonic jazz.

In 1926, Henry Osborne Osgood published *So This Is Jazz,* one of the earliest books specifically on jazz music and the foremost example of the Whiteman-influenced style of jazz criticism. "This book is," Osgood wrote, "so far as I know, the first attempt to set down a connected account of the origin, history and development of jazz music."[86] An enthusiastic supporter of Paul Whiteman, Osgood lionized the bandleader as the primary example of real jazz. "For if it hadn't been for his ambition and initiative," Osgood wrote of Whiteman, "jazz would still be the same old tum-tum fox-trot music, with its eternal monotony."[87] Osgood's emphasis on symphonic jazz never emerged as the predominant focus for later jazz historians, and in general, Osgood's devotion to Whiteman almost seemed passé in 1926. During this same period two other critics began casually organizing a new framework of jazz criticism. Working separately, Gilbert Seldes and Carl Van Vechten broke from the segregated and narrow jazz narrative posited by Osgood, and throughout their work, these two critics helped couple a respect for African American culture with their appreciation of mainstream jazz artists. Despite expressing "reservations of the Negro's artistic potential," Seldes in particular maintained that black artists played a larger creative role in jazz history than earlier scholars had allowed.[88] Likewise, Van Vechten's admiration for black artists tended to include a slightly patronizing attitude.

Inspired by Whiteman's Aeolian Hall concert, Van Vechten wrote a series of articles on George Gershwin, but the transplanted Iowan quickly fell under the spell of the Harlem Renaissance, a cultural rebirth of black America at least partially directed by wealthy white patrons.[89]

The work of Seldes and Van Vechten established the early pattern of mainstream critical acceptance of jazz: an acknowledgement of black agency tied to an artistic attachment to white musicians. In conjunction with the emerging critical discourse on jazz music, magazines devoted to jazz began to appear in the 1930s. This nascent jazz press helped expand and invigorate the audience for jazz and "absorbed and catalyzed the throbbing populist energy unleashed by swing's youth audience."[90] In 1934, *Down Beat*—originally a "trade sheet for Chicago dance band musicians"—emerged as the most important national magazine devoted to jazz music.[91] That same year in France, Hugues Panassie published *Le jazz hot*, "the most important full-scale study of jazz," largely creating a market for legitimate studies of jazz.[92] Although Paul Whiteman's popularity served in part as an inspiration for these new critics, these writers also surfaced during the early 1930s as the culture of ambivalence gave way to a gradual acceptance of the new cultural framework.

The economic devastation of this period had both immediate and long-lasting impacts on the music business, and Paul Whiteman's band directly experienced certain difficulties that foreshadowed the coming storm of the 1930s. The Depression called into question both the cost of the film as well as its box-office capabilities. At its opening in early 1930, *The King of Jazz* brought in respectable receipts, but demand for the movie dropped off quickly as customers became much more cautious with their discretionary income. This growing consumer tightness also affected the marketability of the band, and after a decade of robust commercial activity, Whiteman's record sales dropped drastically. In addition, venue promoters shied away from establishing extended concert schedules with the band. The economic circumstances of the period also forced a redistribution of the band's pay-roll, and Whiteman could no longer afford to offer star musicians the considerable salaries that he had throughout the 1920s.[93] The Depression thus affected the musical structure of the band, as Whiteman failed to renew contracts with key members of his orchestra, and this reduced payroll compelled Whiteman to cut the Rhythm Boys from his roster.[94]

Despite the short-term actions made by Whiteman as he attempted to ride out the immediate effects of the economic collapse, the Great Depression could not be escaped. The Depression had tremendous political and cultural ramifications, and these pressures eventually resulted in a new style of jazz music.[95] Between 1917 and 1929, the successes of the record, radio, and film industries; the development and expansion of urban culture; the careers of popular jazz performers such as Rudy Vallee and Paul Whiteman; and the eventual emergence of jazz criticism converged to generate a new and thoroughly modern sound.[96] But after the collapse, the success of jazz music and musicians was in jeopardy as record sales collapsed and consumers refused unnecessary entertainment expenses. At its height in 1927, the record industry boasted sales of $104 million. Five years later, record sales stood at a mere $6 million.[97] The economic crisis hastened corporate integration, and in the late 1930s, the Radio Corporation of America (RCA) and the Columbia Broadcasting System (CBS) purchased Victor and Columbia Records—the two largest radio corporations now owning the two largest record labels.[98] In addition, the repeal of Prohibition implied that club owners no longer needed to hire jazz bands to attract customers. As a result, musicians' unions had reduced influence as slashed monthly fees retained members but emptied coffers.[99] The new economics of the jazz scene in the early 1930s affected all musicians, but the Great Depression directly challenged the jazz careers of white middle-class musicians. These musicians chose occupations outside of mainstream society and were then confronted with what one scholar argues "was the greatest test of their dedication to jazz careers."[100] Despite these hardships, the Great Depression only accelerated many of the musical changes affecting jazz over the last half decade, and together, the cultural, social, and musical developments of the 1920s helped spawn a new style of jazz in the 1930s.

As the Great Depression affected the consolidation of business, the economic situation of the early 1930s hastened the commercialization of jazz as musicians took jobs that once seemed beneath them in the music industry. Musicians who had once criticized more commercial music—even music played by generally respected artists such as Duke Ellington—came to see this style of music more positively once Depression-era bills continued to pile up.[101] Connected to the jazz of the past, this new genre known as "swing" reflected the modern age as it connected an integrated commercial approach to an expanded big band sound.[102] In large measure, swing developed from the big band sound realized by the New York bands of Fletcher Henderson and Duke Ellington. These bandleaders established the swing template of large bands (twelve- to fifteen-piece groups) divided into distinct sections of brass, reed, and rhythm instruments performing a riff-based syncopated music that also allowed for solo improvisation. By the 1930s, various musicians had simplified the complexities inherent in the arrangements of Henderson and Ellington to produce a streamlined music that emphasized concise riffs and a steady rhythmic pulse. In many ways, the musical developments of the early 1930s simply accentuated the ideas first set forth by Fletcher Henderson and Duke Ellington: larger bands playing arrangements that emphasized group riffs and limited, individual solos. The Swing Era of big band jazz served as a reduction of the New York scene of the late 1920s. Riffs became simpler, bolder; melodies became more concise; and the rhythm section became the basic instrumental base for bands, especially once recording techniques improved, allowing for better low-frequency fidelity. The Great Depression accelerated much of this change as bands pursued a more commercial sound in the wake of greater competition and decreased job security.[103]

The primary articulation of this new sound—and the musician most closely associated with the commercial possibilities of this music—was Benny Goodman. Born in Chicago in 1909, Goodman grew up in a large, working-class family with first-generation immigrant parents.[104] As a working-class Jewish Chicagoan, Goodman exemplified the role of the outsider disconnected from mainstream culture. He combined this outsider social status with a professional musical education, and as a young boy, commenced a lifelong obsession with practicing his clarinet.[105] Goodman studied both with his synagogue band as well as a local Hull House group, and by the age of ten he received clarinet instruction from Franz Schoepp, a clarinetist who also tutored members of the Chicago Symphony Orchestra.[106] Goodman's training combined with a burgeoning interest in hot jazz to produce a prodigiously talented and confident clarinet player.[107] Younger by almost a decade than most of the first wave of jazz players such as Louis Armstrong and Bix Beiderbecke, Goodman epitomized a new generation of jazz musicians as he combined classical training with jazz improvisation. Unlike Whiteman with his fumbling attempts at a classical-jazz fusion, Goodman naturally incorporated classical techniques into jazz performance. First learning jazz from listening to phonograph records, Goodman garnered quick respect with his improvisational abilities in a variety of musical settings.[108] By the late 1920s, Goodman had developed as a strong hot-jazz clarinet player, and his prodigious combination of technical skillfulness and instrumental versatility made him one of the most sought-after clarinetists of the period.[109]

An integral part of Goodman's success—and the success of jazz acceptance in general—was his relationship to his manager, John Hammond. A wealthy Yale University dropout, Hammond proved an incalculable boon for Goodman's career as he helped to extend the musician's audience throughout the 1930s. Hammond personified the stereotypical white college student drawn to the foreign sounds of jazz music and resembled in many ways earlier jazz enthusiasts such as Carl Van Vechten. Rather than simply listening to jazz records or attending jazz concerts, Hammond and his new cohort of white intellectuals became intimately involved in the business, and during the late 1920s and early 1930s, a number of wealthy white jazz aficionados entered the jazz scene as managers. Black artists managed by wealthy white men—most notably Louis Armstrong and Joe Glaser, and Duke Ellington and Irving Mills—experienced considerable success, but also fell victim to inequitable business arrangements. Hammond's relationship to Goodman differed somewhat from these other associations, most obviously in its lack of an implicit racial hierarchy.[110] In addition to managing artists, Hammond operated as a cultural gatekeeper, especially with the increased power of national radio broadcasts. Organized network radio produced an audience captive to the tastes of corporate executives, and Hammond gladly served as the cultivator of a national jazz soundtrack.[111] Hammond, through his position with Columbia Records, actively advanced the careers of other jazz artists during this period, helping to promote musicians like Bessie Smith, Billie Holiday, and Count Basie.[112] More important, Hammond's prodigious musical knowledge coupled with his power within the recording industry brought swing music to a larger audience.[113]

With Hammond's assistance, Goodman discovered a national audience on the radio, and in 1934 the clarinetist began a stint as bandleader on *Let's Dance,* a three-hour radio program sponsored by the National Broadcasting Company (NBC).[114] In conjunction with providing a larger audience, this program—which went out to fifty affiliate stations—granted Goodman financial security during the worst years of the Great Depression. Goodman used the resources proffered by NBC to create a formidable band with inventive arrangements and innovative soloists.[115] During his tenure on the radio, Goodman perfected his style of swing music with the addition of drummer Gene Krupa and arranger Fletcher Henderson, musicians introduced to the clarinetist by Hammond.[116] Krupa, the most famous member of Goodman's band, eschewed an overt swing feel, maintaining instead a stomping-on-the-beat style centered on the snare, tom-tom, and kick drums. A bass-heavy drummer, Krupa used cymbals sparingly and focused more on providing a solid—if occasionally ostentatious—foundation for Goodman's band.[117] Emphasizing flashy solos over modest fills, a driving stomp over a nuanced swing, Krupa's thundering, crowd-pleasing roar underpinned many of Goodman's most successful swing recordings in the 1930s.

In addition to Krupa, John Hammond also coordinated the meeting between Goodman and Fletcher Henderson (who had been musically idle for several years), and Henderson successfully wedded his arrangements to the strengths of Goodman's band.[118] Henderson extended the elements he had first developed in New York, and with Goodman's band the arranger established a musical schematic based around the reed section, with saxophones providing the basic components of the song augmented with crisp brass passages and a strong rhythm section. More than any specific instrumental change, however, Henderson contributed a sensitivity to dynamics, and many of his most successful arrangements merged contrasts in tone and volume with the powerful rhythm section. These elements coalesced in "King Porter Stomp," perhaps the greatest example of the swing synergy between Goodman and Henderson.[119] Besides a pounding rhythm section, stimulating solos, and several overt shifts in dynamics, "King Porter Stomp" utilized an innovative arrangement that emphasized textural contrasts such as underpinning a high octave clarinet solo with low-pitched trombones. Also, as an African American, Henderson's position in Goodman's band represented a growing tolerance for integrated units, and Goodman's group served as a nationally recognized example of black and white jazz musicians working in tandem.[120]

In early 1935, Goodman signed a recording contract with Victor Records, a career boon particularly after NBC canceled the *Let's Dance* program the following month. Between his radio exposure and record sales, Goodman escaped much of the economic turmoil of the period, and the clarinetist expanded this success by embarking on a national tour later in 1935. The early engagements on this 1935 tour proved less than successful as audiences clamored for Goodman's dance hits instead of his more experimental compositions.[121] Despite popular radio broadcasts, audiences failed to embrace the style of swing music performed by Goodman, and slow ticket sales forced the band to consider a return to New York. Once the band reached California, however, audience reception began to change, and Goodman noticed that audiences were warming to the music. In Los Angeles, the band encountered the largest crowds of the entire tour, with jazz enthusiasts lining up around the block for tickets to the concerts.[122] The dancers in Los Angeles craved the hot Henderson-arranged music Goodman had recently recorded, and the opening night at the Palomar vindicated Goodman's swinging style of jazz.[123] Goodman's revolution in sound had found an audience—the crowds at the Palomar in 1935 signified the acceptance of jazz music.[124] For one night everything came together, and Goodman's triumph at the Palomar introduced America to the Swing Era. For the next several years, musicians such as Goodman, Chick Webb, Glenn Miller, and Count Basie discovered tremendous success as the public clamored for more swing music. Two decades removed from its subcultural origins, jazz in the late 1930s defined American popular music. "Never again," jazz historian Ted Gioia notes, "would popular music be so jazzy, or jazz music so popular."[125]

The Palomar concert thrust Goodman into the national spotlight, giving the clarinetist the boost to build upon his success throughout 1935. More significant, the show fulfilled jazz music's manifest destiny as jazz garnered an audience interconnected through record sales, radio broadcasts, and film appearances. In less than two decades, jazz music developed from an unrecorded form of southern black folk culture to a compelling articulation of modern American values with a mainstream audience. As Chicago (with its recording studios), New York City (with its radio broadcasts), and Los Angeles (with its film industry) transmitted jazz to the nation, a number of critics emerged denouncing the music as destructive to American values and morals. The transformation of American culture in the 1920s forced people into a new set of relationships—socially, regionally, and politically—and the anxiety generated by this cultural shift fomented heated attacks on jazz music. This jazz debate over the direction of American society reflects the larger culture of ambivalence that characterized the nation during the 1920s. The rapidity with which jazz music infused America, therefore, underscored both the growing acceptance of a new order as well as fervent rejection of all things modern. As jazz began to creep into mainstream American culture, members of various disparate communities panicked and rebelled against the popular new music. Divergent in demographics and reasoning, this jazz-fueled tension connected to a large number of themes rooted in the growing concern over the emergence of modern America. Fear and hostility framed much of this debate as many

Americans reacted negatively to the influence of urban society, the prevalence of technological innovation, the promotion of forms of black culture, and the development of new standards of morality and femininity. By the mid-1930s, the jazz frontier was settled as records, radio broadcasts, and films transmitted jazz to the nation. Benny Goodman's performance in Los Angeles completed the circuit begun by Paul Whiteman as another white midwesterner brought jazz music to a national audience. In a larger sense, however, Goodman represented the culmination of the entire story of jazz—from its subcultural origins, through its stylistic evolution, subsequently culminating in its enormous popularity. Goodman fused first-rate musicianship with the rhythmic inventiveness of New Orleans jazz and produced a modern jazz expression instilled with traditional instrumentation and verve. His popularity, however, stemmed not only from his musical accomplishment but also from the revolution in values that took place during the previous decade. A newly liberated youth culture adopted Goodman as their symbol, and swing music served as the national soundtrack for an entire generation.[126] Goodman personified the age of swing, and his music served as the primary articulation of a new culture transformed by the larger shift in values that created modern America. The Swing Era thus completed the musical arc begun in the rural South as a folk music predominantly performed by African Americans came to represent the quintessential expression of American culture during the Great Depression.

CONCLUSION

"Twenty Years of Jazz": Benny Goodman and Jelly Roll Morton, 1938

On January 16, 1938, Benny Goodman and his band performed at Carnegie Hall in New York City. Fourteen years after Paul Whiteman's experiment at the Aeolian Hall, Goodman gathered an adaptable ensemble that underscored the clarinetist's talents with leading small as well as large jazz configurations. In addition to a group of talented musicians—including drummer Gene Krupa and trumpeter Harry James—Goodman had corralled perhaps the finest jazz arranger of the period, Fletcher Henderson, to update several standards for the event. Opening with "Don't Be That Way," Goodman's band exploded onto the stage with strong ensemble work, blaring solos, and a propulsive rhythm section.[1] Riding a smooth riff with trumpet and saxophone counterpoint, Goodman's band sounded assured as they introduced themselves to the historically well-heeled audience at Carnegie Hall. Goodman took an early clarinet solo before Gene Krupa slyly stole the attention of the audience with his bass accents and snare work. Following energetic solos by Babe Russin on tenor saxophone and Harry James on trumpet, the band launched into a long group decrescendo emphasizing the group's dynamic discipline as well as Goodman's command. Crowd-pleaser Krupa disrupted the calm, however, hitting a raucous drum break to bring the band back to a powerful conclusion. The crowd loudly approved, and over the next two hours, the band held court at Carnegie Hall with Goodman's band producing some of the strongest jazz music of the Swing Age.

With this dexterous introduction, the band navigated "Sometimes I'm Happy" (arranged by Fletcher Henderson) and "One O'Clock Jump" (made famous by Count Basie) before Goodman shifted gears to a prepared section entitled "Twenty Years of Jazz," a planned tribute to the group's jazz forbearers. Through the performance of five songs, the band limned a brief schematic of jazz music highlighting individual songs as well as specific bands and musicians.[2] The first song, "Sensation Rag," touched on the ragtime and New Orleans roots of jazz with a composition written by Ed Edwards in 1917. This piece was popular during the early years of recorded jazz with performances by the Original Dixieland Jazz Band, the New Orleans Rhythm Kings, Bix Beiderbecke, Red Nichols, and Sidney Bechet.[3] With a song so closely identified with the beginnings of recorded jazz, Goodman began his history lesson not in the rhythms of New Orleans but in the recording studios of New York, marking the beginning of the jazz story with its commercial promise. A specific tribute to Bix Beiderbecke followed, with the band performing a Will Marion Cook composition, "I'm Coming Virginia," a piece well connected to the trumpet player. Beiderbecke, who had died in 1931, cast a strong shadow across the Goodman band as he inspired a generation of young white musicians to enter the jazz world. The third piece further underscored the influence of white musicians on jazz with "When My Baby Smiles at Me," a song with strong personal connotations for Goodman, who had been inspired immensely by the career of the song's composer, Ted Lewis. Overall, these three songs reflected the influence white jazz musicians had on Goodman, but the history segment continued with two numbers associated with black bands. Harry James, Goodman's white trumpet player, approximated Louis Armstrong on "Shine," a song that dated back to 1910 but had been a sizable hit for Armstrong in the 1920s; and the band concluded the segment with "Blue Reverie," a Duke Ellington composition from 1936.[4] For this number, Goodman invited Ellington sidemen Johnny Hodges, Harry Carney, and Cootie Williams to play with the band, an inclusion that signified the first major integrated jazz performance.[5] Connecting backward to the musical antecedents of jazz as well as anticipating the future with an integrated band, the Carnegie Hall concert signaled the acceptance of jazz music as a mainstream (and uniquely American) musical expression.

The importance of this concert was not lost on the musicians, the audience, or the various critics involved in the event. Goodman fretted over the song selection in the weeks prior to the show, crowds lined up outside of the venue on a blustery day hopeful to obtain entrance to the sold-out show, and the *New York Times* published a long review of the concert the following morning. Further illustrating the importance of the evening, sound engineers recorded the program and sent one of the copies to the Library of Congress.[6] And everyone, it seemed, approved of the performance—with the glaring exception of the *New York Times* music critic Olin Downes. Fourteen years earlier, Downes had enthused over Paul Whiteman's 1924 Aeolian Hall concert, and in 1938, Downes attempted to place Goodman into a similar context. Downes confided to his readers that he attended the concert "expecting a new, original, and elemental kind of music; one that we had been told marks a novel and original form of expression." Unhappy with the results, Downes wrote, "This is not the sort of thing that Paul Whiteman triumphed in introducing to the polite musical world some fourteen years ago in this city." "Whiteman has been practically canonized by the younger generation," Downes contended, "and relegated to last by the Goodmans, Dorseys, Duke Ellingtons and such of the present." Labeling Goodman's music as "a curious reduction, almost disintegration of music into its component elements," Downes argued, "there is hardly an attempt at beauty of tone, and certainly none at construction of melody." In addition, Downes disavowed any inclusion of innovative or novel musical elements in Goodman's music. "These are effects and devices as old as the hills to any one who has listened in the last fifteen years to jazz music," he wrote, "they are merely carried to extremes."[7]

The audience, however, enthusiastically welcomed Goodman and his band, and "it took some minutes to establish quiet." "The audience broke out before the music stopped," Downes wrote, "in crashing applause and special salvos as one or another of the heroes of the orchestra rose in his place to give his special and ornate contribution to the occasion." Downes conceded that the music represented only one component of the evening's importance: "We went to discover a new, original, thrilling music. We stayed to watch a social and physical phenomenon." Downes admitted that he "may be a hopeless old-timer, sunk in the joys of Whiteman jazz, unable to appreciate the starker, modern product."[8] Despite the reservations of Downes, the year 1938 signified the high point of the Swing Era. The popularity of swing helped resuscitate the ailing record industry, and by the late 1930s total record sales exceeded 50 million units with sales of over 17 million swing records in particular. That same year, two million listeners regularly tuned into Benny Goodman's radio program three times a week.[9] Many Americans, with the obvious exception of Olin Downes, tended to like jazz in its popular incarnation, and the record-buying, radio-listening audiences helped make jazz music tremendously profitable.

Several months after Goodman's Carnegie Hall triumph, Jelly Roll Morton recounted his interpretation of jazz history to Alan Lomax, and these two events—Goodman's New York success and Morton's New Orleans narrative—illustrate the complexity of jazz history as well as the rapidity in which jazz emerged as a nationally accepted popular music.[10] In 1938, Morton, the prematurely old chronicler of jazz prehistory who drew up a fragmented map of blurred borders and shadowy limits, struggled to escape the indifferent response to a career two decades past its prime. Perennially out of fashion, Morton's music existed on the wrong side of what constituted popular music; ahead of his time for most of his life, by the late 1930s, Morton's music seemed hopelessly antique. In contrast, Goodman stood as the crisp representative of modern jazz, a musician who had fused together the lessons of the jazz past to create an altogether new and very commercial musical expression. As Goodman reiterated the past in order to charge ahead, Morton—who would be dead in three years—fought to (re)define his legacy in a story that had all but erased him.

Two outsiders with two convergent histories, Jelly Roll Morton and Benny Goodman underscore the intrinsic elements of jazz: a music based on a rhythmic pulse and harmonic structure at once primitive and modern, and a music born out of cultural tension, a racial-ethnic-regional hybrid capable of connecting disparate groups of listeners. Morton, a dispossessed Creole struggling through egotism to construct a career positioned somewhere between two racially distinct worlds, and Goodman, a lower-class Jewish Chicagoan drawn to the fascinating and foreboding sounds of a foreign culture, both found resonance through jazz music and represented the music's connective potential. Outsiders connected to other outsiders, and this newly invented subculture of jazz artists and audiences thrived along the larger fault lines threatening to transform mainstream American culture. By the late 1930s, jazz (in its mass-produced incarnation of swing) had emerged as the popular expression of modernity, and through record sales, radio broadcasts, and motion pictures, a music by and for outsiders served as a fundamental connecting unit of American culture.

Less than four decades had elapsed between jazz music's apex of popu-larity during the Swing Era and its whispered origins in the 1890s, when two pioneers separately tinkered with two musical genres. A transplanted Texan, Scott Joplin methodically perfected a piano style that showcased a near-mathematical technique coupled with a rolling melodicism that invig-orated late-nineteenth-century American music. During this same period, W. C. Handy discovered an expression of the rural South that upended the popular music conventions of the time. Cleaning up the rhyme scheme while retaining the music's harmonic uniqueness, Handy successfully merged a form of black folk music with Tin Pan Alley song structures to produce a commercially viable style of the blues. Both ragtime and the blues prefigured the syncopated rhythms and harmonic intricacies of jazz, but these early forms also connected to a burgeoning marketing arrange-ment through the sale of sheet music and piano rolls (and eventually pho-nograph records). This element of profitability would define in large mea-sure jazz music, but ragtime and the blues existed outside of the mass commercial culture that developed alongside jazz music.

As Joplin and Handy formulated their careers, a different set of musi-cians noisily conceived of an altogether new style of music. In and around New Orleans, black, white, and Creole musicians constructed a music based in improvisation that reflected the urban and rural anomalies present in a city still strongly sutured to the countryside. Buddy Bolden, Jack Laine, and Jelly Roll Morton all contributed to the rapidly emerging jazz form—either through musical innovation, instrumental instruction, or composi-tional experimentation—and these musicians helped construct a novel form of cultural expression. A transient form of dance music, the music performed by New Orleanians at the dawn of the twentieth century hardly had a name much less commercial viability. New Orleans, however, signi-fied the confluence of elements that sparked the jazz revolution, and throughout the twentieth century, musicians, critics, and audiences would continually revisit and rediscover the city and its place in jazz history. Later musicians would extend and reconfigure the lessons of ragtime, the blues, and the early jazz of New Orleans, and this early formational period con-tinually cast a sharply defined shadow across the Jazz Age.

Although New Orleans failed to serve as the urban center of jazz develop-ment during the 1920s, many of the city's musicians rose to prominence with careers in larger cities. Three cities in particular played important roles in the gradual diffusion of jazz, and although musicians performed jazz in other cities during this period, Chicago, New York City, and Los Angeles combined dynamic jazz scenes with technological innovation to transmit jazz to the nation. In the early 1920s, for instance, Chicago replaced the undocumented sounds of New Orleans with commercially viable recordings, a step that helped connect jazz to the marketplace. Small bands dominated the Chicago jazz scene, and trumpeter Louis Armstrong, in particular, endeavored to redefine the parameters of the music. His recording of "West End Blues," for example, combined traditional instrumentation with a new sense of melody and harmony to connect jazz back to New Orleans as well as provide a modern context for jazz improvisation.

Despite the fact that Chicago maintained arguably the most dynamic jazz scene during this period and the recording industry began to make connections on a regional scale, the city remained somewhat disconnected from mainstream culture. In contrast, New York City represented the center of the ever-expanding entertainment world, and the city's jazz musicians had greater access to a national audience through radio broadcasts. Connected to a powerful and urban black community, New York's jazz scene featured larger bands, playing more complicated arrangements, to a more diverse audience than bands in Chicago. Duke Ellington personified in many ways the New York jazz style, and throughout the late 1920s and early 1930s, Ellington's band held a prominent spot at the Cotton Club, the premier white club in the city. Ellington's music drifted away from the improvisational focus of Chicago jazz as the composer began to emphasize the more elaborate melodies, harmonies, and rhythms attainable by a larger, twelve- to fifteen-piece band. The jazz styles of New Orleans and Chicago served less as stylistic templates for the New York scene than as an ancestral mode of musical expression. Also, New York removed the regional boundaries that limited earlier jazz scenes by transmitting jazz music to a national audience through radio broadcasts.

This pattern of national diffusion continued with the emerging jazz scene of Los Angeles. The jazz performed in Los Angeles related much more explicitly to mainstream musical forms, and the prominent musicians working in southern California focused less on improvisation than on commercial viability. A relatively small black community provided a different social context for the jazz played in Los Angeles, and in general, diffusion rather than musical innovation defined the jazz contributions of the area. Hollywood gravitated immediately to the jazz community that did exist in Los Angeles, and the early film industry quickly adapted jazz music to their artistic goals. In 1927, Hollywood brought jazz to a national audience with the release of *The Jazz Singer,* the first major talking picture. Movie studios also released a number of jazz-themed musical shorts to accompany longer films, and many local musicians found lucrative employment in Hollywood during the late 1920s. Although a different style of jazz, the Los Angeles musical scene had a massive impact on the acceptance of jazz as the film industry projected the music to the nation.

As jazz reached a larger and more diverse audience through record sales, radio broadcasts, and motion pictures, the music encountered a massive backlash. Many critics of jazz posited the music as detrimental to the traditional American values of morality, thrift, and responsibility, while other jazz opponents feared the supposed impact of African American values on the nation. Black critics, too, feared that Americans would generally view jazz as a mode of black expression, and many of these black detractors struggled to distance the African American community from the more outrageous elements of the emerging jazz culture. Much of this criticism, though rooted in specific, if anecdotal, evidence of moral degradation, signified a reaction to the larger cultural transformation that had started to redefine American life since the 1890s. The tensions stemming from the increased roles gained by many women and African Americans as well as growing concerns over industrialization and urbanization therefore provided much of the context for the jazz debate. The larger social and cultural changes that helped produce a national audience for jazz, in other words, also fueled the subsequent controversy as more Americans came into contact with jazz.

By the 1930s, however, jazz seemed much less threatening as many Americans began to accept the modern order. During this period, two musicians attempted a melding of respectable music with jazz rhythms, and though separated by ten years and differing in emphasis, the careers of Paul Whiteman and Benny Goodman helped make jazz an acceptable expression of American culture. While Whiteman endeavored to force jazz into a classical context through such ambitious pieces as George Gershwin's *Rhapsody in Blue,* Goodman streamlined jazz into a well-rehearsed and arranged soundtrack for dancing. Classically trained, Goodman appreciated the technical elements of traditional music, but the Chicagoan also sought out a large audience by centering his band on a stomping rhythm section. By the mid-1930s, Goodman's music had attained a nationwide audience through record sales, radio broadcasts, and tours, and the Swing Era helped complete the musical arc begun in the rural South as a folk music predominantly performed by African Americans emerged as the quintessential expression of American culture during the Great Depression. Created by (and reflective of) the larger pattern of modernization reconfiguring the nation between the 1890s and the 1930s, jazz music thus serves as an unambiguous articulation of the cultural transformation of America in the early twentieth century.

NOTES

INTRODUCTION: A SONG IS BORN

1. *A Song Is Born,* dir. Howard Hawks (Goldwyn, 1948).
2. Hawks used many of the same sets and crew as well as the basic screenplay from his 1941 film *Ball of Fire.* The only real distinction scriptwise between the two films concerned the earlier film's focus on linguists discovering slang, rather than musicologists discovering jazz.
3. For a discussion of the broad definitions and implications of "culture," see Raymond Williams, *Culture and Society, 1780–1950* (New York: Columbia University Press, 1983).
4. Warren Susman, *Culture as History: The Transformation of American Society in the Twentieth Century* (New York: Pantheon Books, 1984), 106.
5. Lawrence W. Levine, "Jazz and American Culture," reprinted in Lawrence W. Levine, *The Unpredictable Past: Explorations in American Cultural History* (New York: Oxford University Press, 1993), 188.
6. Neil Leonard, *Jazz and the White Americans: The Acceptance of a New Art Form* (Chicago: University of Chicago Press, 1962).
7. See, for example, Burton W. Peretti, *The Creation of Jazz: Music, Race, and Culture in Urban America* (Urbana: University of Illinois Press, 1992); Charles Hersch, *Subversive Sounds: Race and the Birth of Jazz in New Orleans* (Chicago: University of Chicago Press, 2007); Charley Gerard, *Jazz in Black and White: Race, Culture, and Identity in the Jazz Community* (Westport, Conn.: Praeger, 1998). See also Michelle R. Boyd, *Jim Crow Nostalgia: Reconstructing Race in Bronzeville* (Minneapolis: University of Minnesota Press, 2008); William Kenney, *Chicago Jazz: A Cultural History, 1904–1930* (New York: Oxford University Press, 1993); and Donald M. Marquis, *In Search of Buddy Bolden: First Man of Jazz* (Baton Rouge: Louisiana State University Press, 1978). For a broader discussion of some of these issues, see Kevin Phinney, *Souled American: How Black Music Transformed White Culture* (New York: Billboard Books, 2005).
8. See, for example, Leroy Ostransky, *Jazz City: The Impact of Our Cities on the Development of Jazz* (Englewood Cliffs, N.J.: Prentice-Hall, 1978); and Kenney, *Chicago Jazz.* Although his focus is on Detroit after World War II, Thomas Sugrue's work on race and urban America has shaped my thinking on these issues. Thomas J. Sugrue, *The Origins of the Urban Crisis: Race and Inequality in Postwar Detroit* (Princeton: Princeton University Press, 1998).
9. Peretti, *The Creation of Jazz;* and Ted Gioia, *The History of Jazz* (New York: Oxford University Press, 1997). See also Thomas J. Hennessey, *From Jazz to Swing: African-American Jazz Musicians and Their Music* (Detroit: Wayne State University Press, 1994); and Kenneth J. Bindas, *Swing That Modern Sound* (Jackson: University Press of Mississippi, 2001). For a more musicological approach to this period, see Gunther Schuller, *Early Jazz: Its Roots and Musical Development* (New York: Oxford

University Press, 1968), and *The Swing Era: The Development of Jazz, 1930–1945* (New York: Oxford University Press, 1989).

10. Kathy J. Ogren, *The Jazz Revolution: Twenties America and the Meaning of Jazz* (New York: Oxford University Press, 1989); David Ake, *Jazz Cultures* (Berkeley: University of California Press, 2002); Hersch, *Subversive Sounds;* and Lawrence B. DeGraaf, "The City of Black Angels: Emergence of the Los Angeles Ghetto, 1890–1930," *Pacific Historical Review* 39 (1970): 323–352.

11. For two recent examples, see Ingrid Monson, *Freedom Sounds: Civil Rights Call Out to Jazz and Africa* (Oxford: Oxford University Press, 2007); and Iain Anderson, *This Is Our Music: Free Jazz, the Sixties, and American Culture* (Philadelphia: University of Pennsylvania Press, 2007). See also John Szwed, *So What: The Life of Miles Davis* (New York: Simon and Schuster, 2004).

12. Thomas Brothers, *Louis Armstrong's New Orleans* (New York: W. W. Norton, 2006). The historical quality of jazz biographies can vary greatly, but there are a number of strong studies that combine intimate portrayals of individual musicians within the larger context of American culture. See, for example, Marquis, *In Search of Buddy Bolden;* James Lincoln Collier, *Benny Goodman and the Swing Era* (New York: Oxford University Press, 1989); and John Chilton, *Sidney Bechet: The Wizard of Jazz* (New York: Oxford University Press, 1987).

13. On a related note, new technologies introduced listeners to the unfamiliar territories of recorded sound and forced Americans into new interactions with music. Along these lines, William Kenney's work on the phonograph and Emily Thompson's study on the cultural impact of technology help elucidate the fundamental connections between mechanical advancement and modernity. William H. Kenney, *Recorded Music in American Life: The Phonograph and Popular Memory, 1890–1945* (Oxford: Oxford University Press, 1999); and Emily Thompson, *The Soundscape of Modernity: Architectural Acoustics and the Culture of Listening in America, 1900–1933* (Cambridge, Mass.: MIT Press, 2002).

14. See, for example, Nathan W. Pearson Jr., "Political and Musical Forces That Influenced the Development of Kansas City Jazz," *Black Music Research Journal* 9:2 (Autumn 1989): 181–192; Frank Driggs and Chuck Haddox, *Kansas City Jazz: From Ragtime to Bebop—A History* (Oxford: Oxford University Press, 2006); and Douglas Henry Daniels, *One O'Clock Jump: The Unforgettable History of the Oklahoma City Blue Devils* (Boston: Beacon Press, 2006).

15. William H. Kenney's book on riverboats and jazz is a fine example of recent historiographical work on the expansion of the jazz narrative. William H. Kenney, *Jazz on the River* (Chicago: University of Chicago Press, 2005).

16. Paul Gilroy, *The Black Atlantic: Modernity and Double Consciousness* (Cambridge, Mass.: Harvard University Press, 1993); Houston A. Baker Jr., *Modernism and the Harlem Renaissance* (Chicago: University of Chicago Press, 1989); Samuel A. Floyd Jr., *The Power of Black Music: Interpreting Its History from Africa to the United States* (New York: Oxford University Press, 1995); Guthrie P. Ramsey Jr., *Race Music: Black Cultures from Bebop to Hip-Hop* (Berkeley: University of California Press, 2003); Joel Dinerstein, *Swinging the Machine: Modernity, Technology, and African American Culture between the World Wars* (Amherst: University of Massachusetts Press, 2003); and Ingrid Monson, *Freedom Sounds: Civil Rights Call Out to Jazz and Africa* (Oxford: Oxford University Press, 2007). Davarian L. Baldwin's recent work on modernism and the Great Migration was also a key source in centering modernism

within the context of urban America. Davarian L. Baldwin, *Chicago's New Negroes: Modernity, The Great Migration, and Black Urban Life* (Chapel Hill: University of North Carolina Press, 2007). See also Paul Allen Anderson, *Deep River: Music and Memory in Harlem Renaissance Thought* (Durham, N.C.: Duke University Press, 2001) (esp. 59–111). For two prominent literary takes on these ideas, see Ishmael Reed, *Mumbo Jumbo* (New York: Atheneum, 1972); and Henry Louis Gates Jr., *The Signifying Monkey: A Theory of African-American Literary Criticism* (Oxford: Oxford University Press, 1989). For a thoughtful examination of these issues within the broader world of art, see Alfred Appel Jr., *Jazz Modernism: From Ellington and Armstrong to Matisse and Joyce* (New Haven: Yale University Press, 2002). Marshall Berman's work is still the classic study of the vastness of the modern experience. Marshall Berman, *All That Is Solid Melts into Air: The Experience of Modernity* (London: Penguin Books, 1982).

17. Ramsey, *Race Music*, 27–30.
18. Charles Nanry, "Jazz and Modernism," *Annual Review of Jazz Studies* 1 (1982): 149.

CHAPTER 1. RAGTIME, THE BLUES, AND THE REORIENTATION OF AMERICAN LIFE

1. Laurence Bergreen would later define the music as "the bastard child of several colliding cultures." Laurence Bergreen, *Louis Armstrong: An Extravagant Life* (New York: Broadway Books, 1997), 51.

2. My argument here is informed by Paul Gilroy's groundbreaking discussion of the idea of the Black Atlantic. Paul Gilroy, *The Black Atlantic: Modernity and Double Consciousness* (Cambridge, Mass.: Harvard University Press, 1993), 1–40, 72–74. Lewis Erenberg offers a more musically specific discussion of the interconnections between jazz and the concepts of movement, migration, and American cultural identity in his work on swing. See, in particular, Lewis Erenberg, *Swingin' the Dream: Big Band Jazz and the Rebirth of American Culture* (Chicago: University of Chicago Press, 1998) as well as Lewis Erenberg, *Steppin' Out: New York Nightlife and the Transformation of American Culture* (Chicago: University of Chicago Press, 1984). On a related note, see also Joel Dinerstein, *Swinging the Machine: Modernity, Technology, and African American Culture between the World Wars* (Amherst: University of Massachusetts Press, 2003), especially 63–104. In addition, Ingrid Monson has established a useful modernist approach in her discussion of jazz during the civil rights movement of the 1950s and 1960s. See, in particular, Ingrid Monson, *Freedom Sounds: Civil Rights Call Out to Jazz and Africa* (Oxford: Oxford University Press, 2007): 3–28.

3. In large measure, the period from the early 1890s to the end of World War I signifies a distinct change in American life, and scholars have labeled this era a "turbulent transition," a "fundamental transformation," a "fundamental shift," and a time of "profound cultural change." Richard Hofstadter, *The Age of Reform: From Bryan to F.D.R.* (New York: Vintage Books, 1955), 7 ("turbulent transition"); Thomas J. Schlereth, *Victorian America: Transformations in Everyday Life* (New York: HarperPerennial, 1991), xv ("fundamental transformation"); Robert H. Wiebe, *The Search for Order, 1877–1920* (New York: Hill and Wang, 1967), vii ("fundamental shift"); and William Leach, *Land of Desire: Merchants, Power, and the*

Rise of a New American Culture (New York: Vintage Books, 1993), 381 ("profound cultural change").

4. Gilroy's *Black Atlantic* (rooted deeply in the work of W. E. B. Du Bois) is the best examination of the tensions involved in African Americans experiencing the coming modern order. See Gilroy, *The Black Atlantic*, 1–40.

5. Nell Irving Painter, *Standing at Armageddon: The United States, 1877–1919* (New York: W. W. Norton, 1987), 116–140; Wiebe, *Search for Order*, 91; and Schlereth, *Victorian America*, 174–175.

6. Frederick Jackson Turner, "The Significance of the Frontier in American History," in John Mack Faragher, *Rereading Frederick Jackson Turner: "The Significance of the Frontier in American History" and Other Essays* (New Haven: Yale University Press, 1999), 31–60. For a discussion of Turner within the context of a "usable past," see Warren Susman, *Culture as History: The Transformation of American Society in the Twentieth Century* (New York: Pantheon Books, 1984), 27–38.

7. The technology and culture of the city remained at the center of the celebration, and as one writer has noted, "The Chicago setting evoked a planned, albeit idealized, urban environment. Its scale, density of buildings, and municipal services all suggested a model metropolis." Schlereth, *Victorian America*, 169.

8. "As a kind of music that grew in popularity in the years following 1893," one historian has written, "ragtime must be examined within the context of these two events and as an example of the changing components of American culture and identity." Susan Curtis, *Dancing to a Black Man's Tune: A Life of Scott Joplin* (Columbia: University of Missouri Press, 1994), 47.

9. Edward A. Berlin, *Ragtime: A Musical and Cultural History* (Berkeley: University of California Press, 1980), 11–13, 26–29, 40–44.

10. Most sources cite November 24, 1868, as Joplin's date of birth, but as Edward Berlin has pointed out, Joplin's widow gave this date in the 1940s and must be "almost certainly incorrect" according to various census figures. Instead, Berlin places his birth about six months earlier that year. See Edward A. Berlin, *King of Ragtime: Scott Joplin and His Era* (New York: Oxford University Press, 1994), 4.

11. Curtis, *Dancing to a Black Man's Tune*, 36. More significantly, Joplin's life in Texarkana allowed for an interracial education that "began the process of education and interaction with whites and blacks that enabled him to create a new and compelling form of music at the end of the century." Curtis, *Dancing to a Black Man's Tune*, 38.

12. Berlin, *King of Ragtime*, 8.

13. Ibid., 12.

14. David A. Jasen and Gene Jones, *Black Bottom Stomp: Eight Masters of Ragtime and Early Jazz* (New York: Routledge, 2002), 3.

15. At least one scholar has argued that this difference may be accounted for by Joplin's unrefined notational skills rather than a compositional dissimilarity. Curtis, *Dancing to a Black Man's Tune*, 210.

16. These social clubs "had among [their] members some of the town's brightest and most enterprising young black men." Berlin, *King of Ragtime*, 34.

17. Edward Berlin offers the most informative study of the Black 400 and the Maple Leaf Clubs. See ibid., 34–44. Berlin mentions that the ragtime pianist Arthur Marshall, among others, flipped the order of the two clubs' creations. Curtis, in her book *Dancing to a Black Man's Tune*, seems to indicate that Tony Williams ran the

Maple Leaf in 1894 (four years earlier than Berlin indicates) and that he later opened the Black 400. Curtis further suggests that the two clubs had waning attendance in the late 1890s, a supposed period of inactivity that coincides with Berlin's date of inception. See Curtis, *Dancing to a Black Man's Tune*, 79–80.

18. Berlin, *King of Ragtime*, 43–44.

19. Ibid., 47.

20. Jasen and Jones, *Black Bottom Stomp*, 17; Berlin, *King of Ragtime*, 51. Ragtime pianist Joshua Rifkin has produced several modern recordings of Joplin's music. For a recent performance of the song that strives to capture Joplin's spirit, see Joshua Rifkin, *Scott Joplin: Piano Rags* (Elektra Records, 1994).

21. "What catches our attention," Berlin writes, "are how single notes may play rhythmic rather than melodic functions." Berlin, *King of Ragtime*, 62.

22. Berlin attempts to piece together a more factual account and succeeds in debunking many of the earlier stories involving Stark "happening upon" the lucky Joplin. Berlin, *King of Ragtime*, 53–54. See also Jasen and Jones, *That American Rag*, 28–31.

23. Joplin's situation offered greater financial stability, and acquiring "a royalty contract for what became the best-known instrumental rag of the period, gave him sufficient income to change the conditions and course of his life." Berlin, *King of Ragtime*, 56.

24. Jasen and Jones, *Black Bottom Stomp*, 16–17.

25. Although it would not make Joplin wealthy, this one song "was probably able to meet most of his basic expenses." Berlin, *King of Ragtime*, 58.

26. Edward A. Berlin, "Cole and Johnson Brothers' *The Evolution of 'Ragtime,'*" *Current Musicology* 36 (1983): 31. See also Berlin, *Ragtime*, 1–60.

27. Jasen and Jones, *Black Bottom Stomp*, 7.

28. David A. Jasen and Gene Jones, *That American Rag: The Story of Ragtime from Coast to Coast* (New York: Schirmer Books, 2000), xxxv.

29. Berlin, *King of Ragtime*, 11. The essential source for the origins and importance of blackface minstrelsy within American society is Eric Lott, *Love and Theft: Blackface Minstrelsy and the American Working Class* (New York: Oxford University Press, 1995).

30. For W. E. B. Du Bois's explanation of "double consciousness," see W. E. B. Du Bois, *The Souls of Black Folk* (New York: W. W. Norton, 1999), 9–16. See also Dickson D. Bruce Jr., "W. E. B. Du Bois and the Idea of Double Consciousness," reprinted in ibid., 236–244; and Gilroy, *The Black Atlantic*, 124–130.

31. Giles Oakley, *The Devil's Music: A History of the Blues* (New York: Da Capo Press, 1997), 21–24; and Jasen and Jones, *That American Rag*, xxxvi–xxxix.

32. Jasen and Jones, *That American Rag*, xxxvii.

33. Ibid., xxxvi–ix. For a larger discussion of the intersecting histories of ragtime, "coon songs," and the theater circuit, see Lynn Abbott and Doug Seroff, *Ragged but Right: Black Traveling Shows, "Coon Songs," and the Dark Pathway to Blues and Jazz* (Jackson: University Press of Mississippi, 2007). See also Eli H. Newberger, "The Transition from Ragtime to Improvised Piano Style," *Journal of Jazz Studies* 3:2 (Spring 1976): 3–18.

34. William Barlow, *"Looking Up at Down": The Emergence of Blues Culture* (Philadelphia: Temple University Press, 1989), 13.

35. James Lincoln Collier, *The Making of Jazz: A Comprehensive History* (Boston: Houghton Mifflin, 1978), 37.

36. William R. Ferris, *Blues from the Delta* (Garden City, N.Y.: Anchor Press, 1978), 35.

37. "The origin and definition of the blues," one writer has noted, "cannot be under-stood independent of the suffering that black people endured in the context of white racism and hate." "The blues," therefore, "tells us about black people's attempt to carve out a significant existence in a very trying situation. The purpose of the blues is to give structure to black existence in a context where color means rejection and humiliation." James H. Cone, quoted in David Meltzer, ed., *Writing Jazz* (San Francisco: Mercury Press, 1999), 43.

38. Collier, *Making of Jazz*, 27.

39. Defining blue notes remains somewhat difficult. Vocalists and some instrumentalists, such as trombonists, can easily bend notes in and out of pitch. Piano players can also at least allude to these tones by either sliding as cleanly as possible into a certain note, or by accenting the seventh chord. Thomas Dorsey, for one, argues that "blues notes are on the piano; been on the piano just like opera and its trills and things. A blue note? There's no such thing as a blue note. Blues don't own no notes." Dorsey both negates the fact that piano players cannot achieve these notes and also argues that the blues is a feeling, not a musical notation device. Meltzer, *Writing Jazz*, 43.

40. "The record was a major breakthrough," one blues historian has argued, "a turning point in blues history." Oakley, *Devil's Music*, 84.

41. "From the time of Mamie Smith's first recordings," one writer notes, "it became possible for anyone in any part of the country to hear the same blues and hear it repeated in exactly the same way and as many times as the listener wanted, until the grooves of the disc were worn smooth." Oakley, *Devil's Music*, 84. Francis Davis refers to "Crazy Blues" as "a synthesis of the blues and black vaudeville." Francis Davis, *The History of the Blues: The Roots, the Music, the People from Charley Patton to Robert Cray* (New York: Hyperion, 1995), 29, 62. It should be noted that the early blues records were entirely of the classic blues genre (mainly sung by women). The country blues of Charley Patton, Son House, and Robert Johnson would not be recorded until the late 1920s.

42. Oakley, *Devil's Music*, 40.

43. W. C. Handy, *Father of the Blues* (New York: MacMillan, 1941), 74.

44. Oakley, *Devil's Music*, 40–41; Davis, *History of the Blues*, 23–28; and Handy, *Father of the Blues*, 73–77 (quotations on 77).

45. Handy, *Father of the Blues*, 77 (italics in original).

46. Ibid., 93–94.

47. "His place in blues history," Giles Oakley argues, "is as a popularizer and publisher rather than as a blues performer." Oakley, *Devil's Music*, 41.

48. Handy, *Father of the Blues*, 120.

49. Amiri Baraka, *Blues People: Negro Music in White America* (New York: Quill, 1963), 148. Baraka, not too surprisingly, has little positive to say about Handy's music, especially since Baraka sees it as only a pale imitation of the more "authentic" blues of Robert Johnson or Charley Patton.

50. "Only the first and third strains of 'St. Louis Blues,'" Davis points out, "employ traditional twelve-bar blues structure." Elsewhere, the song contains "an unambiguous tango." Davis, *History of the Blues*, 59.

51. For a military band version of the tune that retains much of Handy's original intent, see Jim Europe's 369th U.S. Infantry Band, "St. Louis Blues," in *Early Jazz, 1917–1923* (Fremeaux & Associes, 2000).

52. Davis, *History of the Blues*, 60.

53. Kay C. Thompson, "Ragtime vs. the Blues," *Jazz Journal* (November 1950): 2. Even Thompson points out that the ragtime blurb speaks more than a little to the confusing nature of genre labels during this period. Still, as Thompson writes, "it was clearly indicative of the degree to which everyone, Handy included, wanted in on Mr. Joplin's ragtime act." Ibid.

54. Baraka, *Blues People*, 90.

55. Gunther Schuller, *Early Jazz: Its Roots and Musical Development* (New York: Oxford University Press, 1968), 62.

56. Ted Gioia, *The History of Jazz* (New York: Oxford University Press, 1997), 20. Despite a brief discussion of ragtime, most of Gioia's emphasis remains squarely on the blues.

57. Jelly Roll Morton, "Maple Leaf Rag," in *Jelly Roll Morton: The Complete Library of Congress Recordings by Alan Lomax* (Rounder Records, 2005).

58. At one point, Morton implies that other piano players played "Maple Leaf Rag" slower out of sloppy fingerwork. In reference to the piece's own composer, Morton argued that "the boy couldn't finger too good." Jelly Roll Morton interview with Alan Lomax, in ibid.

CHAPTER 2. NEW ORLEANS AND THE CREATION OF EARLY JAZZ

1. Jelly Roll Morton, "I Created Jazz in 1902," *Down Beat* (August 1938): 3. The African American press also picked up on the story; see *Baltimore Afro-American*, April 23, 1938, 10. Both the magazine and newspaper considerably edited Morton's letter, an early version of which is in the Historic New Orleans Collection. See MSS 507, "Jelly Roll Morton Correspondence," William Russell Collection, Folder 1, Historic New Orleans Collection Museum and Research Center, New Orleans, Louisiana. Also partially reprinted in Ralph de Toledano, *Frontiers of Jazz* (Gretna, La.: Pelican Publishing, 1994), 104–107; and William Russell, ed., *"Oh, Mister Jelly," A Jelly Roll Morton Scrapbook* (Copenhagen: JazzMedia, 1999), 171. In their recent biography of the piano player, Howard Reich and William Gaines argue that a friend of Morton's actually composed the letter following a lengthy conversation with the piano player. See Howard Reich and William Gaines, *Jelly's Blues: The Life, Music, and Redemption of Jelly Roll Morton* (New York: Da Capo Press, 2003), 155–157.

2. A version of this chapter was published as "New Orleans and the Creation of Early Jazz" in 2006 (*Popular Music and Society* 29:3 [July 2006]: 299–315). In 2007, I also presented a portion of this piece at the American Historical Association Annual Meeting in Atlanta, Georgia, under the title "From Jim Crow to Jelly Roll: Segregation and the Origins of Jazz in New Orleans."

3. Alan Lomax, *Mister Jelly Roll: The Fortunes of Jelly Roll Morton, New Orleans Creole and Inventor of Jazz* (Berkeley: University of California Press, 1973), 8. The standard book on early African connections to Louisiana is Gwendolyn Midlo Hall, *Africans in Colonial Louisiana: The Development of Afro-Creole Culture in the Eighteenth Century* (Baton Rouge: Louisiana State University Press, 1992). See also Lawrence Gushee, *Pioneers of Jazz: The Story of the Creole Band* (Oxford: Oxford University Press, 2005), 4–7; 293–295. For a brief introduction to Spanish rule in

Louisiana and the creation of Afro-Louisianan culture, see Ned Sublette, *The World That Made New Orleans: From Spanish Silver to Congo Square* (Chicago: Lawrence Hill Books, 2008), 5–7.

4. Morton routinely gave 1885 as his year of birth, thus making him seventeen in 1902, a convincing age for his claim of creating jazz. "An 1885 birth date," Giddens writes, "made his famous claim of having single-handedly invented jazz in 1902 seem a tad more plausible." Gary Giddens, *Visions of Jazz: The First Century* (New York: Oxford University Press, 1998), 69.

5. "As I can understand," Morton continued, "my folks were in the city of New Orleans long before the Louisiana Purchase. And all my folks came directly from the shores—or not the shores, I mean from France. That's across the world, in the other world. And they landed here in the New World years ago." Jelly Roll Morton interview with Alan Lomax, reprinted in transcript form in *Jelly Roll Morton: The Complete Library of Congress Recordings by Alan Lomax.* This box set includes all of the Library of Congress interviews between Lomax and Morton (along with the audio material remastered from the original tapes, transcripts from unrecorded interviews by Lomax, a book featuring an excellent essay by jazz scholar John Szwed, and a variety of printed facsimiles of Lomax's notes). See *Jelly Roll Morton: The Complete Library of Congress Recordings by Alan Lomax* (Rounder Records, 2005). The quoted material begins on page 8 of the transcript. For years the only easy access to this material was through edited editions of the music released by the different record labels. These recordings, however, omitted most if not all of the interview material in order to present only the songs Morton performed. Unedited versions of the interview material circulated on various LP and CD collections, all of which have been made obsolete by the Rounder collection from 2006.

6. "I didn't want to be called Frenchy," Morton declared. Lomax, *Mister Jelly Roll*, 3. See Phil Pastras, *Dead Man Blues: Jelly Roll Morton Way Out West* (Berkeley: University of California Press, 2001), 15, 105; and David Ake, *Jazz Cultures* (Berkeley: University of California Press, 2002), 180 n.23.

7. In an interesting twist on the rather complex assortment of sexual and ancestral names entwined in Morton's new identity, the piano player notes that "the King of Spain didn't do anything, it was the queen, Isabella." Lomax, *Mister Jelly Roll*, 4. Later, Morton discusses his trepidation at claiming the piano as his instrument because he "didn't want to be called a sissy." Ibid., 6. Pastras alludes to Morton's possible homosexuality in Pastras, *Dead Man Blues*, 105. See also "Winin' Boy Blues, Pt. 1" and "Winin' Boy Blues, Pt. 2," *Jelly Roll Morton: The Complete Library of Congress Recordings by Alan Lomax* (discs 3 and 7). Lomax, among others, sanitized much of Morton's language. In his various versions of "Make Me a Pallet on the Floor," for example, Morton progressively enhanced the vulgarity of his lyrics in each take. See "Make Me a Pallet on the Floor" (parts 1–4), *Jelly Roll Morton: The Complete Library of Congress Recordings by Alan Lomax* (disc 4).

8. "He sought," one recent scholar has noted, "to enrich blues with the gaudy melodies and thumping euphoria of ragtime." Giddens, *Visions of Jazz*, 71.

9. Created in 1897 by city officials in an attempt to control prostitution, Storyville encompassed an area of several blocks north of the French Quarter, and it served as a playground for white and Creole New Orleanians. Despite date discrepancies, Morton more than likely did play in and around Storyville, an area he referred to as "the District" or "Tenderloin." Black people could find service employment in

Storyville, but in general local African Americans congregated a few blocks west of this main area in a district informally known as "Black Storyville." See Marquis, *In Search of Buddy Bolden*, 50. For the "Spanish tinge," see Hersch, *Subversive Sounds*, 143–146; and Sublette, *The World That Made New Orleans*, 124.

10. James L. Collier, one of the more iconoclastic jazz scholars of the last few decades, also errs in his emphasis on Storyville. Even after noting that only piano players could find regular work in the district, Collier writes, "yet Storyville did provide employment for musicians, and it gave those who worked there an opportunity to develop their skills and refine the music itself." James Lincoln Collier, *The Making of Jazz: A Comprehensive History* (Boston: Houghton Mifflin, 1978), 64. Leroy Ostransky makes a similar point, arguing that "a considerable part of the musical synthesis [of New Orleans] took place in Storyville" (Leroy Ostransky, *Jazz City: The Impact of Our Cities on the Development of Jazz* [Englewood Cliffs, N.J.: Prentice-Hall, 1978], 32). In addition, an important early source of (mis)information is Stephen Longstreet, *Sportin' House: A History of New Orleans Sinners and the Birth of Jazz* (Los Angeles: Sherbourne Press, 1965).

11. Joy J. Jackson, *New Orleans in the Gilded Age: Politics and Urban Progress, 1880–1896* (Baton Rouge: Louisiana State University Press, 1969), 9, 11.

12. Thomas J. Hennessey, *From Jazz to Swing: African-American Jazz Musicians and Their Music* (Detroit: Wayne State University Press, 1994), 20; Burton W. Peretti, *The Creation of Jazz: Music, Race, and Culture in Urban America* (Urbana: University of Illinois Press, 1992), 24–25. Barker quote in Nat Shapiro and Nat Hentoff, eds., *Hear Me Talkin' to Ya: The Story of Jazz as Told by the Men Who Made It* (New York: Dover Publications, 1966), 4.

13. See Ostransky, *Jazz City*, 1–40. For an overview of the racial issues both discussed and ignored within jazz historiography, see Charles Hersch, *Subversive Sounds: Race and the Birth of Jazz in New Orleans* (Chicago: University of Chicago Press, 2007), 6–10.

14. "New Orleans," Rudi Blesh writes, "offered a special combination of musical ingredients not to be found elsewhere." Rudi Blesh, *Shining Trumpets: A History of Jazz* (New York: Da Capo Press, 1975), 174.

15. The somewhat common term "Black Creole" (or "Creole of Color") denotes this third group who "were a mixture of nationalities—French, Spanish, Haitian, and African." Donald M. Marquis, *In Search of Buddy Bolden: First Man of Jazz* (Baton Rouge: Louisiana State University Press, 1978), 74. To lessen confusion, this study will use the term "Creole" only in connection to its third definition except where noted. This usage does not signify a simplification of New Orleans society, but rather should be viewed as an attempt at clarification. See also Sublette, *The World That Made New Orleans*, 79–80.

16. For definitions of Creole society, see Ted Gioia, *The History of Jazz* (New York: Oxford University Press, 1997), 33; John Chilton, *Sidney Bechet: The Wizard of Jazz* (New York: Oxford University Press, 1987), 2; Martin T. Williams, *Jazz Masters of New Orleans* (New York: Macmillan, 1967), 9–10; Jackson, *New Orleans in the Gilded Age*, 14–15; and David A. Jasen and Gene Jones, *Black Bottom Stomp: Eight Masters of Ragtime and Early Jazz* (New York: Routledge, 2002), 127–128. Complicating matters further, "the word Creole became common parlance for any light-skinned Negro." Chilton, *Sidney Bechet*, 2.

17. Peretti, *Creation of Jazz*, 36.

18. Ibid., 38.

19. The concept of jazz as a "folk music" continues to be a source of confusion (if not irritation) for some scholars and listeners. In the early years of jazz, however, labels and musical genres proved incredibly flexible. For the first few decades of its existence jazz continued to be regarded as folk, or blues, or ragtime, or some combination of the three. Furthering this complexity, jazz musicians routinely performed blues compositions, blues musicians played folk songs, and writers and critics debated endlessly where the lines should be drawn. Overall, Jelly Roll Morton's entire career proves the arbitrary nature of labels—as does the rather broad taxonomy presented in *A Song Is Born*—and for the purposes of this study I generally use the term "folk" to denote the close connections between performer and audience that defined early jazz as well as to provide a contrast with the jazz commercialism that began to occur in the 1920s. For a brief discussion of some of these issues, see Elijah Wald, *Escaping the Delta: Robert Johnson and the Invention of the Blues* (New York: Amistad, 2004), 62–63; 230–235. See also Ake, *Jazz Cultures*, 39–40.

20. Collier has argued repeatedly that early jazz should be seen as a commercial music connected to a professional class of musicians. See James Lincoln Collier, *Jazz: The American Theme Song* (New York: Oxford University Press, 1993), 92; and Collier, "The Faking of Jazz," *New Republic* 193 (November 18, 1985): 33–40. Bruce Raeburn, in contrast, argues that early jazz existed somewhere between folk tradition and commercialism. See Bruce Raeburn, "New Orleans Style: The Awakening of American Jazz Scholarship and Its Cultural Implications," Ph.D. dissertation, Tulane University, 1991, 25.

21. Quoted in Marquis, *Searching for Buddy Bolden*, 103. See also his comment, "a student should learn to read music first," quoted in Peretti, *Creation of Jazz*, 103.

22. Quoted in Hersch, *Subversive Sounds*, 104. For his comments on Creoles and jazz, see Hersch, *Subversive Sounds*, 102–104. See also Shapiro and Hentoff, *Hear Me Talkin' to Ya*, 18–19.

23. Marquis, *The Search for Buddy Bolden*, 139–140. See also Peretti, *Creation of Jazz*, 29.

24. Interview with Lomax included in *Jelly Roll Morton: The Complete Library of Congress Recordings by Alan Lomax*, 146. In the same interview, Picou (who made a point to refer to the cornet player as "a light brown-skinned man") reiterated the famed power of Bolden's volume: "he used to blow that cornet that you could hear him for blocks" (ibid.).

25. Krin Gabbard, in his excellent essay on musical quoting, notes that the solo was so influential that Charlie Parker—a musician not normally associated with the sounds of early jazz—signified on Picou on his 1945 recording, "Warming Up a Riff." Krin Gabbard, "The Quoter and His Culture," in Reginald T. Buckner and Steven Weiland, eds., *Jazz in Mind: Essays on the History and Meanings of Jazz* (Detroit: Wayne State University Press, 1991), 104, 110 n.24. Charles Hersch explicitly argues that Picou did *not* originate the solo. Hersch, *Subversive Sounds*, 160–164. See also Thomas Brothers, *Louis Armstrong's New Orleans* (New York: W. W. Norton, 2006), 230, 265.

26. Pointing out the differences between brass band performances and the blues, Creole Leonard Bechet remarked: "Picou is a very good clarinet player, but that ain't a hot clarinet player. All he can play is that 'High Society.' He plays music, but he brags so much about—he claims that 'High Society.' That's what he claims, that that's him." Interview with Leonard Bechet, transcript in *Jelly Roll Morton: The Complete Library of Congress Recordings by Alan Lomax*, 150.

27. Picou made several comments about his first introduction to the blues, each with vaguely contradictory narratives. Burton Peretti cites one story of Picou meeting up with a bass player who taught him the blues near the railroad tracks. In an interview with Alan Lomax, however, Picou makes clear that he was taught by an African American female singer (though her bass-playing husband was present as well). In addition, Charles Hersch mentions the origin story confusion in his discussion of Picou. Hersch, *Subversive Sounds*, 228 n.63.

28. "He realized early," Richard Sudhalter has written in his study of white jazz musicians, "that anyone organizing a social event that needed music would have to turn to someone who could supply musicians to order, in groups large and small." Richard M. Sudhalter, *Lost Chords: White Musicians and Their Contribution to Jazz, 1915–1945* (New York: Oxford University Press, 1999), 12. "Jack had as many as three brass bands at once," Ramsey writes, "with a few dance bands thrown in for good measure." Frederic Ramsey, *Jazzmen* (New York: Harcourt Brace Jovanovich, 1977), 43.

29. Hennessey, *From Jazz to Swing*, 20.

30. One oft-repeated myth concerns the Spanish-American War and the increased availability of brass instruments. Collier, for example, notes that the discharged soldiers returning home sold their instruments to local pawnshops. Collier, *Making of Jazz*, 63–64. Connie Atkinson, among others, dismisses this claim and argues that a history of brass bands exists in New Orleans and dates back almost a century before the Spanish-American War. Also, she notes, few (if any) soldiers left the service through New Orleans. Atkinson made these comments at a panel discussion entitled "The Myths of New Orleans Music History," sponsored by the New Orleans International Music Colloquium and conducted during the French Quarter Festival, New Orleans, Louisiana, April 11, 2003.

31. William John Schafer, *Brass Bands and New Orleans Jazz* (Baton Rouge: Louisiana State University Press, 1977), 2.

32. By the 1890s, when Laine began performing with the Reliance, the primary lead instrument was the cornet, the louder, easier-to-tune replacement of the bugle. Schafer, *Brass Bands*, 6.

33. Ibid., 6–8.

34. Schafer argues that no real improvisation occurred until around 1900. He cites, in particular, one member of a brass band who argues that once Bolden became popular more and more bands began performing improvisational tunes. Ibid., 25.

35. For an overview of white musicians in New Orleans, see Hersch, *Subversive Sounds*, 109–117.

36. Blesh, *Shining Trumpets*, 183. "He was," Louis Armstrong noted, "just a one-man genius that was ahead of 'em all." Shapiro and Hentoff, *Hear Me Talkin' to Ya*, 39.

37. Marquis, *In Search of Buddy Bolden*, 29–30. Scholars rarely questioned Bolden's literacy, and in fact one of the most prominent myths involving Bolden relates to his supposed authorship of "The Cricket," a local gossip sheet. Novelist Michael Ondaatje used many of these myths in the fictional retelling of Bolden's life (which came out before the Marquis study). See Michael Ondaatje, *Coming through Slaughter* (New York: Vintage International, 1976).

38. String bands usually included violin and string bass players along with a guitarist and a horn and reed player. Rather than an orchestral sound, these bands produced music not unlike early country or blues bands.

39. For an overview of early black musicians in New Orleans, see Hersch, *Subversive Sounds,* 88–98.

40. Marquis, *In Search of Buddy Bolden,* 112, 117–122.

41. Gioia, *History of Jazz,* 34.

42. Shapiro and Hentoff, *Hear Me Talkin' to Ya,* 35.

43. Although the rumor of a Bolden wax cylinder routinely surfaces, no hard evidence exists to connect the cornet player to a specific recording. See Marquis, *In Search of Buddy Bolden,* 44.

44. Gathering together many of the early myths of Congo Square, Henry Kmen has attempted a sober (if brief) reassessment of the significance of the area. See Henry L. Kmen, "The Roots of Jazz and the Dance in Place Congo: A Re-Appraisal," *Yearbook for Inter-American Musical Research* 8 (1972): 5–16. See also Hersch, *Subversive Sounds,* 39–40; and Sublette, *The World That Made New Orleans,* 120–121, 274–283.

45. "The historians of jazz," Henry Kmen notes sarcastically, "rode a long way from Congo Square to Buddy Bolden and jazz—most of it on a magic carpet." Kmen, "The Roots of Jazz," 15.

46. White ethnic groups also experienced violent encounters during this period. In 1891, in particular, a New Orleans mob lynched eleven Italian Americans suspected in the murder of a police superintendent. Richard Gambino, *Vendetta: A True Story of the Worst Lynching in America, the Mass Murder of Italian-Americans in New Orleans in 1891, the Vicious Motivations Behind It, and the Tragic Repercussions That Linger to This Day* (New York: Doubleday, 1977).

47. William Ivy Hair, *Carnival of Fury: Robert Charles and the New Orleans Race Riot of 1900* (Baton Rouge: Louisiana State University Press, 1976), 106–107.

48. "The first half-decade of the 1890s," one writer noted succinctly, "was a time of crisis and change in New Orleans." Jackson, *New Orleans in the Gilded Age,* 258. For *Code Noir,* see Ake, *Jazz Cultures,* 15–18.

49. The most complete study of the Robert Charles story remains Hair, *Carnival of Fury.* See also Joel Williamson, *A Rage for Order: Black-White Relations in the American South since Emancipation* (New York: Oxford University Press, 1986), 133–141; and Brothers, *Louis Armstrong's New Orleans,* 14–15.

50. Williamson, *Rage for Order,* 136.

51. Ibid., 133.

52. Lomax, *Mister Jelly Roll,* 57.

53. The complete transcriptions of Lomax's interviews with Morton underscore the importance of the Robert Charles riot to Morton. Even if the piano player was not present (as he claims that he was), Morton talks at length about the details surrounding the Charles affair: "Robert Charles was very orderly, seeming, to everybody. . . . Never had any trouble before. But this arose him to fury. And through this killing, it started a great New Orleans riot. People, innocent people of all kinds, were killed." See *Jelly Roll Morton: The Complete Library of Congress Recordings by Alan Lomax,* 24–26.

54. Hair argues that the anger of lower-class whites toward more economically successful, middle-class Creoles only complicated an already tenuous social arrangement. Hair, *Carnival of Fury,* 71–72.

55. Virginia R. Dominguez, *White by Definition: Social Classification in Creole Louisiana* (New Brunswick, N.J.: Rutgers University Press, 1986), 136.

56. William Ivy Hair, in his study of the Robert Charles riot and its impact on the racial contours of New Orleans, provides a good overview of the complex situation that gave rise to the conflagration as well as the violent aftershocks that reverberated throughout the city during this period. See Hair, *Carnival of Fury*, 183–200. See also Williamson, *A Rage for Order*, 133–141; and Brothers, *Louis Armstrong's New Orleans*, 282–284.

57. Chilton, *Sidney Bechet*, 2. See also Ake, *Jazz Cultures*, 24–37.

58. Williams, *Jazz Masters of New Orleans*, 136.

59. Chilton, *Sidney Bechet*, 5–7.

60. This first soprano sax was a curved model with a regular saxophone shape. A few years later in London, Bechet purchased the more distinctive (and currently standard) straight model of the sax. See ibid., 45.

61. Harry O. Brunn, *The Story of the Original Dixieland Jazz Band* (Baton Rouge: Louisiana State University Press, 1960), xv. Although one of the only full-length studies of the Original Dixieland Jazz Band, Brunn's work devolves too easily into a rather hagiographic portrait of the band.

62. Oddly, LaRocca's father also played cornet, but the elder LaRocca did not want his son to become a professional musician. Ibid., 2–5.

63. Ibid., 30. "LaRocca," Brunn writes, "avers that the word 'jazz' was changed because children, as well as a few impish adults, could not resist the temptation to obliterate the letter 'j' from the poster." Ibid., 57. For the origins of the term, see Gushee, *Pioneers of Jazz*, 297–302. Also see Robert Walser, ed., *Keeping Time: Readings in Jazz History* (New York: Oxford University Press, 1999), 13, 53; David Meltzer, ed., *Reading Jazz* (San Francisco: Mercury House, 1993), 37–70; and Macdonald Smith Moore, *Yankee Blues: Musical Culture and American Identity* (Bloomington: Indiana University Press, 1985), 185.

64. Brunn, *Story of the Original Dixieland Jazz Band*, 26–50.

65. *New York Times*, February 2, 1918. At one point prior to 1917, some posters even used the term "jasz." Brunn, *Story of the Original Dixieland Jazz Band*, 52.

66. Brunn, *Story of the Original Dixieland Jazz Band*, 64.

67. Original Dixieland Jazz Band, "Livery Stable Blues" (Columbia Records, 1917) on *Early Jazz, 1917–1923* (Fremeaux & Associes, 2000). Brunn points to "The Holy City" as the hymn that inspired LaRocca. Brunn, *Story of the Original Dixieland Jazz Band*, 70.

68. Brunn, *Story of the Original Dixieland Jazz Band*, 71.

69. LaRocca quoted in Hersch, *Subversive Sounds*, 178. In the 1950s, LaRocca wrote a number of letters to various critics and scholars who dismissed his old band. See Brunn, *Story of the Original Dixieland Jazz Band*, 250–251. LaRocca, as Hersch points out, continued to make more virulent racist comments as he got older. "I'm a segregationist," LaRocca made clear in 1959, "and a die-hard one because I don't think the colored man has earned his place, so far." Quoted in Hersch, *Subversive Sounds*, 183.

70. Gunther Schuller, for example, argues that "the ODJB reduced New Orleans Negro music to a simplified formula. It took a new idea, an innovation, and reduced it to a kind of compressed, rigid format that could appeal to a mass audience." Schuller, *Early Jazz*, 180.

71. Like most of these early jazz musicians, Oliver's date and place of birth as well as his early life remain shrouded in mystery. See Giddens, *Visions of Jazz*, 77.

72. Despite his individual achievements, Giddens writes, "what [Oliver] could do better than anyone else was drive an ensemble that specialized in improvised polyphony." Giddens, *Visions of Jazz*, 80.

73. Collier, *Making of Jazz*, 85.

74. "If Storyville hadn't closed," two influential early jazz scholars argued, "a lot of the musicians would have stayed on in New Orleans" (Ramsey and Smith, *Jazzmen*, 58). In contrast, Danny Barker argues "that there were always, in New Orleans, both before and after Storyville closed, there were always so many musicians, so many great cats all the way down the line." Shapiro and Hentoff, *Hear Me Talkin' to Ya*, 66–67.

75. Gioia, *History of Jazz*, 45. See also Barry Kernfeld, ed., *The New Grove Dictionary of Jazz* (New York: St. Martin's Press, 1994), 88, 319, 615–617, 649, 670, 804, 833, 917, 935, 942, 945.

76. Gioia, *History of Jazz*, 45. "As a mainstream tradition," Gunther Schuller argues, "the New Orleans style in its earliest form did not survive the 1920s." Schuller, *Early Jazz*, 86.

77. Ramsey and Smith have referred to the New Orleans Rhythm Kings as "the most important white band after the Dixieland Jazz Band." Ramsey and Smith, *Jazzmen*, 57.

78. Rick Kennedy, *Jelly Roll, Bix, and Hoagie: Gennett Records and the Birth of Recorded Jazz* (Bloomington: Indiana University Press, 1994), 75–77.

79. Much confusion surrounds the names of two of the principal players in the New Orleans Rhythm Kings. Leon Ropollo, for example, is often referred to as Leon Rapollo, and Georg Brunis apparently altered the spelling of his given name (George Brunies) after consulting a numerologist. "Milenberg Joys" refers (through a misspelling) to the Lake Pontchartrain town of Milneburg, Louisiana. See Hersch, *Subversive Sounds*, 80–85; Kernfeld, *New Grove Dictionary of Jazz*, 163, 1061. Also see "Producer's Note," *New Orleans Rhythm Kings and Jelly Roll Morton* (Berkeley, Calif.: Fantasy Records, 1992), 4 (liner notes to compact disc).

80. New Orleans Rhythm Kings and Jelly Roll Morton, "Milenberg Joys" (Gennett Records, 1923) on *New Orleans Rhythm Kings and Jelly Roll Morton* (Fantasy, 1992). I am referring here to the first take of "Milenberg Joys"—included on both the vinyl and compact disc versions of *New Orleans Rhythm Kings and Jelly Roll Morton*. The compact disc adds a fourth take of the song that boasts a cleaner sound, but the solos are not as strong and Morton's playing is less audible.

81. The New Orleans Rhythm Kings, however, never capitalized on these 1923 sessions and the group disbanded in the mid-1920s. Morton, in contrast, would hit his creative peak three years later with his Red Hot Peppers recordings in 1926.

82. Giddens, *Visions of Jazz*, 70.

CHAPTER 3. CHICAGO AND THE RECORDING OF JAZZ IN THE 1920S

1. For these sessions the Creole Jazz Band consisted of Joe Oliver (cornet), Louis Armstrong (cornet), Honore Dutrey (trombone), Lil Hardin (piano), Bill Johnson (bass), and Warren "Baby" Dodds (drums). Liner notes for Louis Armstrong, "Louis Armstrong/King Oliver" (Milestone Records, 1992). See also Laurence Bergreen, *Louis Armstrong: An Extravagant Life* (New York: Broadway Books, 1997), 218, 499.

2. Rick Kennedy, *Jelly Roll, Bix, and Hoagie: Gennett Records and the Birth of Recorded Jazz* (Bloomington: Indiana University Press, 1994), 29. According to legend, Armstrong's cornet proved too loud, and engineers moved the young musician to a spot fifteen feet away from the rest of the band in order to achieve a decent mix. If true—Dodds never mentions the incident, and Armstrong changed it during his life—the story attests to the lack of balance control in acoustic recordings. Armstrong may have been placed a few feet behind Oliver, but the idea of Armstrong blaring, somewhat self-consciously, from the corner of the studio is more myth than reality. Ibid., 64.

3. Bergreen, *Louis Armstrong*, 215–217.

4. King Oliver's Creole Jazz Band, "Snake Rag" (Gennett Records, 1923) on *Louis Armstrong and King Oliver* (Milestone Records, 1992).

5. Kennedy, *Jelly Roll, Bix, and Hoagie*, 65–66.

6. Brian Priestly, *Jazz on Record: A History* (London: Elm Tree Books, 1988), 15–16. Shortly after the Gennett sessions, Oliver's band recorded "Snake Rag" for OKeh and emphasized the ragtime rhythm even further. Bergreen, *Louis Armstrong*, 217–220, 499.

7. Leroy Ostransky, *Jazz City: The Impact of Our Cities on the Development of Jazz* (Englewood Cliffs, N.J.: Prentice-Hall, 1978), 83. See also Davarian L. Baldwin, *Chicago's New Negroes: Modernity, the Great Migration, and Black Urban Life* (Chapel Hill: University of North Carolina Press, 2007), 23–25.

8. For a concise examination of Chicago as a quintessential jazz city, see Ostransky, *Jazz City*, 62–99. See also William Howland Kenney, *Chicago Jazz: A Cultural History, 1904–1930* (New York: Oxford University Press, 1993), xi–xv, 3–60; Baldwin, *Chicago's New Negroes*, 2–19, 21–52.

9. For one version of the story, see Gary Giddins, *Satchmo: The Genius of Louis Armstrong* (New York: Da Capo Press, 1988), 44.

10. The 1966 interview was later published as Louis Armstrong, *Louis Armstrong, A Self-Portrait* (New York: Eakins, 1971), 28. See also Louis Armstrong, *Satchmo: My Life in New Orleans* (New York: Prentice-Hall, 1954), 229–232; Bergreen, *Louis Armstrong*, 175–177; Grossman, *Land of Hope*, 114–116.

11. In his detailed study of the Great Migration, James Grossman outlines the various racial, informational, and economic obstacles facing African Americans traveling to the North for the first time by rail. See, in particular, Grossman, *Land of Hope*, 98–119.

12. See Armstrong, *Satchmo*, 191–211; Bergreen, *Louis Armstrong*, 144–154; Thomas Brothers, *Louis Armstrong's New Orleans* (New York: W. W. Norton, 2006), 249–255; Giddins, *Satchmo*, 41–44.

13. Armstrong, *Satchmo*, 211.

14. Crouched next to the phonograph, Beiderbecke would meticulously transpose the horn parts he heard to the piano. Without formal lessons, Bix would teach himself the cornet parts by playing the piano transcription that he had worked out. This novel method of instruction—resulting in an unorthodox embouchure and fingering style—provided Beiderbecke with a singular cornet sound that forced many other aspiring musicians to obsess over the records that he created. Kennedy, *Jelly Roll, Bix, and Hoagie*, 92. See also William Howland Kenney, *Recorded Music in American Life: The Phonograph and Popular Memory, 1890–1945* (New York: Oxford University Press, 1999), 15–16.

15. One writer has claimed that the "greatest single event in Chicago's early jazz history was the arrival of King Oliver in Chicago." Ostransky, *Jazz City*, 107.

16. Ibid., 111. See also Derek Vaillant, *Sounds of Reform: Progressivism and Music in Chicago, 1873–1935* (Chapel Hill: University of North Carolina Press, 2003), 173–176.

17. Allan H. Spear, *Black Chicago: The Making of a Negro Ghetto, 1890–1920* (Chicago: University of Chicago Press, 1967), 11–27, 91–110, 129–146; St. Clair Drake and Horace R. Clayton, *Black Metropolis: A Study of Negro Life in a Northern City* (New York: Harcourt, Brace, 1945) 58–64, 174–214, 379–397; Dempsey J. Travis, *An Autobiography of Black Jazz* (Chicago: Urban Research Institute, 1983), 13–17, 35–40.

18. Travis, *Autobiography of Black Jazz*, 39–40. See also Vaillant, *Sounds of Reform*, 208–213. None of the clubs in Bronzeville exist today, and most of the Stroll is currently the site of the Illinois Institute of Technology.

19. *Chicago Defender*, January 12, 1924, 9. See also Kenney, *Chicago Jazz*, 15, 26–27; Spears, *Black Chicago*, 81–82, 114–115, 134–136, 184–185; and St. Clair, *Black Metropolis*, 400–412.

20. Peyton wrote for the *Defender* from September 26, 1925 to July 27, 1929. My comments on Peyton are based on an examination of his columns during this period. Missing columns include: November 14, 1925; December 25, 1926; December 31, 1926; July 6, 1929; and portions of December 24, 1927, and December 22, 1928.

21. *Chicago Defender*, April 21, 1928, 8. See also ibid., October 24, 1925, 6; October 31, 1925, 6; December 5, 1925, 6; December 26, 1925, 6; January 9, 1926, 9; January 30, 1926, 6; March 20, 1926, 6; March 27, 1926, 6; July 31, 1926, 7; September 11, 1926, 6; November 6, 1926, 7; November 20, 1926, 6; December 11, 1926, 6; December 18, 1926, 6; January 8, 1927, 7; January 22, 1927, 6; February 26, 1927, 7; May 7, 1927, 8; June 11, 1927, 8; October 8, 1927, 8; October 29, 1927, 10; December 10, 1927, 10; December 17, 1927, 10; January 28, 1928, 8; March 2, 1928, 8; March 10, 1928, 8; March 17, 1928, 10; April 7, 1928, 10; April 28, 1928, 8; June 9, 1928, 10; July 14, 1928, 8; and August 4, 1928, 8. Peyton also warned of a poor musical education, and he believed that many of the ills he saw in jazz musicians stemmed at least in part from subpar teachers. See ibid., October 24, 1925, 6; February 20, 1926, 6; July 17, 1926, 7; December 3, 1927, 8; and April 13, 1929, 10. See also Kathy J. Ogren, *The Jazz Revolution: Twenties America and the Meaning of Jazz* (New York: Oxford University Press, 1989), 115–116.

22. *Chicago Defender*, September 26, 1925, 8.

23. Ibid., October 10, 1925, 6.

24. Ibid., October 24, 1925, 6.

25. Ibid., August 7, 1926, 7. In fact, advertisements for Armstrong's recordings often ran adjacent to "The Musical Bunch." See, e.g., ibid., September 11, 1926, 6.

26. Ibid., December 12, 1925, 7; ibid., February 5, 1927, 2; ibid., June 16, 1928, 10. In various other shorter pieces, Peyton also spoke on the history of jazz within the scope of African American music. See, e.g., ibid., May 29, 1926, 7; ibid., October 2, 1926, 6; ibid., August 11, 1928, 9; ibid., August 18, 1928, 11; ibid., November 3, 1928, 10; ibid., November 17, 1928, 10.

27. Ibid., December 12, 1925, 7.

28. Ibid., April 9, 1927, 9; and ibid., July 16, 1927, 8. See also ibid., March 10, 1928, 8.

29. Ibid., February 5, 1927, 2.

30. Ibid., June 16, 1928, 10.

31. "The style of jazz the public has gone wild about," Peyton wrote in 1926, "is that which Paul Whiteman, Vincent Lopez, the late James Reese Europe, Leroy Smith, and Fletcher Henderson's orchestras are putting out—beautiful melodies, garnished with eccentric figurations propelled by strict rhythm." Ibid., February 27, 1926, 7.

32. Ibid., March 12, 1927, 8. For definitions of "good jazz" see ibid., February 20, 1926, 6; ibid., February 27, 1926, 7; ibid., August 7, 1926, 7; and ibid., December 29, 1928, 10.

33. Ibid., May 19, 1928, 10. See also ibid., February 20, 1926, 6; ibid., May 22, 1926, 6; ibid., December 4, 1926, 7; ibid., May 28, 1927, 8; ibid., October 22, 1927, 8; ibid., October 29, 1927, 10; and ibid., July 7, 1928, 9.

34. Ibid., October 8, 1927, 8.

35. Ibid., October 31, 1925, 6.

36. Ibid., January 9, 1926, 6. See also ibid., October 17, 1925, 6; ibid., January 2, 1926, 6; and ibid., February 27, 1926, 7.

37. Ibid., February 5, 1927, 6 (quotation); and ibid., March 9, 1929, 10. See also ibid., October 24, 1925, 6; ibid., September 18, 1926, 7; ibid., May 21, 1927, 8; ibid., May 12, 1928, 10; ibid., August 11, 1928, 8; and ibid., November 3, 1928, 10.

38. Ibid., September 18, 1926, 7.

39. Ibid., July 16, 1927, 8.

40. Ibid., November 6, 1926, 7. For his views on jazz in movie theaters see also ibid., April 14, 1928, 10; ibid., October 6, 1928, 10; ibid., July 28, 1928, 8; and ibid., November 24, 1928, 10. On the controversy surrounding the Vitaphone, see ibid., November 27, 1926, 8; ibid., February 19, 1927, 6; ibid., October 27, 1928, 10; and ibid., May 4, 1929, 9.

41. Ibid., March 12, 1927, 8.

42. Ibid., July 21, 1928, 10.

43. See the advertisements for *125 Jazz Breaks for Cornet* and *50 Jazz Choruses* in ibid., August 27, 1927, 8.

44. Kennedy, *Jelly Roll, Bix, and Hoagie*, 14–27.

45. Ibid., 50. See also Rust, *Jazz on Record*, 1–2, 4–5.

46. "In an ironic and incongruous twist of fate," one scholar notes, "the Original Dixieland Jazz Band . . . was the first to make commercial recordings of this distinctly African American music." Gioia, *History of Jazz*, 37.

47. Record companies designated most releases by black entertainers and for a predominantly black audience as "race records." The companies lumped into this category a wide range of styles including blues, jazz, and gospel. Gioia, *History of Jazz*, 17.

48. "Victor's sales of phonograph players and records by the end of 1921 had reached an astounding $50 million." Kennedy, *Jelly Roll, Bix, and Hoagie*, 26.

49. Ibid., 27.

50. Ibid., 74.

51. Ibid., 36–39. Kennedy notes that "though Klan literature was circulated in the factory, the Gennetts did not publicly support the organization." Ibid., 38.

52. Ibid., 90.

53. Chicago actually hosted two major events in 1926. Earlier that February, the South Side Elks Lodge sponsored a smaller gala event. The highlight, at least according to the *Defender*, was a demonstration by Armstrong's Hot Five of how phonograph records were made. The band recorded a song on stage and then played back the recorded results for the audience. See Kenney, *Chicago Jazz*, 124.

54. Mildred Ann Henson, "Coliseum Will Resemble a Scene from 'Arabian Nights'"; and Bob Hawley, "Thousands to be Given as Prize Awards," both in *Chicago Defender*, June 12, 1926, 1. For more on the gala, see also Robert S. Abbott, "Music Hath Charms," 1, 4; and other articles on pp. 1 and 2, also in *Chicago Defender*, June 12, 1926.

55. Henson, "Coliseum Will Resemble a Scene From 'Arabian Nights.'" See also Kenney, *Recorded Music in American Life*, 121–123.

56. "Their success at the OKeh ball would be an indication of the eventual victory of Chicago recordings over the actual live sounds of the period." Thomas J. Hennessey, *From Jazz to Swing: African-American Jazz Musicians and Their Music, 1890–1935* (Detroit: Wayne State University Press, 1994), 67.

57. Henson, "Coliseum Will Resemble a Scene From 'Arabian Nights.'"

58. *Chicago Defender*, June 12, 1926, special music section, 4. See also ibid., May 22, 1926, 6.

59. Ibid., June 19, 1926, 6.

60. "He was in the process of developing the vocabulary of modern jazz," one biographer has written, "taking it out of sleepy New Orleans and sticking it right in the fast-beating heart of Chicago." Bergreen, *Louis Armstrong*, 200.

61. For Armstrong's 1924 trip to New York, see Bergreen, *Louis Armstrong*, 236–259; Ilsa Storb, *Louis Armstrong: The Definitive Biography* (New York: Peter Long, 1999), 25–26; and Mike Pinfold, *Louis Armstrong: His Life and Times* (New York: Universe Books, 1987), 40–47. For his return to Chicago, see Bergreen, *Louis Armstrong*, 260–310.

62. Bergreen, *Louis Armstrong*, 262–265.

63. Louis Armstrong, "Heebie Jeebies" (OKeh Records, 1925), on *Louis Armstrong: The Complete Hot Five and Hot Seven Recordings* (Columbia, 2000). Storb, *Louis Armstrong*, 32–33; Pinfold, *Louis Armstrong*, 52–53; and Alyn Shipton, *A New History of Jazz* (London: Continuum, 2001), 142.

64. Milton Mezzrow and Bernard Wolfe, *Really the Blues* (New York: Citadel Press, 1990), 119–120.

65. *Chicago Defender*, April 17, 1926, 6.

66. Ibid., March 19, 1927, 8.

67. Ibid., June 18, 1927, 8. See also ibid., November 7, 1925, 8; ibid., November 21, 1925, 6; ibid., December 12, 1925, 7; ibid., March 20, 1926, 6; ibid., April 10, 1926, 6; ibid., September 25, 1926, 6; ibid., April 16 1927, 9; ibid., July 2, 1927, 8; ibid., July 16, 1927, 8; ibid., December 31, 1927, 6; ibid., April 28, 1928, 8; ibid., April 27, 1929, 8; and ibid., May 4, 1929, 9.

68. Bergreen, *Louis Armstrong*, 307. Armstrong's career after 1928 remains controversial, and in fact, Bergreen is one of the few writers to place a positive spin on the issue by implying that Armstrong had a clear musical direction. Gunther Schuller, on the other hand, argues that Armstrong basically forsook his jazz roots (and talent) and settled for the more financially lucrative path of recording popular, commercial music. Schuller, *Early Jazz*, 131.

69. The complete lineup featured Louis Armstrong (trumpet), Earl Hines (piano), Fred Robinson (trombone), Jimmy Strong (clarinet/tenor saxophone), Don Redman (clarinet/alto saxophone), Mancy Carr (banjo), and Arthur "Zutty" Singleton (drums).

70. Bergreen, *Louis Armstrong*, 304.

71. Ibid.

72. Ibid., 291.

73. Louis Armstrong, "West End Blues" (OKeh Records, 1928), on *Louis Armstrong: The Complete Hot Five and Hot Seven Recordings* (Columbia, 2000). During that same session (June 28, 1928), the band also recorded "Don't Jive Me" and "Sugar Foot Strut." Jos Willems, *All of Me: The Complete Discography of Louis Armstrong* (Lanham, Md.: Scarecrow Press, 2006), 55–56.

74. Robert O'Meally argues that the piece "might be used to mark the modern period in American expression." Robert G. O'Meally, "An Appreciation of Armstrong's Hot Five and Seven Recordings," *Louis Armstrong: The Complete Hot Five and Hot Seven Recordings* (New York: Columbia Records, 2000), 67 (liner notes to compact discs). The "introductory free-tempo cadenza," Gunther Schuller has written, "was for a time one of the most widely imitated of all jazz solos. It made Armstrong a household name, and to many Europeans it epitomized jazz." Schuller, *Early Jazz*, 115. See also Storb, *Louis Armstrong*, 39–40; Kenney, *Recorded Music in American Life*, 19–20; and Shipton, *New History of Jazz*, 142–143.

75. "No one had ever made music like these recordings," one Armstrong biographer wrote, "and no one, not even Louis, would ever manage to again." Bergreen, *Louis Armstrong*, 306.

76. William Kenney refers to records as "structures of sound" and industrial commodities. Kenney, *Recorded Music in American Life*, xvii, 15.

77. Kenney, *Chicago Jazz*, 155–156. See also Vaillant, *Sounds of Reform*, 271–272.

78. For a detailed discussion of some of the reform activities centered on Chicago nightlife in the early twentieth century, see Vaillant, *Sounds of Reform*, 184–233.

79. Kennedy, *Jelly Roll, Bix, and Hoagy*, 192. By the early 1930s, Paramount Records, the premier label for blues artists, had disappeared, and having bought out a number of their smaller rivals such as Victor and OKeh, Columbia Records and the Radio Corporation of America reclaimed control of the recording industry.

80. Although radio broadcasts would be central to the New York jazz story, African American musicians in Chicago, of course, also had access to radio opportunities. See, in particular, William Barlow, "Black Music on the Radio during the Jazz Age," *African American Review* 29:2 (Summer 1995): 325–328.

CHAPTER 4. NEW YORK CITY AND THE BROADCASTING OF JAZZ IN THE 1920S

1. Fletcher Henderson, "Sugarfoot Stomp" (Columbia Records, 1925), on *A Study in Frustration* (Columbia Records, 1994). See also Jeffrey Magee, *The Uncrowned King of Swing: Fletcher Henderson and Big Band Jazz* (Oxford: Oxford University Press, 2005), 85–89.

2. Frank Driggs, "Liner Notes," Fletcher Henderson, on *A Study in Frustration* (Columbia Records, 1994), 24.

3. Ted Gioia, *The History of Jazz* (New York: Oxford University Press, 1997), 111. Collier sums up the arrangement pattern simply as "one section played the melodic lead, or dominating riff, which the other sections either answered during

the pauses in the line or punctuated with brief rhythmic figures." James Lincoln Collier, *The Making of Jazz: A Comprehensive History* (Boston: Houghton Mifflin, 1978), 182. See also Samuel A. Floyd Jr., *The Power of Black Music: Interpreting Its History from Africa to the United States* (Oxford: Oxford University Press, 1996), 113–114.

4. "'Sugar Foot Stomp,' recorded often and also published as a stock," Magee writes, "became a mainstay of the jazz repertory, and Redman's arrangement became the model on which other bands based their versions into the 1940s." Magee, *The Uncrowned King of Swing*, 89.

5. Gunther Schuller, *Early Jazz: Its Roots and Musical Development* (New York: Oxford University Press, 1968), 263.

6. Schuller argues that the tune had several obvious flaws and proclaims it "a record of very mixed quality." However, the composer also notes the forward-thinking elements of the arrangement (most notably the drumming), and he states that "in 1925, the band was not ready to make such quasi-intellectual ideas succeed." Schuller, *Early Jazz*, 262–263.

7. Magee's recent study on Henderson is the most complete look at the musician's life and compositions. Magee, *The Uncrowned King of Swing*.

8. Richard Hadlock, *Jazz Masters of the 20s* (New York: Macmillan, 1972), 194–195, 198–199; Samuel B. Charters and Leonard Kunstadt, *Jazz: A History of the New York Scene* (Garden City, N.Y.: Doubleday, 1962), 166; Gioia, *History of Jazz*, 191. Gioia notes that Henderson "drew primary inspiration *not* from New Orleans and Chicago, but from [the] currents of popular music and dance that were sweeping New York." Gioia, *History of Jazz*, 107.

9. James Lincoln Collier, *Jazz: The American Theme Song* (New York: Oxford University Press, 1993), 21–22.

10. Schuller pronounces the Hell Fighters as "in a real sense . . . the first big band." Schuller, *Early Jazz*, 249. In contrast, Gioia pointedly notes that Europe's music "stood out as a late flowering of the ragtime style, rather than as a harbinger of the Jazz Age." Gioia, *History of Jazz*, 106. See also Kathy J. Ogren, *The Jazz Revolution: Twenties America and the Meaning of Jazz* (New York: Oxford University Press, 1989), 35–39.

11. Although it was commercially unsuccessful, Samuel Floyd argues persuasively for the composition's primary position in the development of African American modernism. Floyd generally sees Joplin as an important (if somewhat overlooked) figure within this intellectual tradition. Floyd, *The Power of Black Music*, 90.

12. David A. Jasen and Gene Jones, *Black Bottom Stomp: Eight Masters of Ragtime and Early Jazz* (New York: Routledge, 2002), 68. "Stride," they note, "had one basic tempo (fast) and one basic mood (hilarity)." Ibid., 102.

13. "The left hand is often relieved of its duty as metronome, set free to join with the right, to provide syncopated countermelodies, and to provide unexpected accents and contrasts with those in the upper octave." Ibid., 72.

14. Jasen and Jones note that Smith possessed an "unparalleled sense of harmony." Ibid., 84.

15. Floyd, *The Power of Black Music*, 110–111.

16. Jasen and Jones, *Black Bottom Stomp*, 102.

17. "His wide-ranging left hand," one writer has observed, "had become, by 1927, a model of metrical accuracy and buoyant swing combined with harmonic daring and tremendous rhythmic power." Hadlock, *Jazz Masters of the 20s*, 155.

18. "To pay for his eating, drinking, and reveling," Jasen and Jones argue, "he sometimes sold himself too cheaply, and he often worked himself too hard." Jasen and Jones, *Black Bottom Stomp,* 103.

19. Gioia, *History of Jazz,* 99.

20. Besides the Original Memphis Five, a few of the more popular bands during this period included the Original Georgia Five, the Original Indiana Five, and the Rialto Versatile Five. Most of these bands featured white musicians with only tangential (if any) connection to the named city or state and played a rather standard form of slightly improvisational jazz. These bands did, however, usually include five members. See Charters and Kunstadt, *Jazz,* 124.

21. Richard M. Sudhalter, *Lost Chords: White Musicians and Their Contribution to Jazz, 1915–1945* (New York: Oxford University Press, 1999), 108. See also Sudhalter, *Lost Chords,* 101–129; and Barry Kernfeld, ed., *The New Grove Dictionary of Jazz* (New York: St. Martin's Press, 1994), 943.

22. Sudhalter, *Lost Chords,* 106.

23. "Black bands," one writer notes, "did not often play at the downtown spots." Leroy Ostransky, *Jazz City: The Impact of Our Cities on the Development of Jazz* (Englewood Cliffs, N.J.: Prentice-Hall, 1978), 178.

24. Ibid., 178, 201.

25. In 1929, one writer has observed, "the cost per person for an evening at Connie's averaged twelve to fifteen dollars; by contrast, at Small's Paradise, the average was about four dollars." Ibid, 201.

26. Ibid., 205.

27. For a good overview of some of the contours of the historiography of the Harlem Renaissance, see Houston A. Baker Jr., *Modernism and the Harlem Renaissance* (Chicago: University of Chicago Press, 1987), 9–14. For a brief examination of the impact of Pan-Africanism on the Harlem Renaissance (from a musical perspective), see Floyd, *The Power of Black Music,* 100–102. See also Ogren, *The Jazz Revolution,* 116–120.

28. Cary D. Wintz, *Black Culture and the Harlem Renaissance* (Houston: Rice University Press, 1988), 1. For commentary on the lack of musical emphasis in Harlem studies, see Paul Allen Anderson, *Deep River: Music and Memory in Harlem Renaissance Thought* (Durham, N.C.: Duke University Press, 2001), 3. See also Floyd, *the Power of Black Music,* 100–107.

29. Nathan Irvin Huggins, *Harlem Renaissance* (New York: Oxford University Press, 1971), 64.

30. Wintz, *Black Culture and the Harlem Renaissance,* 17.

31. See ibid., 20; and Ann Douglas, *Terrible Honesty: Mongrel Manhattan in the 1920s* (New York: Farrar, Straus, and Giroux, 1995), 73.

32. On Harlem's lack of a middle class, see Wintz, *Black Culture and the Harlem Renaissance,* 26.

33. Magee, *The Uncrowned King of Swing,* 32–35.

34. Philip K. Eberly, *Music in the Air: America's Changing Tastes in Popular Music, 1920–1980* (New York: Hastings House, 1982), 43.

35. The standard history on radio development in the United States is still Erik Barnouw, *A Tower in Babel: A History of Broadcasting in the United States,* vol. 1 (New York: Oxford University Press, 1966); quote on 41. See also William Barlow, "Black Music on Radio during the Jazz Age," *African American Review* 29:2 (Summer 1995): 325–328.

36. Barnouw, *Tower in Babel*, 189.

37. For the Radio Act of 1927, see Robert W. McChesney, *Telecommunications, Mass Media, and Democracy: The Battle for the Control of United States Broadcasting, 1928–1935* (New York: Oxford University Press, 1993), 12–18.

38. Kingsley Welles, "The Listeners' Point of View," *Radio Broadcast* 7:6 (October 1925): 754.

39. Susan Smulyan, *Selling Radio: The Commercialization of American Broadcasting, 1920–1934* (Washington, D.C.: Smithsonian Institution Press, 1994), 29.

40. Barnouw, *Tower in Babel*, 126. "*Potted Palm*," William Barlow notes, "was an industry term for classical and semi-classical concert music played by amateur musicians, who volunteered their services to the stations free of charge." Barlow, "Black Music on Radio during the Jazz Age," 326.

41. Barnouw, *Tower in Babel*, 129–131.

42. Eberly, *Music in the Air*, 24–25.

43. Ibid., 31.

44. John Edward Hasse, *Beyond Category: The Life and Genius of Duke Ellington* (New York: Simon and Schuster, 1993), 101.

45. A number of local clubs used similar "southern" images, but the Cotton Club's size and popularity distinguished it from the others. Other clubs included Club Kentucky, Club Alabam, and the Plantation Café. See Mark Tucker, *Ellington: The Early Years* (Urbana: University of Illinois Press, 1995), 110.

46. Hasse, *Beyond Category*, 101–103.

47. Edward "Duke" Ellington, *Music Is My Mistress* (Garden City, N.Y.: Doubleday, 1973), 23–30.

48. Tucker, *Ellington*, 75.

49. Ibid., 74–80. See also Mark Tucker, "The Renaissance Education of Duke Ellington," in *Black Music in the Harlem Renaissance: A Collection of Essays*, ed. Samuel A. Floyd Jr. (New York: Greenwood Press, 1990).

50. Tucker, *Ellington*, 81, 83–84, 92–95.

51. Ibid., 99.

52. Gioia, *History of Jazz*, 107–108.

53. "Ellington's subsequent five-year engagement at the Cotton Club, with its network wire," one scholar argues, "not only launched the career of one of America's leading musical originals, it also made possible the first important national propagation of popular music by a black group." Eberly, *Music in the Air*, 47.

54. For a concise examination of the shift to swing, see Joel Dinerstein, *Swinging the Machine: Modernity, Technology, and African American Culture between the Wars* (Amherst: University of Massachusetts Press, 2003), 56–62.

55. The New Orleans soloist "was playing his line over a pulse that went, effectively, at half the speed of the one the swing soloist was working against." Collier, *Making of Jazz*, 191.

56. "The recordings," one music scholar has noted, "made by the Washingtonians between November 1924 and October 1926 had reflected Ellington's status as a relative newcomer to New York's competitive musical scene." Tucker, *Ellington*, 211.

57. Duke Ellington, "The Creeper" (Vocalian Records, 1926), on *The Okeh Ellington* (Columbia Records, 1991).

58. Tucker, *Ellington*, 222–223.

59. A. H. Lawrence, *Duke Ellington and His World: A Biography* (New York: Routledge, 2001), 84.

60. Duke Ellington, "Mood Indigo" (Columbia Records, 1930), on *Ellington Indigos* (Columbia Records, 1989).

61. Lawrence, *Duke Ellington and His World*, 165.

62. Schuller, *Early Jazz*, 340–343. Hasse notes the original title of the piece. Hasse, *Beyond Category*, 142.

63. Schuller, *Early Jazz*, 340.

64. Lawrence, *Duke Ellington and His World*, 165.

65. Marshall Berman, *All That Is Solid Melts into Air: The Experience of Modernity* (New York: Penguin Books, 1988), 5.

66. "The phonograph record," Albert Murray writes, "has served as the blues musician's equivalent to the concert hall almost from the outset. It has been in effect his concert hall without halls, his *musee imaginaire*, his comprehensive anthology, and also his sacred repository and official archive." Albert Murray, *Stomping the Blues*, 183–184.

67. Ellington, *Music Is My Mistress*, 79.

68. *Black and Tan,* dir. Dudley Murphy (Paramount, 1929).

69. Lawrence, *Duke Ellington and His World*, 149–151.

CHAPTER 5. LOS ANGELES AND THE DIFFUSION OF EARLY JAZZ

1. *Check and Double Check,* dir. Melville Brown (RKO, 1930).

2. The most complete study of *Check and Double Check* is in Klaus Stratemann, *Duke Ellington Day by Day and Film by Film* (Copenhagen: JazzMedia, 1992), 29–44.

3. Ibid., 35. "Seeing the film today," Stratemann writes, "it is not difficult to determine the reasons for the disappointment of black audiences." Ibid. The film also failed to make much of an impression on white audiences, forcing the studio to cancel a planned sequel. After this disappointment, Gosden and Correll appeared as Amos and Andy only in small roles until eventually replaced by black actors for the television series produced in the early 1950s.

4. Ibid.; Krin Gabbard, *Jammin' at the Margins: Jazz and the American Cinema* (Chicago: University of Chicago Press, 1996), 167–168. The black press also noted this burnt cork decision. See *Baltimore Afro-American*, August 3, 1930, 8.

5. Some confusion surrounds Ellington's involvement with this number. Stratemann argues that the "rather saccharine" arrangement fails to connect to Ellington's work during this period. See Stratemann, *Duke Ellington,* 36–37. In the movie, the song begins with a seemingly tacked-on growling trumpet introduction before commencing with a fairly standard popular song arrangement. This incongruence coupled with the appearance of the Rhythm Boys lends credibility to Stratemann's claim.

6. Lawrence B. DeGraaf, "The City of Black Angels: Emergence of the Los Angeles Ghetto, 1890–1930," *Pacific Historical Review* 39 (1970): 330.

7. "The modern black community," DeGraaf argues, "began not with the founding party, but with the land boom of 1887–1888 which increased the Negro population in the city to 1,258, or 2.5% of the total in 1890." Ibid., 327.

8. "Between 1900 and 1920," DeGraaf notes, "the volume of Negro migration to the city increased sharply, causing the Negro population to multiply more than sevenfold." Ibid., 330. See also Catherine Parsons Smith, *Making Music in Los*

Angeles: Transforming the Popular (Berkeley: University of California Press, 2007), 139–144.

9. Michael B. Bakan, "Way Out West on Central: Jazz in the African-American Community of Los Angeles before 1930," in Jacqueline C. DjeDje and Eddie S. Meadows, eds., *California Soul: Music of African Americans in the West* (Berkeley: University of California Press, 1998), 32. Bakan's essay remains the most complete and valuable study of early Los Angeles jazz. For a more general overview of African American music in the city, see Smith, *Making Music in Los Angeles,* 166–186.

10. In 1920, only twenty-eight black residents were employed as salesmen out of a total of 11,341 workers, a statistic that reflects the imbalance of African Americans in the nonprofessional, white-collar job sector. DeGraaf, "City of Black Angels," 342.

11. Ibid., 350. Percussionist Lionel Hampton presents a different perspective on local racism in his autobiography, noting that "Hollywood was a pretty town, but I didn't think much of the attitude towards blacks there. It was my first real experience with discrimination." Comparing the city to Chicago, Hampton argued that "in Chicago, the black population was so big that you could live and go to school and work and never even have to talk to a white person." Lionel Hampton with James Haskins, *Hamp: An Autobiography* (New York: Warner Books, 1989), 28–29.

12. DeGraaf, "City of Black Angels," 351. See also Lonnie G. Bunch, "A Past Not Necessarily Prologue: The Afro-American in Los Angeles," in Norman M. Klein and Martin J Schiesl, eds., *Twentieth Century Los Angeles: Power, Promotion, and Social Conflict* (Claremont, Calif.: Regina Books, 1990), 103.

13. Dates for this early period remain somewhat elusive, but both Bakan and Gushee tend to place the Creole Band in Los Angeles in 1908. Certainly by 1911, members of the band began appearing in the city directory. More important than individual dates, however, is the fact that jazz scholars routinely ignore Los Angeles in the early history of jazz, viewing it as more of a footnote than a connected scene. Despite various contradictions and incongruities, Los Angeles maintained a rather thriving ragtime and early jazz scene throughout the 1910s and 1920s. See Bakan, "Way Out West on Central," 31; Lawrence Gushee, *Pioneers of Jazz: The Story of the Creole Band* (Oxford: Oxford University Press, 2005), 71–94; and ibid., "New Orleans–Area Musicians on the West Coast, 1908–25," *Black Music Research Journal* 9:1 (1989): 9.

14. Again, dates remain quite unclear, and Morton conceivably could have been in the area earlier than 1912, the earliest date usually given for his arrival. See Bakan, "Way Out West on Central," 35.

15. Ibid., 41.

16. Although their careers developed separately, Morton's and Ory's travel patterns mirrored one another during this period. In 1922, for example, Morton left California for Chicago, a move paralleled by Ory two years later. For these musicians, Los Angeles served as a tangential way station for the eventual relocation to Chicago. See ibid., 40–41.

17. "Because of the European art music background of most local players and the conservative aesthetic sensibilities of Los Angeles's black establishment," one scholar notes, "well-schooled local musicians with limited skills in improvisation tended to enjoy greater professional success than hot-blowing improvisers from New Orleans, Chicago, and elsewhere." Ibid., 39.

18. Ibid., 29.

19. "Jazz thrived in Los Angeles," Bakan summarizes, "where an interesting mix of local players, New Orleans expatriates, and itinerant and resident musicians from all over the country contributed to an active and exciting musical culture." Ibid., 34.

20. The band, Bakan argues, "became one of the busiest groups in Los Angeles through the first half of the twenties, posing the most serious competition to bands led by newly arriving New Orleans musicians." Ibid., 34, 44–47 (quote on 34).

21. The lack of phonographic evidence also makes defining the jazz scene in Los Angeles difficult. Unlike in Chicago and New York, where a wide range of bands found themselves in the recording studio, relatively few Los Angeles bands preserved their sound on wax.

22. Bakan, "Way Out West on Central," 57. See also Tom Stoddard, *Jazz on the Barbary Coast* (Chigwell, Essex: Storyville Publications, 1982), 55–57.

23. "These early experiences," Bakan notes, "provided the Spikes brothers with a solid foundation for their contributions to African-American vaudeville in the 1920s." Bakan, "Way Out West on Central," 57. During this period, the Spikeses toured with Hattie McDaniel, the comedienne who went on to appear in *Gone With the Wind*. Floyd Levin, "The Spikes Brothers: A Los Angeles Saga," *Jazz Journal* 4:12 (December 1951): 12.

24. Bakan, "Way Out West on Central," 57; Albert J. McCarthy, *Big Band Jazz* (New York: Putnam, 1974), 168; Levin, "The Spikes Brothers," 12. See also Steven L. Isoardi, *The Dark Tree: Jazz and the Community Arts in Los Angeles* (Berkeley: University of California Press, 2006), 24–26.

25. McCarthy, *Big Band Jazz,* 168.

26. "The stomps, blues, rags African-American jazz bands played on the latest race records and in the integrated clubs along Central Avenue, in the chic, segregated nightspots of Hollywood, and in other parts of town," Bakan writes, "represented the cutting edge of West Coast music for black and white audiences alike." Bakan, "Way Out West on Central," 56.

27. Reb Spikes' Majors and Minors, "My Mammy's Blues," (1927), on *Jazz in California, 1923–1930* (Timeless Records, 1997). Brian Rust gives the lineup as including George Morgan (trumpet), W. B. Woodman (trombone), "Slocum" (clarinet), Roland Bruce (violin), Fritz Weston and "Gordon" (piano), George Craig (drums), and unknown musicians on second trumpet, second trombone, alto sax, tenor sax, tuba, and banjo. See Brian Rust, "Liner Notes," *Jazz in California, 1923–1930* (Timeless Historical Records, 1997), n.p. Levin gives Slocum's name as Adam Mitchell. Levin, "The Spike Brothers," 13.

28. "It is virtually impossible," Bakan argues, "to discuss any aspect of early jazz in Los Angeles without some reference to [the Spikes brothers]." Bakan, "Way Out West on Central," 54. In a similar vein, McCarthy writes that "there was no corner of jazz activity in Los Angeles in which one or other of the brothers was not deeply involved." McCarthy, *Big Band Jazz,* 168. Not all references to the brothers, however, remained positive, as McCarthy also reports that "in 1925 the orchestra received unwelcome publicity and the 16th September issue of Variety reported that three of its members had been arrested for contributing to the delinquency of three under-age white girls." McCarthy, *Big Band Jazz,* 168.

29. Sonny Clay's Plantation Orchestra, "Jambled Blues," (1925), on *Jazz in California, 1923–1930* (Timeless Records, 1997).

30. McCarthy, *Big Band Jazz*, 172–173. See also Rust, "Liner Notes," n.p. Seven months after "Jambled Blues," the band recorded a version of Jelly Roll Morton's "Chicago Breakdown." Again, the band performs a very composed form of improvised jazz, with instrumental breaks.

31. "Of all the California bands recording during the late 'twenties and early 'thirties," one writer argues, "Paul Howard's was the one most obviously in the mainstream of contemporary big band development." McCarthy, *Big Band Jazz*, 169. Paul Howard moved to Los Angeles from Ohio in 1911 as a teenager. Barry Kernfeld, ed., *The New Grove Dictionary of Jazz* (New York: St. Martin's Press, 1994), 542.

32. Paul Howard's Quality Serenaders, "Cuttin' Up," (1930), on *Jazz in California, 1923–1930* (Timeless Records, 1997).

33. "The arrangements," Albert McCarthy notes, "are functional and efficient, while the ensemble passages are played with technical expertise." Though certainly accurate, this description tends to downplay the obvious differences between the work of the Quality Serenaders and, for example, one of Sonny Clay's bands. McCarthy, *Big Band Jazz*, 172. See also Bakan, "Way out West on Central," 61–64.

34. The lineup for these 1930 sessions included: George Orendorff and Earl Thompson (trumpets), Lawrence Brown (trombone), Charlie Lawrence and Lloyd Reese (clarinet and alto sax), Paul Howard (tenor sax), Reginald Forsythe (piano), Thomas Valentine (banjo), James Jackson (tuba), and Lionel Hampton (drums, vocals). See Brian Rust, "Liner Notes," n.p.

35. A slighter facsimile of Louis Armstrong, Lionel Hampton plays the scat lines more as a humorous aside than as an instrumental solo. Hampton also scatted on several other Howard songs including "Moonlight Blues," "Stuff," and "California Swing." Hampton, of course, would rise to fame later with the Benny Goodman band.

36. Born in Atlanta in 1906, George Orendorff played with Howard from 1925 to 1930 before leaving to play with Les Hite throughout the next decade. The trumpet player shines on most of Howard's recordings, and as Brian Rust notes, "open or muted, he drives the band along with an attack that never becomes frenzied." See Brian Rust, "Liner Notes," n.p. For biographical information see Kernfeld, *New Grove Dictionary of Jazz*, 939.

37. McCarthy described the club as "an exclusive and inordinately expensive room much favored by the leading film stars of the time." McCarthy, *Big Band Jazz*, 170.

38. "In the 1920s," Ted Gioia argues, "there was no 'West Coast jazz,' if by that one means a distinctive regional style." Ted Gioia, *West Coast Jazz: Modern Jazz in California, 1945–1960* (New York: Oxford University Press, 1992), 8. See also Bakan, "Way Out West on Central," 39.

39. Robert Sklar, *Movie-Made America: A Cultural History of American Movies* (New York: Vintage Books, 1994), 10.

40. Edison based his work primarily on the experiments of two men, Eadweard Muybridge and Etienne Jules Marey, who had separately developed unique aspects of early film production. See ibid., 5–10.

41. Edison first publicly unveiled the kinetoscope at the Columbian Exposition in 1893, a machine that involved "a peep-show viewer capable of showing unenlarged 35mm. black-and-white pictures with a maximum running time of about ninety seconds." Ibid., 13.

42. On the impact of the kinetoscope on vaudeville, see ibid., 13–14. For the turning away of the middle-class audience, see ibid., 18–19. For an examination of the Victorian

ideals at odds with early film and the resultant reform movement, see Lary May, *Screening Out the Past: The Birth of Mass Culture and the Motion Picture Industry* (Chicago: University of Chicago Press, 1983), 43–59.

43. The Biograph Company proved an exception, as it maintained a patent for a different type of camera. This exception lasted only until 1908 when the constant lawsuits by Edison and threats of bankruptcy forced Biograph into the Edison fold. One concise history of the early business pattern of the film industry is in Sklar, *Movie-Made America*, 33–47.

44. Ibid., 41–47.

45. Ibid., 42.

46. May, *Screening Out the Past*, 60–95; Sklar, *Movie-Made America*, 57–61.

47. For the early history of Hollywood, see May, *Screening Out the Past*, 167–99; and Sklar, *Movie-Made America*, 67–85.

48. Sklar, *Movie-Made America*, 69.

49. "Along with cheap land," May writes of the studio heads, "they found a civic administration that helped break strikes in the studios and protected their interests as well." May, *Screening Out the Past*, 182.

50. "Hollywood," May argues, "showed how middle-class ideals could be regenerated to fit the modern age." Ibid., 198.

51. May elaborates greatly on the idea of Hollywood's creation of a new frontier; see ibid., 198–199.

52. *The Jazz Singer*, dir. Alan Crosland (Warner Brothers, 1927). Filming took place over the summer of 1927 with everything filmed in California except for external location shots of New York City. For the background to the film as well as the movie's working script, see Robert L. Carringer, ed., *The Jazz Singer* (Madison: University of Wisconsin Press, 1979). The two best pieces of criticism of the film are Michael Rogin, "Blackface, White Noise: The Jewish Jazz Singer Finds His Voice," *Critical Inquiry* 18 (Spring 1992): 417–453; and Gabbard, *Jammin' at the Margins*, 14–19, 35–44.

53. This finale appears only in the film, as Raphaelson ends his story with Robin serving as cantor. "The triumphant but slightly incoherent 'Mammy' finale," Gabbard notes, "was added to the film by Warners if only for the sake of a more upbeat ending." Gabbard, *Jammin' at the Margins*, 41. See also Carringer, *The Jazz Singer*, 26.

54. The sound technology—known as Vitaphone—was cost-prohibitive for a number of smaller theaters, impelling Warner Brothers to distribute a silent version of the film as well. Carringer, *The Jazz Singer*, 140.

55. A number of theaters that usually switched out movies every week showed *The Jazz Singer* for two months straight. Richard Barrios, *A Song in the Dark: The Birth of the Musical Film* (New York: Oxford University Press, 1995), 39.

56. Carringer, *The Jazz Singer*, 20. See also Barrios, *A Song in the Dark*, 39.

57. In 1921, D. W. Griffith included a musical number and a "short talking prologue" to his film, *Dream Street*. This film, Richard Barrios argues, "is left to history as the first major—if brief—use of recorded sound in a feature film." Barrios, *A Song in the Dark*, 15. Technically, the majority of *The Jazz Singer* was also silent as music and speaking appeared in only one-quarter of the film.

58. Ibid., 34.

59. Rogin, "Blackface, White Noise," 420.

60. The generally astute Rogin, for example, maintains that "the most obvious fact about *The Jazz Singer,* unmentioned in all the critical commentary, is that it contains no jazz." Ibid., 14. Gabbard, who agrees with most of Rogin's larger points, counters Rogin rather forcefully, noting that "although *The Jazz Singer* ought not win praise for eliminating blacks from its presentation of 'jazz,' the film should not be held responsible for using the term in the same way that most whites would have understood it in the 1920s." Gabbard, *Jammin' at the Margins,* 17.

61. Rogin, "Blackface, White Noise," 430.

62. In one scene, Jakie's father demands of his son, "What you mean, coming in my house and playing on my piano your music from the streets—your jazz?" Carringer, *The Jazz Singer,* 96. Also, in the foreword to the play, Raphaelson argues that "jazz is prayer." Quoted in Carringer, *The Jazz Singer,* 23.

63. Bruce M. Tyler, *From Harlem to Hollywood: The Struggle for Racial and Cultural Democracy, 1920–1943* (New York: Garland, 1992), 88.

64. Carrington, *The Jazz Singer,* 63, 83, 120.

65. Race certainly plays a role in any blackface performance, but the point made here centers on the primary intent of this particular use of blackface, which was not meant to denigrate or humiliate African Americans. Rogin elaborates quite well on the subject of blackface throughout his article, "Blackface, White Noise."

66. "Blackface," Rogin maintains, "is the instrument that transfers identities from immigrant Jew to American." Ibid., 434.

67. Again, black newspapers related the blackface story, but most members of the white audience would have been unaware of the use of makeup. See, e.g., *Baltimore Afro-American,* August 3, 1930, 8.

68. McCarthy, *Big Band Jazz,* 177.

69. In his catalog of jazz films, David Meeker lists over forty films produced between 1917 and 1930 that maintained some connection (however tenuous) to jazz music. See David Meeker, *Jazz in the Movies* (London: Talisman, 1981).

70. Hazel V. Carby, "It Jus Be's Dat Way Sometime: The Sexual Politics of Women's Blues," reprinted in Robert G. O'Meally, ed., *The Jazz Cadence of American Culture* (New York: Columbia University Press, 1998), 469–482. For a discussion on women and modern consumer culture, see Roland Marchand, *Advertising the American Dream* (Berkeley: University of California Press, 1986), 175–188.

71. Aubrey Scotto, *A Rhapsody in Black and Blue* (Paramount, 1932). Immediately prior to this film, Armstrong appeared (in partial cartoon form) in a Betty Boop animated film in which he also performs "I'll Be Glad When You're Dead, You Rascal You." Thomas Robert Cripps, *Slow Fade to Black: The Negro in American Film, 1900–1942* (New York: Oxford University Press, 1977), 229.

72. For an interesting take on Armstrong's connection to the song "Shine," see Alfred Appel Jr., *Jazz Modernism: From Ellington and Armstrong to Matisse and Joyce* (New Haven: Yale University Press, 2002), 31–32, 135, 140, 142–146.

73. Armstrong's acceptance of popular music over the music he performed in Chicago represents the most controversial part of his career. Most critics tend to dismiss Armstrong after 1930 as merely a "popular entertainer," no longer capable of brilliant jazz. One reason for the shift concerned Armstrong's damaged lip that made his horn playing difficult. Still, his singing always represented a crowd-pleasing element of his shows, and part of Armstrong's decision certainly dealt

with the possibility of a larger audience. Critics, however, were angrier about his choice of music, which most of them saw as watered-down, vaudeville-style pop music. Although not completely unfounded, Armstrong steadfastly argued that he placed no boundaries on music, unlike the critical pedants angry with him. For a brief survey of the critical response, see Gabbard, *Jammin' at the Margins*, 206–209.

74. Ibid., 6.

75. "The matriarchy," Cripps notes, "that rose as a function of male unemployment and the blues sounds of the 'race records' were made to seem mutual enemies." Cripps, *Slow Fade to Black*, 233.

76. *Cab Calloway's Hi-De-Ho*, dir. Fred Waller (Paramount, 1932).

77. "Heebie Jeebies," *At the Jazz Band Ball: Early Hot Jazz, Song and Dance* (Yazoo Video, 2000).

78. Linda Dahl, *Stormy Weather: The Music and Lives of a Century of Jazzwomen* (New York: Pantheon Books, 1984), 129. Dahl and Kernfeld refer to New Orleans as their native city, but one other scholar has shown that the family most likely moved to New Orleans in 1914, when the young girls were between five and seven years old. See Kernfeld, *New Grove Dictionary of Jazz*, 140; and Colin Larkin, ed., *The Encyclopedia of Popular Music* (London: Muse, 1998), 677.

79. Dahl, *Stormy Weather*, 129–130.

80. See Larkin, *Encyclopedia of Popular Music*, 677–678. Connee, in particular, influenced a generation of singers (both black and white) with her bluesy, syncopated style, and Ella Fitzgerald, for one, frequently cited Boswell as a strong influence on her own singing style. Larkin, *Encyclopedia of Popular Music*, 678.

81. *The Musical Doctor* (Paramount, 1932).

82. The megaphone served as Vallee's trademark, and the instrument allowed for both a smooth timbre as well as a method of projection for radio transmission. His appeal, Michael Pitts argues, "lay in his supremely radiophonic voice, a perfect match for the mikes, amps, and loudspeakers of the period." Michael Pitts et al., *The Rise of the Crooners* (Lanham, Md.: Scarecrow Press, 2002), 33.

83. "Indeed," Pitts notes, "there was nothing very sexy in his face, hair, or body. He was the epitome of the clean-cut college boy." Ibid., 33. Rather oddly, Vallee "claimed his sex appeal was due to a phallic quality deep in his throat." Ibid., 21.

84. Later in the film, Vallee employs a "Televisor," a device allowing the doctor to check on (and sing to) all of his patients while standing in his office.

85. "Because they required little investment," one writer argues, "and because the risk of failure and its impact on their careers was borne almost exclusively by the black performers, the studios could grind them out regularly." Cripps, *Slow Fade to Black*, 219.

CHAPTER 6. AN AMERICAN MUSIC

1. For a description of the show, see Don Rayno, *Paul Whiteman: Pioneer in American Music*, vol. 1, *1890–1930* (Lanham, Md.: Scarecrow Press, 2003), 71–86; Henry Osborne Osgood, *So This Is Jazz* (1926; reprint ed., New York: Da Capo Press, 1978), 129–142; Thomas A. DeLong, *Pops: Paul Whiteman, King of Jazz* (Piscataway, N.J.: New Century, 1983), 3–11; Paul Allen Anderson, *Deep River: Music and Memory in Harlem Renaissance Thought* (Durham, N.C.:

Duke University Press, 2001), 231–235; Neil Leonard, *Jazz and the White Americans: The Acceptance of a New Art Form* (Chicago: University of Chicago Press, 1962), 80–81; and Joshua Berrett, *Louis Armstrong and Paul Whiteman: Two Kings of Jazz* (New Haven: Yale University Press, 2004), 59–67. Berret, in particular, provides a good discussion on the general shift in musical tastes and connects the Aeolian Hall concert to the premiere of Stravinsky's *Rite of Spring* that had occurred two weeks earlier.

2. James Reese Europe had already organized a similar concert several years earlier. See Rayno, *Paul Whiteman*, 75. For a contemporary discussion of the fusion of jazz and concert music, see Alfred V. Frankenstein, *Syncopating Saxophones* (Chicago: Robert O. Ballou, 1925), 41–43. See also Mary Herron Dupree, "'Jazz,' the Critics, and American Art Music in the 1920s," *American Music* 4:3 (Fall 1986): 288–294.

3. The press release is reprinted in David Meltzer, ed., *Reading Jazz* (San Francisco: Mercury House, 1993), 166–167. Although supposedly Whiteman's words, Hugh C. Ernst, Whiteman's manager, wrote the release. See Robert Walser, *Keeping Time: Readings in Jazz History* (New York: Oxford University Press, 1999), 39–40.

4. The best analysis of the 1924 concert and the attendant issues of race and culture is Gerald Early, "Pulp and Circumstance: The Story of Jazz in High Places," in Robert O'Meally, ed., *The Jazz Cadence of American Culture* (New York: Columbia University Press, 1998), 398–430. "If, however," Early writes, "Whiteman's concert is a jazz history of the world or a history of the jazz world, it is a revisionist history that has excised the presence of blacks as creators of this music." Ibid., 409. For a discussion of Whiteman's connection to issues of race, jazz, and modernity, see Joel Dinerstein, *Swinging the Modern* (Amherst: University of Massachusetts Press, 2003), 50–53.

5. Members of the audience apparently failed to see the joke, and Whiteman was stunned to hear the loud ovation for the tune. See James Lincoln Collier, *The Reception of Jazz in America: A New View* (Brooklyn, N.Y.: Institute for the Study of American Music, 1988), 32.

6. Rayno, *Paul Whiteman*, 84. For a studio version of the song, see Paul Whiteman, *"The King of Jazz": His Greatest Recordings, 1920–1936* (ASV Records, 1996).

7. Originally scored for only two pianos, Gershwin composed the piece in a rush. Whiteman had scheduled the concert late in 1923, and Gershwin dated the final manuscript of *Rhapsody in Blue* January 7, 1924. During the writing process, Gershwin would hand off hastily penciled sheets of music to Grofe, who would then arrange the piece for the full orchestra. Rayno, *Paul Whiteman*, 77. For a studio version of the song (with Gershwin playing piano), see Whiteman, *"The King of Jazz."*

8. Olin Downes, "A Concert of Jazz," *New York Times,* February 13, 1924, 16.

9. "This concert," one of Whiteman's biographers notes, "was the culmination of [Whiteman's] many years of attempting to merge jazz and symphonic music, and *Rhapsody in Blue*, in every sense, epitomized this union." Rayno, *Paul Whiteman,* 85.

10. Ibid., 86.

11. See DeLong, *Pops,* 12–29; Rayno, *Paul Whiteman,* 35–51; and Berrett, *Louis Armstrong and Paul Whiteman,* 1–20.

12. Rayno, *Paul Whiteman,* 197–198.

13. DeLong, *Pops,* 110–113.

14. See Rayno, *Paul Whiteman*, 43; and Collier, "Reception," 15.

15. See Lawrence W. Levine, "Jazz and American Culture," reprinted in Lawrence W. Levine, *The Unpredictable Past: Explorations in American Cultural History* (New York: Oxford University Press, 1993), 180.

16. Levine refers to jazz as "one of the houses of refuge in the 1920s for individuals who felt alienated from the central culture." Levine, "Jazz and American Culture," 181.

17. Macdonald Smith Moore, *Yankee Blues: Musical Culture and American Identity* (Bloomington: Indiana University Press, 1985), 105. Daniel Singal presents a definition of modernism similar to Moore's use of the word "jazz." "Modernism," Singal writes, "should properly be seen as a *culture*—a constellation of related ideas, beliefs, values, and modes of perception—that came into existence during the mid to late nineteenth century." Daniel Joseph Singal, "Towards a Definition of American Modernism," *American Quarterly* 39:1 (Spring 1987): 7, 12–14. See also Stanley Coben, "The Assault on Victorianism in the Twentieth Century," *American Quarterly* 27:5 (December 1975): 616–618.

18. Charles Nanry, "Jazz and Modernism," *Annual Review of Jazz Studies* 1 (1982): 149. "Jazz," he argues, "embodied the dynamic tension at the very core of modern life, the tension between the individual 'particularized' creator (the soloist) and the group (the ensemble), with its simultaneous demands for improvisation on the one hand and discipline and coordination on the other." Ibid. Daniel Singal also articulates this idea of cultural blending. Jazz, he argues, "blends the primitivism of its African origins with modern sophistication." Singal, "Towards a Definition of American Modernism," 14.

19. For an amplification of this theme of increased activity as part of the new modern order, see John Higham, "The Reorientation of American Culture in the 1890s," in John Weiss, ed., *The Origins of Modern Consciousness* (Detroit: Wayne State University Press, 1965), 27–30. For the general antimodern sentiment, see T. J. Jackson Lears, *No Place of Grace: Antimodernism and the Transformation of American Culture, 1880–1920* (Chicago: University of Chicago Press, 1981). See also Dupree, "'Jazz,' the Critics, and American Art Music in the 1920s," 296–298.

20. Quoted in Robert Walser, ed., *Keeping Time: Readings in Jazz History* (New York: Oxford University Press, 1999), 44.

21. Warren Susman, *Culture as History: The Transformation of American Society in the Twentieth Century* (New York: Pantheon Books, 1984), 107. In a related argument, Macdonald Moore argues that "jazz challenged the Yankee musical mission because it achieved an instant popularity that illuminated white nervousness over the rapid ethnic transformation of Northern cities and because trained musicians and critics, both abroad and at home, paid serious attention to it." Moore, *Yankee Blues*, 82.

22. "Some critics perceived jazz as the antimusic of robots and riveting machines, the technology of urban civilization." Moore, *Yankee Blues*, 108.

23. Anne Shaw Faulkner, "Does Jazz Put the Sin in Syncopation?" *Ladies Home Journal*, August 1921, 16, 34; reprinted in Walser, *Keeping Time*, 32–36; quote on 33. For an opposite approach to jazz in the workplace, see Munich Fuller Barnard, "Jazz Is Linked to the Factory Wheel," *New York Times*, December 30, 1928, Magazine Section, 4.

24. "Jazz Bands Here and Abroad," *New York Times*, December 12, 1924, 20.

25. Ibid. "Writing about jazz," another writer maintained, "naturally brings to mind other regrettable sounds that only too often irritate the radio listener who wants to hear something else." This writer also compared jazz to aggravating outbursts of static, but concluded that static at least existed "in the nature of things electrical." "Far Harder to Bear Than Static," *New York Times,* January 12, 1925, 14.

26. Neil Leonard, *Jazz and the White Americans: The Acceptance of a New Art Form* (Chicago: University of Chicago Press, 1962), 30.

27. Paul Fritz Laubenstein, "Jazz—Debit and Credit," *Musical Quarterly* 15:3 (October 1929): 614.

28. Moore, *Yankee Blues,* 119. "Whatever jazz may be in the future," one writer argued, "at present to us it is a thing poor indeed." "He Has No Scorn For Jazz," *New York Times,* January 28, 1925, 16.

29. Robert M. Stults, "The Jazz Problem," *The Etude* (1924), reprinted in Walser, *Keeping Time,* 53.

30. "Drawing a Line for Jazz," *New York Times,* December 10, 1922, sec. 8, 4.

31. Will Earhart, "The Jazz Problem," *The Etude* (1924), reprinted in Walser, *Keeping Time,* 49. "A man in an epileptic fit," he continued, "certainly loosens a large amount of energy; but it is ludicrously foggy thinking to appraise such energy as strength."

32. Stephen Wise, "The Jazz Problem," *The Etude* (1924), reprinted in Walser, *Keeping Time,* 51–52.

33. Frank Damrosch, "The Jazz Problem," *The Etude* (1924), reprinted in Walser, *Keeping Time,* 44.

34. "Jazz," he continued, "with its degrading influence takes the place of the sincerity and sweetness of the class." "Damrosch Assails Jazz," *New York Times,* April 17, 1928, 26. A similar argument took place in France during this period, and the *New York Times* published an account of a French audience mad at the jazzing of the "Marseillaise." Although this deliberation took place in France, the commentary reflects the contemporary national scene to such a degree that the *Times* seemingly felt the need to publish the account. The uproar surrounding the incident, the newspaper reported, "indicated that however popular jazz may be with a large part of the public everywhere, it is felt to be a low form of music and that to put a national anthem in it is an insult to patriots." "A Virtuous Revolt against Jazz," *New York Times,* February 2, 1926, 26.

35. Earhart, "The Jazz Problem," *The Etude* (1924), reprinted in Walser, *Keeping Time,* 49.

36. Ibid.

37. "Drawing a Line for Jazz," *New York Times,* December 10, 1922, sec. 8, 4.

38. "Music Clubs against Jazzing of Classics," *New York Times,* December 6, 1927, 29.

39. "Musician Is Driven to Suicide by Jazz; Wouldn't Play It, Couldn't Get Employment," *New York Times,* April 7, 1922, 1.

40. Frank Damrosch, "The Jazz Problem," *The Etude* (1924), reprinted in Walser, *Keeping Time,* 44.

41. "Where the ideal Victorian middle-class woman," one writer notes, "was shrouded in colorless and sexless drapery, fit inside constructs of corsets, layered wrapping, hobbled high-button shoes, the Flapper projected an undomesticated look celebrating sexual abandon and androgyny." "Where the Victorian's body was unimaginable beneath the fortress of her garb," he continued, "the Flapper's

thin and shape-hugging dress announced the body as an emblem of youth and sexuality on display and dancing to the accompaniment of 'jazz.'" David Meltzer, ed., *Reading Jazz* (San Francisco: Mercury House, 1993), 73. See also Kenneth A. Yellis, "Prosperity's Child: Some Thoughts on the Flapper," *American Quarterly* 21:1 (Spring 1969): 48–49.

42. The flapper "bobbed her hair, concealed her forehead, flattened her chest, hid her waist, dieted her hips away and kept her legs in plain sight." Yellis, "Prosperity's Child," 44.

43. Ibid., 47.

44. Ibid., 48.

45. See Paula S. Fass, *The Damned and the Beautiful: American Youth in the 1920s* (New York: Oxford University Press, 1979), 303–306. "Much of the outcry," Eric Porter writes, "had to do with sex," and critics connected jazz music to unrestrained dancing, public lewdness, and eventual sexual relations. "The rhythmic qualities of jazz," he continues, "the participatory elements of the performance, and the physical aspects of the dancing associated with it spoke of unrestrained sexual energies, which had long been projected onto black bodies by Europeans and white Americans." Eric C. Porter, *What Is This Thing Called Jazz? African American Musicians as Artists, Critics, and Activists* (Berkeley: University of California Press, 2002), 9.

46. Faulkner, reprinted in Walser, *Keeping Time,* 33.

47. Ibid., 32.

48. *New York Times,* May 7, 1926, 10.

49. *New York Times,* October 30, 1922, 14.

50. "Both Jazz Music and Jazz Dancing Barred from All Louisville Episcopal Churches," *New York Times,* September 19, 1921, 17.

51. "Couples retiring to automobiles and remaining there during dances were frowned on," the local church organization argued, "[and] a reasonable check must be made for the community good." Ibid.

52. *New York Times,* May 7, 1926, 10.

53. "Says Jazz Threatens Christian Civilization," *New York Times,* December 16, 1934, E2.

54. Ibid., October 30, 1922, 14.

55. Ibid.

56. Ibid.

57. Moore, *Yankee Blues,* 105.

58. Frank Damrosch, "The Jazz Problem," *The Etude* (1924), reprinted in Walser, *Keeping Time,* 44.

59. For a jazz-centered discussion of the black migration patterns out of the South, see Leroy Ostransky, *Jazz City: The Impact of Our Cities on the Development of Jazz* (Englewood Cliffs, N.J.: Prentice-Hall, 1978), 82–99.

60. H. E. Krehbiel, *Literary Digest* 64 (January 12, 1920): 40. See also, Leonard, *Jazz and the White Americans,* 36; and Moore, *Yankee Blues,* 85.

61. Moore, *Yankee Blues,* 108. "Some whites feared jazz," Porter writes, "because it was rooted in black culture, because it played a role in facilitating interracial contact, and because it symbolized, in racially coded terms, the intrusion of popular tastes into the national culture." "At a moment," he continues, "when many young people (and young women in particular) were throwing off the constraints of Victorian

sexual mores, anxieties over white juvenile sexuality dovetailed with fears of black sexuality and, especially, of the impact black culture might have on the sexual behavior of young whites." Porter, *What Is This Thing Called Jazz?* 9.

62. John Higham, *Strangers in the Land: Patterns of American Nativism, 1860–1925* (New Brunswick, N.J.: Rutgers University Press, 1988), 155–157.

63. Each of the following quotes comes from the article, "Warns White Races They Must Drop Jazz," *New York Times,* September 20, 1927, 4.

64. The trombone, he argued, "is made to bray like an ass, guffaw like a village idiot and moan like a cow in distress." The trumpet, "associated in poetry with seraphim, is made to screech and produce sounds like drawing a nail on slate, tearing calico or the wailing of a nocturnal tomcat." Ibid.

65. "The treatment of jazz by Negro writers," one scholar argues, "reveals that it is not considered the kind of cultural achievement of the race that ought to be mentioned or recommended." Morroe Berger, "Jazz: Resistance to the Diffusion of a Culture-Pattern," *Journal of Negro History* 32:4 (October 1947): 466. Berger's essay is still an important touchstone within the discussion of jazz acceptance by national audiences. In addition, the salaciousness of the blues—in the earthy churn of the rhythms and the coarse suggestiveness of the lyrics—dismayed most black intellectuals during the 1920s, and with the important exceptions of Zora Neale Hurston and Langston Hughes, the blues represented only the lowbrow articulation of black musical expression. See, for example, Huggins, *Harlem Renaissance,* 222–223. "Conformity to New Negro standards," Ramsey argues, "necessarily meant a unfavorable attitude toward the lifeblood of African-American music-making: blues, jazz, and other vernacular idioms." Guthrie P. Ramsey Jr., "Cosmopolitan or Provincial? Ideology in Early Black Music Historiography, 1867–1940," *Black Music Research Journal* 16:1 (Spring 1996): 27–28.

66. J. A. Rogers, "Jazz at Home," in Alain Locke, ed., *The New Negro* (1927; reprint ed., New York: Touchstone, 1992), 217. Musically, this essay remains a jumbled arrangement of arguments, and although Rogers's thesis dovetails generally with Peyton's emphasis on ragtime, Rogers also tends to conflate jazz with the blues. "The Negroes who invented it," Rogers writes of jazz, "called their songs the 'Blues.'" Ibid. Locke's *The New Negro,* Guthrie explains, "advanced the ideals and goals that characterized [the Harlem Renaissance]—chief among them, economic, social, and cultural equity with white citizens—to be achieved through the creation and dissemination of great works of literary, musical, and visual art." Ramsey, "Cosmopolitan or Provincial?" 23. For a good discussion of Alain Locke's connection to jazz music, see Anderson, *Deep River,* 155–166.

67. "Jazz is rejuvenation," Rogers contended, "a recharging of the batteries of civilization with primitive new vigor." Rogers, "Jazz at Home," 224. In large measure, Rogers's take on jazz reflects the newfound energy that fueled much of the transformation to modernity. See Higham, "The Reorientation of American Culture in the 1890s," 27–30.

68. "The jazz spirit, being primitive demands more frankness and sincerity," Rogers wrote, "[and] just as it already has done in art and music so eventually in human relations and social manners, it will no doubt have the effect of putting more reality in life by taking some of the needless artificiality out." Rogers, "Jazz at Home," 223. For a discussion of the Primitive elements in jazz, see Huggins, *Harlem Renaissance,* 89–92. For the connections between modernism and the Harlem

Renaissance, see Houston A. Baker, "Modernism and the Harlem Renaissance," *American Quarterly* 39:1 (Spring 1987): 84–97; Gerald Early, "Three Notes toward a Cultural Definition of the Harlem Renaissance," *Callaloo* 14 (Winter 1991): 136–149; Gilbert Osofsky, "Symbol of the Jazz Age: The New Negro and Harlem Discovered," *American Quarterly* 17:2 (Summer 1965): 229–238; and Nathan I. Huggins, *The Harlem Renaissance* (New York: Oxford University Press, 1971), 9–11, 89–92.

69. See Porter, *What Is This Thing Called Jazz?* 5.

70. "The socio-political views of many Renaissance writers," Ramsey writes, "together with their narrow notion of 'great art,' prevented them from unequivocally (or perhaps just publicly) embracing the music of the cabarets, theaters, and speakeasies." Ramsey, "Cosmopolitan or Provincial?" 23.

71. "Harlem intellectuals promoted Negro art," Nathan Huggins maintains, "but one thing is very curious, except for Langston Hughes, none of them took jazz—the new music—seriously." Huggins, *Harlem Renaissance,* 9. For a brief discussion of Hughes's "music inflected verse," see Arnold Rampersad and David Roessel, eds., *The Collected Poems of Langston Hughes* (New York: Vintage Classics, 1994), 3–7. For a different take on the African American response to jazz, see Kathy J. Ogren, *The Jazz Revolution: Twenties America and the Meaning of Jazz* (New York: Oxford University Press, 1989), 125–138.

72. Porter, *What Is This Thing Called Jazz?* 11.

73. Huggins, *Harlem Renaissance,* 10–11.

74. "Jazz," Huggins writes, "was definitely not the 'high art' that James Weldon Johnson and Alain Locke were hoping for." Ibid., 198. "Jazz," Huggins also notes, " was infectious entertainment and not an ingredient of high civilization." Ibid., 64.

75. *New York Times,* May 7, 1926, 10.

76. Between 1922 and 1941, in *The Etude, The Musician,* and *Musical Quarterly,* one-third of the articles rejected all forms of jazz except the sweetest records by Paul Whiteman, and one-third saw that it had a very limited place in American culture. Berger argues that an unapologetically positive article on jazz did not appear until 1935. Berger, "Jazz: Resistance to the Diffusion of a Culture-Pattern," 471–472. In contrast, James Lincoln Collier argues that most magazines and newspapers published articles favorable, or at least not virulently against, jazz music. See Collier, *The Reception of Jazz in America.*

77. *The King of Jazz,* dir. John Murray Anderson (Universal, 1930). See Berrett, *Louis Armstrong and Paul Whiteman,* 89–94.

78. Budget problems continued to plague the film throughout production. The original budget stood at $1.5 million, but that figure increased rapidly once the primary filming commenced. For the preshooting history of the film, see Rayno, *Paul Whiteman,* 233–242; and Richard Barrios, *A Song in the Dark: The Birth of the Musical Film* (New York: Oxford University Press, 1995), 181–182.

79. Rayno, *Paul Whiteman,* 243.

80. These vaudevillian-style skits featured humorous songs, romantic ballads, broad jokes, and synchronized dancing. Rather than instrumental prowess, these skits and short pieces emphasized the hokier elements of the band's stage show. One skit, for example, focused on a musician's ability to play a song on a bicycle pump, and another setup had a musician pretending to play his girlfriend like an instrument.

81. "The cartoon," Krin Gabbard argues, "ultimately portrays Whiteman as bringing music to Africa." Krin Gabbard, *Jammin' at the Margins: Jazz and the American Cinema* (Chicago: University of Chicago Press, 1996), 11.

82. In reference to this cartoon Gabbard notes that "there are constant allusions to African Americans, and much of the film explicitly invokes minstrelsy, the film's grand predecessor in the ambivalent appropriation of blackness by whites." Ibid., 10. In one brief skit later in the film, Whiteman carries in his arms a black child.

83. "A more elaborate, more thorough denial of the African American role in jazz," Gabbard argues, "is difficult to imagine." Ibid.; see 10–14 for entire film (directed by John Murray Anderson). At least one scholar admits to the implicit racism of the film, but still contends that *The King of Jazz* represents a triumph in film musicals. In his book on musical film, Richard Barrios (very much aware of the racial elements of this movie) argues that the movie was "in its way a glorious, unrepeatable stunt." Writing about one of the musical numbers, Barrios contends that "setting aside some deplorable stereotypes the sequence is a delight." Barrios, *A Song in the Dark,* 183.

84. Whiteman was not alone when he connected this disparate grouping of songs to the creation of jazz. J. A. Rogers, in his contribution to Alain Locke's *The New Negro*, argues, "Jazz has always existed. It is in the Indian war-dance, the Highland fling, the Irish jig, the Cossack dance, the Spanish fandango, the Brazilian *maxixe,* the dance of the whirling dervish, the hula of the South Seas, the *danse du venture* of the Orient, the *carmagnole* of the French Revolution, the strains of Gypsy music, and the ragtime of the Negro." "Jazz proper, however," he adds, "is something more than all these." J. A. Rogers, "Jazz at Home," in Alain Locke, ed., *The New Negro* (New York: Touchstone Press, 1992), 217. Also, despite the lack of African Americans in the "Melting Pot" scene, Richard Barrios writes, "that aside, it's an exciting succession of sounds and images, song and dance of many (European) nations blended into a literal large pot." Barrios, *A Song in the Dark,* 186. For an excellent discussion of the image of the melting pot and the role of cultural pluralism, see Anderson, *Deep River,* 128–137.

85. Rayno, *Paul Whiteman,* 246.

86. Osgood, *So This Is Jazz,* vii.

87. Ibid., 123. Interestingly, Osgood notes that "Whiteman's program was modern, using the word in the sense of 'recent,' but it was only the *Rhapsody in Blue* that had even a touch of modernity in style." Ibid., 143.

88. Macdonald Smith Moore, *Yankee Blues: Musical Culture and American Identity* (Bloomington: Indiana University Press, 1985), 94. Seldes and Van Vechten, Moore writes, "gravitated to jazz at least in part because of the black sexuality they associated with it." Ibid., 104. See also Ogren, *The Jazz Revolution,* 139–161.

89. "Van Vechten," Moore notes, "wove himself throughout the history of jazz, noting his every presence and rationalizing every absence." Moore, *Yankee Blues,* 96. See also John Remo Gennari, "The Politics of Culture and Identity in American Jazz Criticism," Ph.D. dissertation, University of Pennsylvania, 1993, 89–91.

90. Gennari, "Politics of Culture and Identity," 130.

91. Ibid., 131. By 1939, *Down Beat* had a national audience of 80,000 readers. Ibid.

92. Scott DeVeaux, "Constructing the Jazz Tradition: Jazz Historiography," *Black American Literature Forum* 35:3 (Autumn 1991): 531. An English translation of *Le jazz hot* (entitled *Hot Jazz*) appeared in 1936.

93. George Gershwin, for example, made $5,000 to appear with the band, and Ross Gorman, Whiteman's star clarinetist, received over $400 a week at the peak of the band's popularity. See Rayno, *Paul Whiteman,* 248; and James Lincoln Collier, *Reception of Jazz in America,* 17.

94. For the effects of the Great Depression on Paul Whiteman, see Rayno, *Paul Whiteman,* 247–248.

95. For the effects of the Great Depression on jazz music, see Ted Gioia, *The History of Jazz* (New York: Oxford University Press, 1997), 135–137; and Burton W. Peretti, *The Creation of Jazz: Music, Race, and Culture in Urban America* (Urbana: University of Illinois Press, 1992), 164–170.

96. "The onset of the Great Depression," one jazz historian writes, "had a chilling effect on the jazz world, as it did on the whole entertainment industry." Gioia, *History of Jazz,* 135.

97. Peretti, *Creation of Jazz,* 164–165.

98. Ibid., 170.

99. Ibid., 164–165.

100. Ibid., 166.

101. Ibid., 167–171.

102. Gunther Schuller, *The Swing Era: The Development of Jazz, 1930–1945* (New York: Oxford University Press, 1989), 5–6.

103. Thomas J. Hennessey, *From Jazz to Swing: African-American Jazz Musicians and Their Music, 1890–1935* (Detroit: Wayne State University Press, 1994), 124–156.

104. For Goodman's early life, see Schuller, *Swing Era,* 10–11; and James Lincoln Collier, *Benny Goodman and the Swing Era* (New York: Oxford University Press, 1989), 1–12.

105. For Goodman's early musical life, see Collier, *Benny Goodman and the Swing Era,* 13–27.

106. Schoepp, Collier writes, "may have been the finest clarinet teacher in the United States at the time." Ibid., 17. See also Gioia, *History of Jazz,* 138–139.

107. Collier, *Benny Goodman and the Swing Era,* 17.

108. Gioia, *History of Jazz,* 139. Although living in Chicago, Goodman was too young to experience many live performances, and the clarinetist would only have been a young teenager during the city's jazz heyday in the early 1920s.

109. Schuller, *Swing Era,* 12–14.

110. Gioia, *History of Jazz,* 139–140; and Collier, *Benny Goodman and the Swing Era,* 93–109. See also, Anderson, *Deep River,* 225–231, 235–247.

111. "The rise of network radio," Gioia notes, "much more than the earlier spread of record players, transformed the general public into passive receptors of entertainment chosen by a few arbiters of taste." Gioia, *History of Jazz,* 137.

112. James Lincoln Collier, *The Making of Jazz: A Comprehensive History* (Boston: Houghton Mifflin, 1978), 261. See also Gennari, "Politics of Culture and Identity," 105–115.

113. Collier, *Making of Jazz,* 261. "John Hammond's achievement," Gennari writes, "was to maintain a strong ideological animus against commercialization even as he spent most of his working days commodifying and marketing the art of his favorite musicians." Gennari, "Politics of Culture and Identity," 105.

114. For the *Let's Dance* radio show, see Collier, *Making of Jazz,* 262; Gioia, *History of Jazz,* 140; Schuller, *Swing Era,* 8–9; and Collier, *Benny Goodman and the Swing Era,* 164–165.

115. "But Goodman, blessed with the *Let's Dance* budget," Collier writes, "was able—indeed required by his employers—to hire the best writers he could." Collier, *Benny Goodman and the Swing Era*, 151.

116. In addition, Goodman added the talented trumpeter Bunny Berigan during this time, and aside from Krupa and Henderson, Hammond also convinced Goodman to hire pianist Jess Stacy and singer Helen Ward. Schuller, *Swing Era*, 8.

117. "Krupa's approach to the drums," Ted Gioia writes, "for all its showmanship, was surprisingly unsyncopated and gleefully ignored the two great hooks of jazz rhythm—accenting the back beat and swinging the down beat—in favor of a relentless on-the-top groove." Gioia, *History of Jazz*, 142–143. Later in this passage, Gioia connects Krupa's quasi-rudimentary style to the origins of jazz drumming. Gunther Schuller refers to Krupa as "an oftimes annoyingly overbearing drummer." Schuller, *Swing Era*, 21.

118. "The special nature of Henderson's contribution," Gioia writes, "lay in his access to a gold mine of material compiled during his own lengthy stint as a bandleader, as well as in his deep sensitivity to the swing style that was about to dominate American airwaves." Gioia, *History of Jazz*, 141.

119. Schuller contends that this song "already embodied all the stylistic elements the Swing Era was to represent at its peak." Schuller, *Swing Era*, 21.

120. Gioia, *History of Jazz*, 143. "In the racially charged atmosphere of the day," Gioia argues, "the symbolic importance of Henderson's role with the Goodman band loomed almost as large as the music itself." Ibid., 141.

121. Goodman's band "was riddled with uncertainty and pressured by middle-American public taste to play the least adventurous part of its repertory." Schuller, *Swing Era*, 20. See also Collier, *Benny Goodman and the Swing Era*, 164–165.

122. For the late airtime of the radio program, see Collier, *Making of Jazz*, 262; Schuller, *Swing Era*, 20; Collier, *Benny Goodman and the Swing Era*, 166; and Gioia, *History of Jazz*, 140.

123. "Swarming the bandstand in their excitement," one scholar notes, "the Los Angeles audience sent a signal, one soon heard all over the nation, that Goodman had tapped into something real." Gioia, *History of Jazz*, 145.

124. "The essential message Goodman received from the young audience that night and in subsequent weeks," one scholar argues, "was that the Fletcher Henderson style arrangements, and Goodman's smart performances of them, had struck home at last." Schuller, *Swing Era*, 21. "A large segment of the public," Schuller continues, "seemed to prefer the best and most advanced arrangements the band had to offer." Ibid.

125. Gioia, *History of Jazz*, 145.

126. "To its adolescent fans," Gennari argues, "swing was theirs." Gennari, "Politics of Culture and Identity," 130. "It was not, then, that Goodman had created a demand for swing," Collier argues, "the demand for something along these lines was already there and already, to an extent, being fed." "What happened," he continues, "was that Goodman's version of the music suited the youthful taste more exactly than did that of his competitors." Collier, *Benny Goodman and the Swing Era*, 166.

CONCLUSION: "TWENTY YEARS OF JAZZ":
BENNY GOODMAN AND JELLY ROLL MORTON, 1938

1. When Goodman heard the new arrangement of "Don't Be That Way," he "decided immediately that this was his icebreaker." Irving Kolodin, Liner Notes, *Benny Goodman at Carnegie Hall—1938—Complete* (Columbia Records, 1999), 12. For other descriptions of the show, see Albert Murray, *Big Band Jazz* (New York: G. P. Putnam's Sons, 1974), 228–229; and James Lincoln Collier, *Benny Goodman and the Swing Era* (New York: Oxford University Press, 1989), 214–229.

2. This section, music critic Irving Kolodin writes, "brought out the family feeling that all good jazz musicians have for their celebrated predecessors, permitting a backward look at such landmarks of the popular music field as the Original Dixieland Jazz Band, Bix Beiderbecke, Ted Lewis, Louis Armstrong, and the perennial Duke Ellington." Kolodin, Liner Notes, *Benny Goodman at Carnegie Hall*, 12.

3. The title, too, was popular, and Joseph Lamb found some success with a similarly titled rag from 1908.

4. For a good discussion of "Shine," see Joel Dinerstein, *Swinging the Machine: Modernity, Technology, and African American Culture between the Wars* (Amherst: University of Massachusetts Press, 2003), 124–125.

5. Goodman had played publicly with black musicians as early as 1936, but the Carnegie Hall concert served as the primary introduction of an integrated band to a large audience. See Turk Van Lake, Liner Notes, *Benny Goodman at Carnegie Hall*, 34. See also Paul Allen Anderson, *Deep River: Music and Memory in Harlem Renaissance Thought* (Durham, N.C.: Duke University Press, 2001), 235–236.

6. Collier, *Benny Goodman*, 218.

7. *New York Times*, January 17, 1938, 11.

8. Ibid.

9. For record sales and broadcasting statistics, see Neil Leonard, *Jazz and the White Americans: The Acceptance of a New Art Form* (Chicago: University of Chicago Press, 1962), 179.

10. "The struggle," one scholar writes concerning the construction of a particular history, "is over possession of that history, and the legitimacy it confers." Scott DeVeaux, "Constructing the Jazz Tradition: Jazz Historiography," *Black American Literature Forum* 35:3 (Autumn 1991): 528.

BIBLIOGRAPHY

COLLECTIONS

Chicago Jazz Archive. Regenstein Library, University of Chicago, Chicago, Illinois.
William Russell Collection. Historic New Orleans Collection. New Orleans, Louisiana.

FILMS

At the Jazz Band Ball: Early Hot Jazz, Song and Dance. Yazoo Video. 2000.
Black and Tan. Dir. Dudley Murphy. Paramount. 1929. 19 minutes.
Cab Calloway's Hi-De-Ho. Dir. Fred Waller. Paramount. 1934. 10 minutes.
Check and Double Check. Dir. Melville Brown. RKO. 1930. 77 minutes.
Hollywood Rhythm: The Paramount Musical Shorts. Vol. 1, *The Best of Jazz and Blues.*
    Kino Video. 2001.
Hollywood Rhythm: The Paramount Musical Shorts. Vol. 2, *The Best of Big Bands and
    Swing.* Kino Video. 2001.
The Jazz Singer. Dir. Alan Crosland. Warner Brothers. 1927. 88 minutes.
King of Jazz. Dir. John Murray Anderson. Universal. 1930. 98 minutes.
The Musical Doctor. Dir. Ray Cozine. Paramount. 1932. 10 minutes.
A Rhapsody in Black and Blue. Dir. Aubrey Scotto. Paramount. 1932. 10 minutes.
A Song Is Born. Dir. Howard Hawks. Goldwyn. 1948. 113 minutes.

PUBLISHED MEMOIRS

Armstrong, Louis. *Satchmo: My Life in New Orleans.* New York: Prentice-Hall, 1954.
Bechet, Sidney. *Treat It Gentle: An Autobiography.* New York: Da Capo Press, 1978.
Buerkle, Jack V., and Danny Barker. *Bourbon Street Black.* New York: Oxford University
    Press, 1973.
Foster, George "Pops," with Tom Stoddard. *Pops Foster: The Autobiography of a New
    Orleans Jazzman.* Berkeley: University of California Press, 1971.
Hampton, Lionel, with James Haskins. *Hamp.* New York: Warner Books, 1989.
Handy, W. C. *Father of the Blues.* New York: MacMillan, 1941.
Lomax, Alan. *Mister Jelly Roll: The Fortunes of Jelly Roll Morton, New Orleans Creole and
    Inventor of Jazz.* Berkeley: University of California Press, 1973.
Mezzrow, Milton, and Bernard Wolfe. *Really the Blues.* New York: Citadel Press, 1990.
Travis, Dempsey J. *An Autobiography of Black Jazz.* Chicago: Urban Research Institute,
    1983.

RECORDINGS

Armstrong, Louis. *The Complete Hot Five and Hot Seven Recordings*. Columbia Records, 2000.

——. *The Hot Fives (and Hot Sevens), Volumes 1–3*. Columbia Records, 1988.

——. *Louis Armstrong and Earl Hines*. Columbia Records, 1988.

——. *Louis Armstrong and King Oliver*. Milestone Records, 1992.

Bechet, Sidney. *Sidney Bechet: Volume 2, 1923–1930*. Masters of Jazz, 1991.

Beiderbecke, Bix. *Volume One: Singin' the Blues*. Columbia Records, 1990.

Blues Masters, Volume 1: Classic Blues Women. Rhino Records, 1993.

Calloway, Cab. *Cab Calloway: Volume 1, 1929–1930*. Masters of Jazz, 1991.

Chicago Hot Bands, 1924–1928. Timeless Records, 1997.

Early Jazz, 1917–1923. Fremeaux and Associes, 2000.

Early Ragtime: Roots and Offshoots. RCA Victor, 1998.

Ellington, Duke. *Ellington Indigos*. Columbia Records, 1989.

——. *The Okeh Ellington*. Columbia Records, 1991.

Goodman, Benny. *Benny Goodman at Carnegie Hall—1938—Complete*. Columbia Records, 1999.

Henderson, Fletcher. *A Study in Frustration: The Fletcher Henderson Story*. Columbia Records, 1994.

Jazz in California, 1923–1930. Timeless Records, 1997.

Johnson, James P. *Snowy Mountain Blues*, Decca Records, 1991.

Lost Chords: White Musicians and Their Contribution to Jazz, 1915–1945. Retrieval Records, 1999.

Morton, Jelly Roll. *Birth of the Hot: The Classic Chicago "Red Hot Peppers" Sessions (1926–27)*. Bluebird Records, 1995.

——. *Jelly Roll Morton: The Complete Library of Congress Recordings by Alan Lomax*. Rounder Records, 2005.

New Orleans Owls. *The Owls' Hoot*. Frog Records, 1994.

New Orleans Rhythm Kings. *New Orleans Rhythm Kings and Jelly Roll Morton*. Fantasy Records, 1992.

New York Columbia Recordings, Volume 1: "Happy Rhythm." Frog Records, 2000.

New York Columbia Recordings, Volume 2: "Go Harlem." Frog Records, 2000.

Original Memphis Five. *The Original Memphis Five Collection, Volume One, 1922–23*. Collector's Classics, 1994.

Parham, Tiny. *Tiny Parham and His Musicians, 1926–1929*. Classics Records, 1992.

Rifkin, Joshua. *Scott Joplin: Piano Rags*. Elektra Records, 1994.

Whiteman, Paul. *"The King of Jazz": His Greatest Recordings, 1920–1936*. ASV Records, 1996.

BOOKS AND ARTICLES

Abbott, Lynn, and Doug Seroff. *Ragged but Right: Black Traveling Shows, "Coon Songs," and the Dark Pathway to Blues and Jazz*. Jackson: University Press of Mississippi, 2007.

Ake, David. *Jazz Cultures*. Berkeley: University of California Press, 2002.

Allen, Walter C. *Hendersonia: The Music of Fletcher Henderson and His Musicians.* Highland Park, N.J.: Walter C. Allen, 1973.

Anderson, Iain. *This Is Our Music: Free Jazz, the Sixties, and American Culture.* Philadelphia: University of Pennsylvania Press, 2007.

Anderson, Maureen. "The White Reception of Jazz in America." *African American Review* 38:1 (Spring 2004): 133–145.

Anderson, Paul Allen. *Deep River: Music and Memory in Harlem Renaissance Thought.* Durham, N.C.: Duke University Press, 2001.

Appel, Alfred, Jr. *Jazz Modernism: From Ellington and Armstrong to Matisse and Joyce.* New Haven: Yale University Press, 2002.

Armstrong, Louis. *Louis Armstrong, A Self-Portrait.* New York: Eakins, 1971.

Austerlitz, Paul. *Jazz Consciousness: Music, Race, and Humanity.* Middletown, Conn.: Wesleyan University Press, 2005.

Badger, R. Reid. "James Reese Europe and the Prehistory of Jazz." *American Music* (Spring 1989): 48–67.

Baker, Houston A., Jr. "Modernism and the Harlem Renaissance." *American Quarterly* 39:1 (Spring 1989): 84–97.

———. *Modernism and the Harlem Renaissance.* Chicago: University of Chicago Press, 1987.

Baldwin, Davarian L. *Chicago's New Negroes: Modernity, The Great Migration, and Black Urban Life.* Chapel Hill: University of North Carolina Press, 2007.

Baraka, Amiri. *Blues People: Negro Music in White America.* New York: Quill, 1963.

Barlow, William. "Black Music on Radio during the Jazz Age." *African American Review* 29:2 (Summer 1995): 325–328.

———. *"Looking Up at Down": The Emergence of Blues Culture.* Philadelphia: Temple University Press, 1989.

Barnouw, Erik. *A Tower in Babel: A History of Broadcasting in the United States.* Vol. 1. New York: Oxford University Press, 1966.

Barrios, Richard. *A Song in the Dark: The Birth of the Musical Film.* New York: Oxford University Press, 1995.

Becker, Howard S. "Professional Jazz Musicians and Their Audience." *American Journal of Sociology* 5 (1951): 136–144.

Berg, Charles. "Cinema Sings the Blues." *Cinema Journal* 17:2 (Spring 1978): 1–12.

Berger, Morroe. "Jazz: Resistance to the Diffusion of a Culture-Pattern." *Journal of Negro History* 32:4 (October 1947): 461–494.

Bergreen, Laurence. *Louis Armstrong: An Extravagant Life.* New York: Broadway Books, 1997.

Berlin, Edward A. "Cole and Johnson Brothers' *The Evolution of 'Ragtime.'*" *Current Musicology* 36 (1983): 21–32.

———. *King of Ragtime: Scott Joplin and His Era.* New York: Oxford University Press, 1994.

———. *Ragtime: A Musical and Cultural History.* Berkeley: University of California Press, 1980.

Berman, Marshall. *All That Is Solid Melts into Air: The Experience of Modernity.* London: Penguin Books, 1982.

Berrett, Joshua. *Louis Armstrong and Paul Whiteman: Two Kings of Jazz.* New Haven: Yale University Press, 2004.

Bindas, Kenneth J. *Swing That Modern Sound*. Jackson: University Press of Mississippi, 2001.

Blesh, Rudi. *Shining Trumpets: A History of Jazz*. New York: Da Capo Press, 1975.

Blesh, Rudi, and Harriet Janis. *They All Played Ragtime*. New York: Oak Publications, 1971.

Bogle, Donald. *Toms, Coons, Mulattoes, Mammies, and Bucks: An Interpretive History of Blacks in American Films*. New York: Continuum, 1994.

Borneman, Ernest. "Jazz and the Creole Tradition." *Jazzforschung* 1 (1969): 99–112.

Boyd, Michelle R. *Jim Crow Nostalgia: Reconstructing Race in Bronzeville*. Minneapolis: University of Minnesota Press, 2008.

Brothers, Thomas. *Louis Armstrong's New Orleans*. New York: W. W. Norton, 2006.

Brown, Lee B. "The Theory of Jazz Music 'It Don't Mean a Thing . . . . ' " *Journal of Aesthetics and Art Criticism* 49:2 (Spring 1991): 115–127.

Broyard, Anatole. " 'Keep Cool Man': The Negro Rejection of Jazz." *Commentary* 11:4 (April 1951): 359–362.

Brubaker, Robert L. *Making Music Chicago Style*. Chicago: Chicago Historical Society, 1985.

Brunn, H. O. *The Story of the Original Dixieland Jazz Band*. Baton Rouge: Louisiana State University Press, 1960.

Buckner, Reginald T., and Steven Weiland, eds. *Jazz in Mind: Essays on the History and Meanings of Jazz*. Detroit: Wayne State University Press, 1991.

Bushell, Garvin. "Garvin Bushell and New York Jazz in the 1920s." *Jazz Review* 2 (February 1959): 9–10.

Bushell, Garvin, with Mark Tucker. *Jazz from the Beginning*. Ann Arbor: University of Michigan Press, 1988.

Butters, Gerald R., Jr. *Black Manhood on the Silent Screen*. Lawrence: University Press of Kansas, 2002.

Carby, Hazel. "In Body and Spirit: Representing Black Women Musicians." *Black Music Research Journal* 11:2 (1991): 177–192.

Carney, Court. "New Orleans and the Creation of Early Jazz." *Popular Music and Society* 29:3 (July 2006): 301–316.

Carringer, Robert L. *The Jazz Singer*. Madison: University of Wisconsin Press, 1979.

Charters, Samuel B., and Leonard Kunstadt. *Jazz: A History of the New York Scene*. Garden City, N.Y.: Doubleday, 1962.

Chilton, John. *Sidney Bechet: The Wizard of Jazz*. New York: Oxford University Press, 1987.

Coben, Stanley. "The Assault on Victorianism in the Twentieth Century." *American Quarterly* 27:5 (December 1975): 604–625.

Collier, James Lincoln. *Benny Goodman and the Swing Era*. New York: Oxford University Press, 1989.

———. "The Faking of Jazz." *New Republic* 193 (November 18, 1985): 33–40.

———. *Jazz: The American Theme Song*. New York: Oxford University Press, 1993.

———. *Louis Armstrong: An American Genius*. New York: Oxford University Press, 1983.

———. *The Making of Jazz: A Comprehensive History*. Boston: Houghton Mifflin, 1978.

Collins, Patricia Hill. *Black Sexual Politics: African Americans, Gender, and the New Racism*. New York: Routledge, 2004.

Cripps, Thomas Robert. *Slow Fade to Black: The Negro in American Film, 1900–1942*. New York: Oxford University Press, 1977.

Crouch, Stanley. *Considering Genius: Writings on Jazz.* New York: Basic Civitas Books, 2006.

Curtis, Susan. *Dancing to a Black Man's Tune: A Life of Scott Joplin.* Columbia: University of Missouri Press, 1994.

Dahl, Linda. *Stormy Weather: The Music and Lives of a Century of Jazzwomen.* New York: Pantheon Books, 1984.

Dance, Stanley. *The World of Duke Ellington.* New York: Scribner's, 1970.

Daniels, Douglas Henry. *One O'Clock Jump: The Unforgettable History of the Oklahoma City Blue Devils.* Boston: Beacon Press, 2006.

Davis, Francis. *The History of the Blues: The Roots, the Music, the People from Charley Patton to Robert Cray.* New York: Hyperion, 1995.

DeGraaf, Lawrence B. "The City of Black Angels: Emergence of the Los Angeles Ghetto, 1890–1930." *Pacific Historical Review* 39 (1970): 323–352.

DeLong, Thomas A. *Pops: Paul Whiteman, King of Jazz.* Piscataway, N.J.: New Century, 1983.

de Toledano, Ralph. *Frontiers of Jazz.* Gretna, La.: Pelican Publishing, 1994.

DeVeaux, Scott. "Constructing the Jazz Tradition: Jazz Historiography." *Black American Literature Forum* 35:3 (Autumn 1991): 525–560.

Dinerstein, Joel. *Swinging the Machine: Modernity, Technology, and African American Culture between the World Wars.* Amherst: University of Massachusetts Press, 2003.

DjeDje, Jacqueline C., and Eddie S. Meadows. *California Soul: Music of African Americans in the West.* Berkeley: University of California Press, 1998.

Dominguez, Virginia R. *White by Definition: Social Classification in Creole Louisiana.* New Brunswick, N.J.: Rutgers University Press, 1986.

Douglas, Ann. *Terrible Honesty: Mongrel Manhattan in the 1920s.* New York: Farrar, Straus, and Giroux, 1995.

Drake, St. Clair, and Horace R. Clayton. *Black Metropolis: A Study of Negro Life in a Northern City.* New York: Harcourt, Brace, 1945.

Driggs, Frank. *Black Beauty, White Heat: A Pictorial History of Classic Jazz, 1920–1950.* New York: William Morrow, 1982.

Driggs, Frank, and Chuck Haddox. *Kansas City Jazz: From Ragtime to Bebop—A History.* Oxford: Oxford University Press, 2006.

Dupree, Mary Herron. "'Jazz,' the Critics, and American Art Music in the 1920s." *American Music* 4:3 (Fall 1986): 287–301.

Eagles, Charles W. "Urban-Rural Conflict in the 1920s: A Historiographical Assessment." *Historian* 49 (November 1986): 26–48.

Early, Gerald. "Three Notes toward a Cultural Definition of the Harlem Renaissance." *Callaloo* 14:1 (Winter 1991): 136–149.

Eberly, Philip K. *Music in the Air: America's Changing Tastes in Popular Music, 1920–1980.* New York: Hastings House, 1982.

Ellington, Edward Duke. *Music Is My Mistress.* Garden City, N.Y.: Doubleday, 1973.

Erenberg, Lewis A. *Steppin' Out: New York Nightlife and the Transformation of American Culture, 1890–1930.* Westport, Conn.: Greenwood Press, 1981.

Everett, Anna. *Returning the Gaze: A Genealogy of Black Film Criticism, 1909–1949.* Durham, N.C.: Duke University Press, 2001.

Fanon, Frantz. *Black Skin, White Masks.* New York: Grove Press, 2008.

Faragher, John Mack. *Rereading Frederick Jackson Turner: "The Significance of the Frontier in American History" and Other Essays.* New Haven: Yale University Press, 1999.

Fass, Paula S. *The Damned and the Beautiful: American Youth in the 1920s.* New York: Oxford University Press, 1977.

Ferris, William R. *Blues from the Delta.* Garden City, N.Y.: Anchor Press, 1978.

Fiehrer, Thomas. "From Quadrille to Stomp: The Creole Origins of Jazz." *Popular Music* 10:1 (January 1991): 21–38.

Floyd, Samuel A., Jr. *Black Music in the Harlem Renaissance: A Collection of Essays.* New York: Greenwood Press, 1990.

———. *The Power of Black Music: Interpreting Its History from Africa to the United States.* New York: Oxford University Press, 1995.

Frankenstein, Alfred. *Syncopating Saxophones.* Chicago: Robert O. Ballou, 1925.

Gabbard, Krin. *Black Magic: White Hollywood and African American Culture.* New Brunswick, N.J.: Rutgers University Press, 2004.

———. *Jammin' at the Margins: Jazz and the American Cinema.* Chicago: University of Chicago Press, 1996.

Gambino, Richard. *Vendetta: A True Story of the Worst Lynching in America, the Mass Murder of Italian-Americans in New Orleans in 1891, the Vicious Motivations Behind It, and the Tragic Repercussions That Linger to This Day.* New York: Doubleday, 1977.

Gates, Henry Louis, Jr. *The Signifying Monkey: A Theory of African-American Literary Criticism.* New York: Oxford University Press, 1989.

Gelatt, Roland. *The Fabulous Phonograph.* Philadelphia: Lippincott, 1955.

Gennari, John. *Blowin' Hot and Cool: Jazz and Its Critics.* Chicago: University of Chicago Press, 2006.

———. "Jazz Criticism: Its Development and Ideologies." *Black American Literature Forum* 25:3 (Autumn 1991): 449–523.

———. "The Politics of Culture and Identity in American Jazz Criticism." Ph.D. dissertation, University of Pennsylvania, 1993.

Gerard, Charley. *Jazz in Black and White: Race, Culture, and Identity in the Jazz Community.* Westport, Conn.: Praeger, 1998.

Gerstner, David A. *Manly Arts: Masculinity and Nation in Early American Cinema.* Durham, N.C.: Duke University Press, 2006.

Giddens, Gary. *Satchmo.* New York: Doubleday, 1988.

———. *Visions of Jazz: The First Century.* New York: Oxford University Press, 1998.

Gilroy, Paul. *The Black Atlantic: Modernity and Double Consciousness.* Cambridge, Mass.: Harvard University Press, 1993.

Gioia, Ted. *The History of Jazz.* New York: Oxford University Press, 1997.

———. *West Coast Jazz: Modern Jazz in California, 1945–1960.* New York: Oxford University Press, 1992.

Gottlieb, Robert, ed. *Reading Jazz: A Gathering of Autobiography, Reportage, and Criticism from 1919 to Now.* New York: Pantheon Books, 1996.

Grant, Barry Keith. " 'Jungle Nights in Harlem': Jazz, Ideology and the Animated Cartoon." *University of Hartford Studies in Literature* 21:3 (1989): 3–12.

Grossman, James R. *Land of Hope: Chicago, Black Southerners, and the Great Migration.* Chicago: University of Chicago Press, 1989.

Gushee, Lawrence. "How the Creole Band Came To Be." *Black Music Research Journal* 8:1 (1988): 83–100.

———. "New Orleans–Area Musicians on the West Coast, 1908–25." *Black Music Research Journal* 9:1 (1989): 1–19.

——. *Pioneers of Jazz: The Story of the Creole Band*. Oxford: Oxford University Press, 2005.

Hadlock, Richard. *Jazz Masters of the 20s*. New York: Macmillan, 1972.

Hair, William Ivy. *Carnival of Fury: Robert Charles and the New Orleans Race Riot of 1900*. Baton Rouge: Louisiana State University Press, 1976.

Hall, Gwendolyn Midlo. *Africans in Colonial Louisiana: The Development of Afro-Creole Culture in the Eighteenth Century*. Baton Rouge: Louisiana State University Press, 1992.

Hansen, Chadwick C. "Social Influences on Jazz Style: Chicago, 1920–30." *American Quarterly* 12:4 (Winter 1960): 493–507.

Hasse, John Edward. *Beyond Category: The Life and Genius of Duke Ellington*. New York: Simon and Schuster, 1993.

Hennessey, Thomas J. "Chicago's Black Establishment." *Journal of Jazz Studies* 2:1 (December 1974): 15–45.

——. *From Jazz to Swing: African-American Jazz Musicians and Their Music*. Detroit: Wayne State University Press, 1994.

Hentoff, Nat, and Albert J. McCarthy. *Jazz*. New York: Reinhart, 1959.

Hersch, Charles. *Subversive Sounds: Race and the Birth of Jazz in New Orleans*. Chicago: University of Chicago Press, 2007.

Higham, John. *Strangers in the Land: Patterns of American Nativism, 1860–1925*. New Brunswick, N.J.: Rutgers University Press, 1988.

Hodeir, Andre. *Jazz: Its Evolution and Essence*. New York: Grove Press, 1956.

Hofstadter, Richard. *The Age of Reform: From Bryan to F.D.R.* New York: Vintage Books, 1955.

Huggins, Nathan Irvin. *Harlem Renaissance*. New York: Oxford University Press, 1971.

Isoardi, Steven L. *The Dark Tree: Jazz and the Community Arts in Los Angeles*. Berkeley: University of California Press, 2006.

Jackson, Joy J. *New Orleans in the Gilded Age: Politics and Urban Progress, 1880–1896*. Baton Rouge: Louisiana State University Press, 1969.

Jarrett, Michael. *Drifting on a Read: Jazz as a Model for Writing*. Albany: State University of New York Press, 1999.

Jasen, David A., and Gene Jones. *Black Bottom Stomp: Eight Masters of Ragtime and Early Jazz*. New York: Routledge, 2002.

——. *That American Rag: The Story of Ragtime from Coast to Coast*. New York: Schirmer Books, 2000.

Jerving, Ryan. "Early Jazz Literature (and Why You Didn't Know)." *American Literary History* 16:4 (2004): 648–674.

——. "Jazz Language and Ethnic Novelty." *Modernism/modernity* 10:2 (2003): 239–268.

Kennedy, Rick. *Jelly Roll, Bix, and Hoagie: Gennett Records and the Birth of Recorded Jazz*. Bloomington: Indiana University Press, 1994.

Kenney, William H. *Chicago Jazz: A Cultural History, 1904–1930*. New York: Oxford University Press, 1993.

——. "James Scott and the Culture of Classic Ragtime." *American Music* (Summer 1991): 149–182.

——. *Jazz on the River*. Chicago: University of Chicago Press, 2005.

——. *Recorded Music in American Life: The Phonograph and Popular Memory, 1890–1945*. New York: Oxford University Press, 1999.

Kernfeld, Barry, ed. *The New Grove Dictionary of Jazz*. New York: St. Martin's Press, 1994.

Klein, Norman M., and Martin J. Schiesl. *Twentieth Century Los Angeles: Power, Promotion, and Social Conflict*. Claremont, Calif.: Regina Books, 1990.

Kmen, Henry L. "The Roots of Jazz and the Dance in Place Congo: A Re-Appraisal." *Yearbook for Inter-American Musical Research* 8 (1972): 5–16.

Knobel, Dale T. *"America for the Americans": The Nativist Movement in the United States*. New York: Twayne, 1996.

Kofsky, Frank. "The Jazz Tradition: Black Music and Its White Critics." *Journal of Black Studies* 1:4 (June 1971): 403–433.

Krehbiel, H. E. *Literary Digest* 64 (January 12, 1920): 40.

Larkin, Colin, ed. *The Encyclopedia of Popular Music*. London: Muse, 1998.

Laubenstein, Paul Fritz. "Jazz—Debit and Credit." *Musical Quarterly* 15:3 (October 1929): 606–624.

Lawrence, A. H. *Duke Ellington and His World: A Biography*. New York: Routledge, 2001.

Lax, John. "Chicago's Black Jazz Musicians in the Twenties: Portrait of an Era." *Journal of Jazz Studies* 1:2 (June 1974): 197–227.

Leach, William. *Land of Desire: Merchants, Power, and the Rise of a New American Culture*. New York: Vintage Books, 1993.

Lears, T. J. Jackson. *No Place of Grace: Antimodernism and the Transformation of American Culture, 1880–1920*. Chicago: University of Chicago Press, 1981.

Le Corbusier (Charles-Édouard Jeanneret-Gris). *When the Cathedrals Were White: A Journey to the Country of Timid People*. New York: Reynal and Hitchcock, 1937.

Leonard, Neil. *Jazz and the White Americans: The Acceptance of a New Art Form*. Chicago: University of Chicago Press, 1962.

Levin, Floyd. "The Spikes Brothers—A Los Angeles Saga." *Jazz Journal* 4:12 (December 1951): 12–15.

Levine, Lawrence W. *Black Culture and Black Consciousness: Afro-American Folk Thought from Slavery to Freedom*. Oxford: Oxford University Press, 2007.

———. "Jazz and American Culture." *Journal of American Folklore* 102: 403 (January–March 1989): 6–22.

———. *The Unpredictable Past: Explorations in American Cultural History*. New York: Oxford University Press, 1993.

Lewis, David Levering. *When Harlem Was in Vogue*. New York: Knopf, 1981.

Lipsitz, George. *Footsteps in the Dark: The Hidden Histories of Popular Music*. Minneapolis: University of Minneapolis Press, 2007.

Locke, Alain, ed. *The New Negro*. 1927. Reprint ed. New York: Touchstone, 1992.

Longstreet, Stephen. *Sportin' House: A History of New Orleans Sinners and the Birth of Jazz*. Los Angeles: Sherbourne Press, 1965.

Lott, Eric. *Love and Theft: Blackface Minstrelsy and the American Working Class*. New York: Oxford University Press, 1995.

———. "'The Seeming Counterfeit': Racial Politics and Early Blackface Minstrelsy." *American Quarterly* 43:2 (June 1991): 223–254.

Magee, Jeffrey. *The Uncrowned King of Swing: Fletcher Henderson and Big Band Jazz*. Oxford: Oxford University Press, 2005.

Marquis, Donald M. *In Search of Buddy Bolden: First Man of Jazz*. Baton Rouge: Louisiana State University Press, 1978.

May, Lary. *Screening Out the Past: The Birth of Mass Culture and the Motion Picture Industry*. Chicago: University of Chicago Press, 1983.

McCarthy, Albert J. *Big Band Jazz*. New York: G. P. Putnam's Sons, 1974.

McChesney, Robert W. *Telecommunications, Mass Media, and Democracy: The Battle for the Control of United States Broadcasting, 1928–1935*. New York: Oxford University Press, 1993.

Meeker, David. *Jazz in the Movies*. New Rochelle, N.Y.: Arlington House, 1977.

Meltzer, David, ed. *Reading Jazz*. San Francisco: Mercury House, 1993.

———. *Writing Jazz*. San Francisco: Mercury House, 1999.

Miller, Marc H., ed. *Louis Armstrong: A Cultural Legacy* Seattle: University of Washington Press, 1994.

Mirriam, Alan P., and Raymond W. Mack. "The Jazz Community." *Social Forces* 38:3 (March 1960): 211–222.

Monson, Ingrid. *Freedom Sounds: Civil Rights Call Out to Jazz and Africa*. Oxford: Oxford University Press, 2007.

Moore, Macdonald Smith. *Yankee Blues: Musical Culture and American Identity*. Bloomington: Indiana University Press, 1985.

Morris, Ronald L. *Wait until Dark: Jazz and the Underworld, 1880–1940*. Bowling Green, Ohio: Bowling Green University Press, 1980.

Morton, Jelly Roll. "I Created Jazz in 1902." *Down Beat* (August 1938): 3.

Moten, Fred. *In the Break: The Aesthetics of the Black Radical Tradition*. Minneapolis: University of Minnesota Press, 2003.

Murray, Albert. *Big Band Jazz*. New York: G. P. Putnam's Sons, 1974.

———. *Stomping the Blues*. New York: McGraw-Hill, 1976.

Nanry, Charles. "Jazz and Modernism." *Annual Review of Jazz Studies* 1 (1982): 146–154.

Newberger, Eli H. "The Transition from Ragtime to Improvised Piano Style." *Journal of Jazz Studies* 3:2 (Spring 1976): 3–18.

Oakley, Giles. *The Devil's Music: A History of the Blues*. New York: Da Capo Press, 1997.

Ogren, Kathy J. *The Jazz Revolution: Twenties America and the Meaning of Jazz*. New York: Oxford University Press, 1989.

Oliver, Paul, ed. *Black Music in Britain: Essays on the Afro-Asian Contribution to Popular Music*. Philadelphia: Open University Press, 1990.

———. *The Meaning of the Blues*. New York: Collier, 1960.

O'Meally, Robert G., ed. *The Jazz Cadence of American Culture*. New York: Columbia University Press, 1998.

O'Meally, Robert G., Brent Hayes Edwards, and Farah Jasmine Griffin, eds. *Uptown Conversations: The New Jazz Studies*. New York: Columbia University Press, 2004.

Ondaatje, Michael. *Coming through Slaughter*. New York: Vintage International, 1976.

Osgood, Henry Osborne. *So This Is Jazz*. 1926. Reprint ed. New York: Da Capo Press, 1978.

Osofsky, Gilbert. *Harlem: The Making of a Ghetto*. New York: Harper and Row, 1968.

———. "Symbol of the Jazz Age: The New Negro and Harlem Discovered." *American Quarterly* 17:2 (Summer 1965): 229–238.

Ostransky, Leroy. *Jazz City: The Impact of Our Cities on the Development of Jazz*. Englewood Cliffs, N.J.: Prentice-Hall, 1978.

Painter, Nell Irving. *Standing at Armageddon: The United States, 1877–1919*. New York: W. W. Norton, 1987.

Pastras, Phil. *Dead Man Blues: Jelly Roll Morton Way Out West*. Berkeley: University of California Press, 2001.

Pearson, Nathan W., Jr. "Political and Musical Forces That Influenced the Development of Kansas City Jazz." *Black Music Research Journal* 9:2 (Autumn 1989): 181–192.

Peretti, Burton W. *The Creation of Jazz: Music, Race, and Culture in Urban America.* Urbana: University of Illinois Press, 1992.

Philpott, Thomas Lee. *The Slum and the Ghetto: Neighborhood Deterioration and Middle-Class Reform, Chicago, 1880–1930.* New York: Oxford University Press, 1978.

Phinney, Kevin. *Souled American: How Black Music Transformed White Culture.* New York: Billboard Books, 2005.

Pinfold, Mike. *Louis Armstrong: His Life and Times.* New York: Universe Books, 1987.

Pitts, Michael, et al. *The Rise of the Crooners.* Lanham, Md.: Scarecrow Press, 2002.

Porter, Eric C. *What Is This Thing Called Jazz? African American Musicians as Artists, Critics, and Activists.* Berkeley: University of California Press, 2002.

Priestly, Brian. *Jazz on Record: A History.* London: Elm Tree Books, 1988.

Raeburn, Bruce. "New Orleans Style: The Awakening of American Jazz Scholarship and Its Cultural Implications." Ph.D. dissertation, Tulane University, 1991.

Ramsey, Frederic, Jr., and Charles E. Smith. *Jazzmen.* New York: Harcourt Brace Jovanovich, 1977.

Ramsey, Guthrie P., Jr. "Cosmopolitan or Provincial? Ideology in Early Black Music Historiography, 1867–1940." *Black Music Research Journal* 16·1 (Spring 1996): 11 42.

———. *Race Music: Black Cultures from Bebop to Hip-Hop.* Berkeley: University of California Press, 2003.

Rayno, Don. *Paul Whiteman: Pioneer in American Music.* Vol. 1, *1890–1930.* Lanham, Md.: Scarecrow Press, 2003.

Reddihough, John. "Jazz in Chicago." *Jazz Monthly* 1:10 (December 1955): 5–9.

Reed, Ishmael. *Mumbo Jumbo.* New York: Atheneum, 1972.

Reich, Howard, and William Gaines. *Jelly's Blues: The Life, Music, and Redemption of Jelly Roll Morton.* New York: Da Capo Press, 2003.

Rogin, Michael. "Blackface, White Noise: The Jewish Jazz Singer Finds His Voice." *Critical Inquiry* 18 (Spring 1992): 417–453.

Russell, William, ed. *"Oh, Mister Jelly," A Jelly Roll Morton Scrapbook.* Copenhagen: JazzMedia, 1999.

Rust, Brian. *Jazz Records, 1897–1942.* New Rochelle, N.Y.: Arlington House, 1978.

Schafer, William John. *Brass Bands and New Orleans Jazz.* Baton Rouge: Louisiana State University Press, 1977.

Schlereth, Thomas J. *Victorian America: Transformations in Everyday Life.* New York: HarperPerennial, 1991.

Schuller, Gunther. *Early Jazz: Its Roots and Musical Development.* New York: Oxford University Press, 1968.

———. *The Swing Era: The Development of Jazz, 1930–1945.* New York: Oxford University Press, 1989.

Shapiro, Nat, and Nat Hentoff, eds. *Hear Me Talkin' to Ya: The Story of Jazz as Told by the Men Who Made It.* New York: Dover Publications, 1966.

Shipton, Alyn. *A New History of Jazz.* London: Continuum, 2001.

Singal, Daniel Joseph. "Towards a Definition of American Modernism." *American Quarterly* 39:1 (Spring 1987): 7–26.

Sklar, Robert. *Movie-Made America.* New York: Random House, 1975.

Smith, Catherine Parsons. *Making Music in Los Angeles: Transforming the Popular.* Berkeley: University of California Press, 2007.

Smulyan, Susan. *Selling Radio: The Commercialization of American Broadcasting, 1920–1934*. Washington, D.C.: Smithsonian Institution Press, 1994.

Southern, Eileen. *The Music of Black Americans*. New York: Norton, 1971.

Spear, Allan H. *Black Chicago: The Making of a Negro Ghetto, 1890–1920*. Chicago: University of Chicago Press, 1967.

Stoddard, Tom. *Jazz on the Barbary Coast*. Chigwell, Essex: Storyville Publications, 1982.

Storb, Ilsa. *Louis Armstrong: The Definitive Biography*. New York: Peter Long, 1999.

Stratemann, Klaus. *Duke Ellington Day by Day and Film by Film*. Copenhagen: JazzMedia, 1992.

Sublette, Ned. *The World That Made New Orleans: From Spanish Silver to Congo Square*. Chicago: Lawrence Hill Books, 2008.

Sudhalter, Richard M. *Lost Chords: White Musicians and Their Contribution to Jazz, 1915–1945*. New York: Oxford University Press, 1999.

Sugrue, Thomas J. *The Origins of the Urban Crisis: Race and Inequality in Postwar Detroit*. Princeton: Princeton University Press, 1998.

Susman, Warren. *Culture as History: The Transformation of American Society in the Twentieth Century*. New York: Pantheon Books, 1984.

Szwed, John. *Crossovers: Essays on Race, Music, and American Culture*. Philadelphia: University of Pennsylvania Press, 2005.

———. *So What: The Life of Miles Davis*. New York: Simon and Schuster, 2004.

Thompson, Emily. *The Soundscape of Modernity: Architectural Acoustics and the Culture of Listening in America, 1900–1933*. Cambridge, Mass.: MIT Press, 2002.

Thompson, Kay C. "Ragtime vs. the Blues." *Jazz Journal* (November 1950): 1–3.

Tirro, Frank. *Jazz: A History*. New York: W. W. Norton, 1977.

Tomlinson, Gary. "Cultural Dialogics and Jazz: A White Historian Signifies." *Black Music Research Journal* 11:2 (1991): 229–263.

Tucker, Mark. *Ellington: The Early Years*. Urbana: University of Illinois Press, 1995.

Tuhkanen, Mikko. "Of Blackface and Paranoid Knowledge: Richard Wright, Jacques Lacan, and the Ambivalence of Black Minstrelsy." *Diacritics* 31:2 (Summer 2001): 9–34.

Tyler, Bruce M. *From Harlem to Hollywood: The Struggle for Racial and Cultural Democracy, 1920–1943*. New York: Garland, 1992.

Ulanov, Barry. *Duke Ellington*. New York: Creative Age Press, 1946.

Vaillant, Derek. *Sounds of Reform: Progressivism and Music in Chicago, 1873–1935*. Chapel Hill: University of North Carolina Press, 2003.

Wald, Elijah. *Escaping the Delta: Robert Johnson and the Invention of the Blues*. New York: HarperCollins, 2004.

Wall, Cheryl A. *Women of the Harlem Renaissance*. Bloomington: Indiana University Press, 1995.

Walser, Robert, ed. *Keeping Time: Readings in Jazz History*. New York: Oxford University Press, 1999.

Wang, Richard. "Researching the New Orleans–Chicago Jazz Connection." *Black Music Research Journal* 8:1 (1988): 101–112.

Weiss, John, ed. *The Origins of Modern Consciousness*. Detroit: Wayne State University Press, 1965.

Welles, Kingsley. "The Listeners' Point of View." *Radio Broadcast* 7:6 (October 1925): 751–758.

Wiebe, Robert H. *The Search for Order, 1877–1920*. New York: Hill and Wang, 1967.

Willems, Jos. *All of Me: The Complete Discography of Louis Armstrong*. Lanham, Md.: Scarecrow Press, 2006.

Williams, Martin T. *Jazz Masters of New Orleans*. New York: Macmillan, 1967.

Williams, Raymond. *Culture and Society, 1780–1950*. New York: Columbia University Press, 1983.

Williamson, Joel. *A Rage for Order: Black-White Relations in the American South since Emancipation*. New York: Oxford University Press, 1986.

Wintz, Cary D. *Black Culture and the Harlem Renaissance*. Houston: Rice University Press, 1988.

Witkins, Robert W. "Why Did Adorno 'Hate' Jazz?" *Sociological Theory* 18:1 (March 2000): 145–170.

Yaffe, David. *Fascinating Rhythm: Reading Jazz in American Writing*. Princeton: Princeton University Press, 2006.

Yellis, Kenneth A. "Prosperity's Child: Some Thoughts on the Flapper." *American Quarterly* 21:1 (Spring 1969): 44–64.

SONG INDEX

GENERAL INDEX

Abbott, Robert S., 63
African Americans
  in Chicago society, 59, 62–64, 66–67
  class distinctions and, 63–68, 80–81, 88
  as entrepreneurs, 18, 26–28, 106–107
  in the film industry, 114, 116–118
  Gennett Records and, 57–58, 70–72
  in Los Angeles society, 103–105
  as music critics, 64–68, 137, 156 (*see also* Peyton, Dave)
  in New Orleans society, 35, 39–41, 42, 43–45, 49–50
  in New York City society (*see* Harlem Renaissance)
  treatment of, in American society, 62–63 (*see also* Jim Crow; labor unions, black; segregation)
  treatment of, in the jazz business, 19, 95
Amos and Andy, 98, 100–101, 181n3
Armstrong, Louis, 60–61, 72–77, 79–80, 151
  arrival in Chicago, 59–60
  career after the 1920s, 176n68, 186n73
  in film, xii (illus.), 2, 115, 116–117
  Gennett recording of, 57–58, 173n2
  public recording demonstration of, 175n53
  "West End Blues" and, 7, 95–96, 155

Ball of Fire (film), 1, 159n2
Baquet, George, 46, 105
Baraka, Amiri, 28, 29, 164n49
Barker, Danny, 34, 171n56, 172n74
Bechet, Sidney, 45–46, 49–51, 151
Beiderbecke, Leon "Bix," 77, 78, 145, 151
  exposure to jazz music and, 60, 61–62, 173n14
  influence on white jazz musicians, 74
  and Whiteman, Paul, 139, 141–142
Bellson, Louis, 2

Berger, Morroe, 192n65, 193n76
Berliner, Emile, 68–69
Biggs, Verona, 63–64, 72
Biograph Company, 185n43
Birth of a Nation (film), 111
Black and Tan (film), 97–99, 100, 116, 117
Black and Tan (Jazz) Orchestra, 106, 108
Black Atlantic, concept of, 14, 161n2, 162n4
"Black Creole" ("Creole of Color"), 35, 44, 167n15. See also Creoles
blackface
  and Armstrong, Louis, 116
  in jazz films, 98–99, 100–103, 112–114, 186n65
  ragtime music and, 22
  and Vallee, Rudy, 119
"blue notes," 25, 30, 164n39
blues
  African American critics of, 137, 192n65
  commercial appeal of, 27
  early history of, 24–26
  early jazz and, 29
  early recordings of, 25–26
  and Handy, W. C., 26–29
  musical categorization of, 25
  New Orleans and, 36, 38, 40, 168n26, 169n27
  New York City and, 83–84
  Peyton, Dave, on, 65
  white approximations on film of, 118, 119
  work songs, connection to, 24, 58
  See also "blue notes"
Bolden, Charles "Buddy," 39–41, 42, 45
  Morton's views on, 44
  and Oliver, Joe, 49
  and Ondaatje, Michael, 169n37
  and Picou, Alphonse, 168n24
Boswell Sisters, 115, 118–119, 187n78

stride piano, 83–85, 109. *See also* Johnson, James P.; Smith, Willie "The Lion"; and Waller, Thomas "Fats"
string bands, 40, 169n38
Susman, Warren, 3, 130
Swing Era, 152, 156–157
swing music
  commercial appeal of, 144–149
  in film, 2
  jazz precursors to, 79–80, 101, 108–109
  radio musicians and, 91
  response to, by mainstream America, 138–139
  See also Swing Era

Tate, Erskine, 61, 73, 79
Tin Pan Alley, 20, 29, 36, 83, 93, 154. *See also* New York City
Tio, Lorenzo, 46
Tizol, Juan, 92, 102
Treemonisha (composition), 20

Vallee, Rudy, 115, 119–120, 144, 187n82
vaudeville
  blues and, 28
  commerce and, 23–25
  development of film and, 110, 113, 118
  jazz performers and, 25–26, 70, 81–82, 83, 84, 93, 140
  racial ideology and, 22–26
  ragtime and, 21–22
  employment on circuits, 61, 82, 92, 100, 105, 119

  See also blackface; jazz: race and; ragtime: racism and
Victorianism, 3, 9, 13–16, 86, 128–129, 133
  See also modernity
Victor Records, 21, 48, 69, 127–128, 144, 147, 177n79
Victor Talking Machine Company, 69

Waller, Thomas "Fats," 83–84
Waters, Ethel, 25
Whiteman, Paul, 156
  at the Aeolian Hall, 125–126
  comparison to Benny Goodman, 150
  critics and, 143, 152
  early career of, 127–128
  in film, 120, 139–142
  as "King of Jazz," 128, 140
  King of Jazz (film) and, 139–142, 193n80
  Peyton and, 65, 66–67
  Rhythm Boys and, 102
white musicians. *See* jazz: white musicians and
women
  modernity and, 133–134
  as musicians, 25
  representations of in jazz films, 115–116, 117, 118–120
  vaudeville theater and, 23
World's Columbian Exhibition (1893), 13, 15, 17, 89